The Ten Commandments

How Our Most Ancient Moral Text Can Renew Modern Life

David Hazony

SCRIBNER

New York   London   Toronto   Sydney

SCRIBNER
A Division of Simon & Schuster, Inc.
1230 Avenue of the Americas
New York, NY 10020

First Scribner hardcover edition September 2010

SCRIBNER and design are registered trademarks of The Gale Group, Inc.,
used under license by Simon & Schuster, Inc., the publisher of this work.

For information about special discounts for bulk purchases,
please contact Simon & Schuster Special Sales at 1-866-506-1949
or business@simonandschuster.com.

The Simon & Schuster Speakers Bureau can bring authors to your live event.
For more information or to book an event contact the Simon & Schuster Speakers Bureau
at 1-866-248-3049 or visit our website at www.simonspeakers.com.

DESIGNED BY ERICH HOBBING

Manufactured in the United States of America

1   3   5   7   9   10   8   6   4   2

Library of Congress Control Number: 2009043129

ISBN 978-1-4165-6235-1
ISBN 978-1-4165-6251-1 (ebook)

For Aba and Ima

Both the tablets and the shattered tablets
were laid in the Ark.

—Babylonian Talmud, Menahot 99a

CONTENTS

The Ten Commandments

THE TEN
COMMANDMENTS
(Exodus 20:2–14)

1.

I am the Lord your God who took you out of Egypt, from the house of slaves.

2.

You shall have no other gods besides me. You shall not make for yourself a carved idol, or any likeness of any thing that is in heaven above, or that is in the earth below, or that is in the water under the earth. You shall not bow down to them, nor serve them. For I the Lord your God am a jealous god, punishing the iniquity of the fathers upon the children unto the third and fourth generations of those that hate me, but showing mercy to thousands of generations of those that love me, and keep my commandments.

3.

You shall not invoke the name of the Lord your God in vain. For the Lord shall not hold blameless one who invokes his name in vain.

4.

Remember the Sabbath day, to sanctify it. Six days you shall labor, and complete all your work. But the seventh will be a Sabbath for the Lord your God. You shall do no work: Neither you, nor your son or your daughter, your man-servant or your maid-servant, your beasts or your stranger in your gates. For in six days the Lord made the heavens, the earth, and the sea, and all that is in them, and he rested on the seventh day. For this reason did the Lord bless the seventh day and sanctify it.

5.

Honor your father and your mother, that you may lengthen your days on the land which the Lord your God has given you.

6.

You shall not murder.

7.

You shall not commit adultery.

8.

You shall not steal.

9.

You shall not bear false witness against your neighbor.

10.

You shall not covet your neighbor's house. You shall not covet your neighbor's wife, nor his man-servant or his maid-servant, his ox or his ass, or anything that is your neighbor's.

Can You Name All Ten?

This book is the product not only of years of exploration of the Bible and the ancient rabbinic teachings, but also of my own failures, triumphs, and lessons learned. Like many of us, I have struggled with a career and the unique pressures of modern life; have loved and failed at love; have endured a complicated childhood and raised children of my own; have lived as both a devoutly religious man and a complete secularist; have struggled to deepen myself spiritually, intellectually, and culturally; have seen war and terrorism and social decay from fairly close up; and have broken one or another of the Ten Commandments too many times. My life has been interesting but far from perfect. I do not presume to preach.

The purpose of this book is not to tell you about all the riches and goodness that come from abandoning our worldly concerns and embracing the Ten Commandments as a simple, divine answer to everything. It is, rather, to share with you my own thoughts about the Hebrew Bible, or Old Testament, and the sense that it has been deeply misunderstood in our world.

My main claim is that the Old Testament's centerpiece, the Ten Commandments, is neither an archaic remnant of a dead past nor an arbitrary set of laws handed down to a hundred generations of hungry supplicants and rebellious fools. The commandments represent, rather, a whole attitude to life, one that recognizes both the weaknesses and the unfathomable potential of humanity—a worldview that has largely been forgotten but has a great deal to offer every one of us today.

I do believe that the Ten Commandments are a blueprint for a good society, and that a proper understanding of what they were originally meant to communicate can lead all of us, regardless of our faith, to a much better place. But to assert this at the outset is probably saying too much, too soon.

Every few years, the Ten Commandments become a major topic of discussion in the Western world. In America, the most public battleground has been the Supreme Court, which has ruled in a series of cases involving the placement of the Ten Commandments in public displays on government grounds. In one case in 2005, they were put on display, alongside eight classic legal works, at courthouses in two Kentucky counties, where they were meant to represent the state's "precedent legal code." In a five-to-four decision, the Court ruled that the display violated the First Amendment's ban on "an establishment of religion" and had to be removed. On the same day, the court ruled on a similar case in Texas—again five-to-four, but this time to permit a six-foot-high statue showing the Ten Commandments on the grounds of the Texas State Capitol.[1]

Though the cases were just different enough in the details to allow the Court to come down on different sides, it was clear that on fundamentals, the justices divided into two roughly even camps—one allowing the display of the Ten Commandments in government institutions, one against.

What were they arguing about? The debate, it turns out, was not about whether the Ten Commandments were a religious text—everyone agreed they were—but whether the kind of religion their display was meant to promote was allowed by law. In his opposition to the Texas display, Justice David Souter pointed to what he saw as the "simple realities that the Ten Commandments constitute a religious statement, that their message is inherently religious, and that the purpose of singling them out in a display is clearly the same."[2]

At the other end was Justice Antonin Scalia, who wrote the dissent in the Kentucky case. In his view, the problem is not that Souter and the other justices misunderstand the Ten Commandments, but that they misunderstand America. To Scalia, America is not like the secular republics of modern-day Europe, where "religion is to be strictly excluded from the public forum." From its founding, American government has actively, officially promoted religion in its broadest sense. The inclusion of "In God We Trust" on the coins, "one nation under God" in the Pledge of Allegiance, and "so help me God" at the end of the witness oath in court—all these are consistent with the basic values of a nation that since its birth has believed, with George Washington, that "reason and experience both forbid us to expect that national morality can prevail in exclusion of religious principle."[3] What is forbidden, in Scalia's view, is not promoting religion but "establishing" it—that is, creating an official religion that excludes people of other faiths from taking part in American civic life. But to promote a nonspecific, Judeo-Christian faith—this, Scalia argues, is essential to the American experience.

What is especially troubling about this debate is how little attention both sides paid to the Ten Commandments' actual contents. They are assumed to be familiar to everyone. What do these commandments have to do with one another? Why these ten and not others? What role were these ten principles origi-

3

nally meant to play, both in religious faith and in public law? How does this particular religious symbol differ from other symbols such as the crucifix, the Star of David, or the crescent? Questions like these were of little interest to the justices of the Court.

How strange: to rule on the meaning of a text without really reading it. Yet the Court's attitude reflects a much wider problem, an enormous gap between how most of us see the Ten Commandments as a symbol, and our familiarity with them as actual teaching. According to one poll, 79 percent of Americans oppose removing the Ten Commandments from public displays (including 60 percent who "strongly oppose" it), whereas 18 percent favor it; but according to another poll, only 40 percent can name more than four of them.[4] We have strong opinions about what we think the Ten Commandments symbolize, but we are surprisingly ignorant of their contents. We know what the Ten Commandments look like but not what they say.

This preference for symbolism over content is especially striking in the context of the broader Western political debate. There is, after all, a great battle under way. Its trenches are the raging, intractable conflicts over abortion, same-sex marriage, euthanasia, pornography, capital punishment, stem-cell research, and profanity in music and film. In the thick of such a struggle, it is inordinately difficult to ask people to take something that looks like yet another front—the Ten Commandments, the textual core of the revelation in the Old Testament—and to think about it independently, to review its merits without the din of the culture wars skewing our judgment. For most people, the Ten Commandments represent not just an expression of old-time religion, but *the* expression of it. They begin, after all, with what looks like a big theological claim ("I am the Lord your God . . .") and go on to make a set of demands, some of which, like the ones about murder and theft, are not just good principles but ought to be laws of every land, while others, like the ban on carving idols or committing adultery, are today often seen as largely a matter of personal choice outside the realm of public law.

For this reason, many have come to see the Ten Commandments as a kind of banner for the forces of darkness in our social battles: They represent an imposition of religion, an archaic archipelago of assertions that do not always fall in line with today's world, and cannot be placed on the lawn of a federal courthouse without undermining the ideals of reason, free discourse, and the secularism of the public square on which Western democracy stands. And because these commandments are often invoked in order to justify the imposition of theocratic norms, it is argued, their placement at the seat of justice represents a dangerous encroachment on everything we have achieved in the modern world.

Others take the opposite position, of course. To them, it is precisely their religious resonance that gives the Ten Commandments such an important role. They are, in the eyes of many, the perfect symbol of everything good that has been threatened by the advent of secularism, of sexual "liberation," of the widespread degradation in the moral norms of our world—community, decency, the church. It is precisely because of the religious values symbolized by the Ten Commandments, it is argued, that they belong in front of a court of law, as one place where the most important truths about man and God are allowed to reside.

In light of all this, many readers will be troubled by the improbable claim on which this book rests: that despite their heavy public association with religion, and despite the fact that they originally appear within a religious context and are treated as sacred by a great many religious people, the Ten Commandments are not really a "religious" text at all—at least not the way we normally use the term. While the Ten Commandments may serve to deepen and enrich our faith, we do not need faith to think about them, understand them, or accept their teachings as true. They are not a mystical text, describing orders of reality inaccessible to our minds without the first step of belief. Nor are they really a work of theology, which is about understanding who or what God is. Nor are they an expression of love or longing for the Divine, as we find in Psalms and some of the prophetic works. Nor are they about prayer or ritual worship. Although they do make statements about God—that he took the Israelites out of Egypt, that he is a "jealous God"—these are a small part of the text, and, as we shall see, do more than anything else to highlight just how much more the Ten Commandments are really talking about us than him, about man's role and purpose in the world rather than who God is or how we ought to relate to him.*

They are, rather, a set of extremely concise statements about the best way to build a good, upright society. They are presented in the Bible as the God-given constitutional core of the Israelite nation, a nation created to serve as an example for mankind. The Ten Commandments are therefore best understood not as a symbol of ancient laws about God and religion, but as a capsule containing profound ideas about human life, ideas that are not always "liberal" or "conservative" but are in fact very deeply Western, ideas that many of us have never fully understood or even imagined to be contained in them, or in ourselves.

Read as a teaching, the Ten Commandments may have a great

---

*I put pronouns referring to God in lowercase. This does not express an opinion about God's divinity or dignity. Rather, it is in my mind a more truthful rendering of the Israelite tradition. The Hebrew language has no capitals, and I think the assertion that God is so distant and impersonal as to justify capitalizing "he" and "him" and "you" and "me" might have come as a surprise to the biblical authors.

deal to offer to both sides of the political and social divide, and may serve to unify rather than to polarize. But if this is the case, then anyone who wants to understand the foundations on which our lives are or could be built, who takes seriously the most profound difficulties afflicting Western life today, who understands that somehow we lack the most important tools to fix what is broken and to improve what works—in short, anyone who still believes that it is possible to make our world into a great one— ought to give the Ten Commandments serious attention and to see whether they constitute a profound, enduring source of wisdom for all mankind.

The Ten Commandments have traveled through the ages, at times on carved representations of ecclesiastical art, or in an epic film, or on the lawn in front of a courthouse, or sometimes just deep in our imaginations, as we envision the biblical stories taught us in childhood. They have survived the turmoil of history for thousands of years—but mostly as a symbol, an indicator of a whole world of meaning that we presume to be, or to have once been, very important. But what do they really mean?

This book offers a theory as to what the Ten Commandments mean. They represent, I suggest, a certain kind of democratic spirit, one that continues to function at the deepest level of our lives but has largely been ignored or forgotten. For our Western world is driven by two different, often complementary, spirits. There is, first, the spirit of *reason,* which promotes rational decision making, dispassionate analysis, creative expression, and open speech, leading us to arrive at good answers in our public and private lives. We have inherited this from the Greeks, by way of the Enlightenment, and it has served us well, helping forge the greatest deliberative discourse and the most technologically advanced society in human history.

But there is a second democratic spirit as well. We may call it the spirit of *redemption*. This spirit, inherited from the ancient Israelites by way of British and early American thought, has given democratic peoples the belief that every individual can change the world for the better, can take action against apathy, ineptitude, and corruption in order to improve his lot and that of his loved ones, and can combine with other individuals to create communities—not just communities of faith but communities dedicated to making things better, communities of action. The spirit of redemption, grounded in the Ten Commandments and expressed throughout the prophetic teachings, calls on us to be dissatisfied with our world, to be vigilant and, when necessary, to do battle against those who aim to harm it, from within or without. It is the idea not only that can good triumph over evil, but that every person has the ability, and therefore the obligation, to take up the struggle.

This democratic ideal—of society as a place not just for rational thought but also for redemptive action—is under constant assault today. We see it, for example, in the low voter turnout for elections throughout much of the democratic world, reflecting a large minority of Westerners who believe either that they cannot change what is wrong, or that changing what's wrong is not so important. We see it in the obsession among many leading scholars to "debunk myths" about our classical heroes—showing that the people we once thought to be exemplars of world-improving action were in fact anything but—without offering new heroes to replace them. We see it in the fashionable, postmodern impulse that replaces liberal tolerance with relativism: By saying that we have "no right to judge" whether the actions of others are good or evil, we undermine the possibility of redemptive action by attacking the whole idea of right and wrong. We see it in the popularity of spiritual teachings that advocate the individual's disassociation from the things of this earth, such that the will to redemptive action is stunted or rendered inoperable. And we see it whenever we feel that sense of public impotence—when elected officials declare our cities to be "ungovernable" because of runaway crime, when genocide continues as world leaders wring their hands, when prominent thinkers decry Western democracy as morally indistinguishable from totalitarianism, when international bodies dedicated to preventing human rights abuses are taken over by the abusers themselves.

This assault has put the spirit of redemption on the defensive. It is being waged on multiple fronts, and it is often the product of the best minds that American and European universities have produced. Although its forms are often intellectualized—reflecting a rich philosophical effort that has spanned the better part of the last century—what unites these attacks is no less a thing of the heart than of the mind. It reflects a different kind of inner sense of how a person ought to feel about himself, his community, and his world: through detachment rather than passionate concern, through an assumption of impotence rather than strength.

In many cases, I fear, it might also imply a certain kind of laziness, a constant, ever-reproducing, and ever-rationalizing search for a way out of the most painful parts of redemptive action: whether it is because of the difficulty in knowing right from wrong in a complex world, or because of the direct contact with the mundane and often repugnant details that all effective action requires, or because of the so-called violence that all real action, it is claimed, entails. What unites these different streams is the sense that on some deeper level, redemptive action is itself a myth, that we no longer really have to take responsibility for what happens around us. Either because we shouldn't, or because we can't.

Creating a redemptive society, in other words, requires far more than education of the mind. It requires education of the spirit. It means instilling in our children a profound inner self-confidence, a psychological health, that recognizes that each of us can be a force for good. It means creating societal frameworks, from family to community to government, that encourage and nurture the redemptive spirit. It means building up exemplary individuals, heroes to inspire the redemptive spirit in each and every one of us. And it means fostering a sense of responsibility toward those around us—our families, our communities, our nations.

Where does this spirit come from, and what can we do to breathe new life into it? Its origins, I have suggested, are not so much in the cautious thinkers of ancient Greece as in the bold actors of ancient Israel. Whereas the earlier Greek mythmakers, of course, also offered a range of dynamic, exciting heroes, only in Israel were such heroes measured by a single God—that is, against a single standard of right and wrong. In the Bible, God himself is, of course, presented as the supreme example of the redemptive spirit, willing a good universe into existence, rescuing the Israelites from oppression at the hands of Pharaoh, showing anger at evil and rewarding the good. And it is this God we are called on to emulate: The Old Testament, throughout its length and breadth, is the story of the successes and failures of one people trying to live up to the redemptive ideal. The kings of Israel are judged according to this standard, and the prophets are the most eloquent advocates for it the world has known.

At the heart of the Hebrew Bible lies the story of the revelation at Mount Sinai in the book of Exodus, when God reveals himself to the Israelites soon after they escape the slavery of Egypt and are on their way to the Promised Land. Led by Moses deep into a forbidding desert, the Israelites are a harried and traumatized lot who probably never would have embarked on such a journey if it were not for the stunning display of divine miracles that keep them in line. Raised as slaves for generations, the greatest miracle of all was not so much the frogs and boils and blood and darkness that they saw God lay on the Egyptians, or the splitting of the Red Sea and the pillars of smoke and fire to lead their way, as the titanic psychological achievement of getting an entire slave nation—six hundred thousand men plus women and children, according to the Bible—to leave Egypt at all.

Two months into their odyssey, racked by hunger and thirst and doubt and bouts of yearning for their enslaved past, the Israelites arrive at the very mountain where Moses had first heard the words of God years earlier during his exile from Egypt. After three days of preparation and purification, they encounter God's very presence, accompanied by a terrifying display of thunder and fire and noise. The experience is so intense that the people, fearing their own deaths in the blast furnace of the Divine, tell Moses to climb the mountain on his own and receive the contents of the revelation on their behalf.

Forty days later, Moses makes his way back down. Having left him for dead, the Israelites have already begun to re-create, by means of a great Golden Calf, the gilded gods they knew back home. Moses now carries in his hands two great tablets of stone, on which God has carved what the Hebrew text calls *aseret hadevarim*—the "Ten Utterances," which through the King James Bible became known in English as the Ten Commandments. These ten statements constitute the core of everything, the essence of the covenant between God and Israel. Indeed, they are so central to the covenant that the text calls them "the Utterances of the Covenant, the Ten Utterances"; the stone tablets are called the "Tablets of the Covenant"; and the ark in which the tablets are later placed is called the "Ark of the Covenant."[5] The Ten Commandments are meant to be the singular symbol of the bond between humanity and the Divine.

Enraged by what he sees before him, the saturnalia of the Golden Calf, the drunken cries of *This is your God, O Israel, that brought you up out of Egypt!,* and faced with the betrayal of everything he has suffered and fought for, Moses cannot contain his anger. He hurls the Tablets of the Covenant at the revelers, shattering them, and then enlists his fellow members of the tribe of Levi to restore order with the sword, grinding the calf into powder and pouring it into the river, making the Israelites drink the admixture as a symbolic act of their rejection, once and for all, of the divinity of man-made things.

This is surprising enough; what happens next, however, is even more so. We might have expected our Old Testament God to rebuke Moses for smashing the words that God carved and throwing them at God's chosen. But instead, he just says to Moses:

> Carve yourself two tablets of stone, like the first ones . . . that you shattered. (Exodus 34:1)[6]

The rabbis of the Talmud would later interpret these words as an endorsement: You were right to shatter them! Moses was right to judge his people unworthy of the Covenant, and to take decisive action to put them back on track.[7] At the same time, having done this, it is now Moses' job to carve a new set, to try again, even in a situation where most people would have abandoned hope and headed back for Egypt, or left the people to die in the desert. Moses goes back up the mountain for another forty days, returns with new tablets, and the people repent.

How are we to understand these twists of plot in Exodus,

both the smashing of the tablets and the creation of new ones? We intuit them to be of more than anecdotal value: There seems to be something crucial about Moses' spontaneous, righteous intervention in the delivery of the Ten Commandments. Is there something in this story that is intimately connected with the purpose of the Ten Commandments themselves?

Both by smashing the tablets and carving new ones, Moses remedies an immediate evil that threatens the entire success of the exodus from Egypt, the divine revelation, and the journey to the Promised Land. The Children of Israel have slid back to their old idolatrous ways—the mental habits of slaves. Moses has to intervene, decisively. Even God's own miracles are no longer enough. In breaking the tablets, Moses is not merely addressing a crisis through high drama. He is carrying out, not in words but in stunning action, the very redemptive spirit that the tablets embody.

How so? To begin with, there is something inherently problematic about the whole God-man relationship implied in the Bible. Seen from a certain perspective, the revelation of the Divine is so overwhelming, so consuming, that it becomes difficult to imagine us mere mortals ever again standing up and doing anything for ourselves. After all, once the Creator of the Universe, all-knowing, all-truth, all-righteousness, is revealed before man in a blast of fire and sound, are we not all of us revealed to be but dust and ashes before the Absolute?

Indeed, in much of the ancient world, this was precisely how mankind was seen. Classical Judaism and Christianity both asserted at times the meaninglessness of human endeavor in the face of God's enormity—as when Ecclesiastes declares, "Vanity of vanities—all is vanity!" (Ecclesiastes 1:2); or when Jesus claims that "my kingdom is not of this world"; or when the traditional Jew supplicates before God on the fast of Yom Kippur:

What are we? What is our life? What is our kindness?
What is our righteousness? What is our salvation? What is our
strength? What is our might? What can we say before you, Lord
our God and God of our forefathers? Are not all the heroes as
naught before you, the renowned as though they never were, the
wise as though devoid of wisdom, and the insightful as though
devoid of insight? For their many deeds are nothing, the days of
their lives vanity before you. Man is not more than a beast, for
all is vanity.[8]

Yet the belief in the utter worthlessness of human action—that
ours is an incurable realm of falsehood, filth, stupidity, and sin,
and that man is impotent in the presence of a controlling God—
does not seem to jibe with the story of the Ten Commandments.
On the contrary: An intense struggle between right and wrong
is taking place before our eyes, where the meaningfulness of
human action and worldly results is taken for granted. God can
do a great deal with his mighty hand and his outstretched arm,
but only when individuals take responsibility for events and act
decisively can real human crises find their resolution.

In smashing the tablets, Moses is teaching us at least as much
as God is. Without redemptive action, humanity cannot be
delivered from its own vices.

Such action may have different kinds of moods or emotions
associated with it. Sometimes it requires tablet-smashing fury
against wrongful deeds, the kind of intensity we associate with
a judge issuing a harsh sentence to a violent criminal, or with the
military defeat of a tyrannical enemy. At other times it requires
the cool, constructive determination of starting over, of carving a second set of tablets in infinite patience with the challenge
at hand. Indeed, the rabbinic sages asserted that the second set
of tablets was in fact superior to the first: Because the first set

were purely the work of God, they were in some way inadequate to the challenge of teaching real people. Only the second
set, carved out by Moses himself, contained a sufficient degree
of human intervention to be an effective answer to the sins of
mankind.[9]

What changed Israel's mind about Moses, we learn, was not
the words of God so much as the deeds of the man: smashing
the tablets, punishing the evildoers, and carving out new tablets
of stone.

We see, then, how the story of the Ten Commandments' delivery to mankind contains some of the central elements of what
I am calling the spirit of redemption. But what about the commandments themselves? In the chapters that follow, I examine
how each of them, in a different way and relating to a different part of life, embodies the same spirit. For this reason, each
chapter is to be read carefully, taking the time to think about
the ideas it contains, to struggle and argue with them, to ask
whether and how they can become a part of our lives.

This approach can be difficult. Often, when encountering
the central texts of Christianity or Judaism, we abandon our
ordinary tools of reading and thinking about what we've read,
whether out of awe, skepticism, revulsion, or fear. In what follows, I ask that we suspend our ingrained interpretive prejudices
and give the Ten Commandments a good, close read—perhaps
for the first time.

This cuts in two ways. Reading the Ten Commandments with
fresh eyes requires overcoming the instinct, common among
many agnostics and atheists and some religious people as well, to
dismiss the text as archaic rather than foundational, as symbolic
of the kind of God-on-the-mountain revelatory symphony that
we thankfully left behind long ago, along with the establishment

of religion and the political authority of religious leaders. But it also means resisting the opposite instinct, common among many religious people, which suggests that because the text is believed to be the Word of God, we cannot really study, question, challenge, or understand it on our own terms. Both instincts are problematic in our attempt to learn important truths from the Ten Commandments, for in both cases we are led away from applying our creative thinking to what is in fact a difficult text. We assume either that we already know what it means, or that we cannot. But there is a world of meaning in the Ten Commandments, an ocean of intention locked in its few verses.

To this end, the book uses three methodological assumptions that have not generally been employed in understanding the Ten Commandments.

The first has to do with why these particular ten statements make up the text. The simple reading of the passage in Exodus suggests that this is meant to be the most important text ever given to man. These stone tablets were so important that they were to be carried in the Ark of the Covenant through the desert, the ark that would later be placed in the Holy of Holies, the most sacred place in the Temple in Jerusalem. The centerpiece of the Israelite faith is a text, containing a set of ideas intended to be the foundation of Israelite civilization and, ultimately, of human civilization as a whole.

Yet if the Ten Commandments are meant to be a blueprint for society, then it follows that each commandment should be read with this in mind. When we look at "You shall not make for yourself a carved idol" or "You shall not covet your neighbor's house," these are clearly meant to be read not simply as specific, technical prohibitions but also expansively and imaginatively, as signifying broader ideas. I look at each commandment as a kind of paradigm for something bigger, a more general state-ment about right and wrong.

It seems clear, for example, that "You shall not steal" can be seen as a prohibition against taking things that are not ours, and also as a larger statement about the importance of respecting and valuing property. This is pretty straightforward—until we dis-cover that according to an ancient rabbinic tradition, the com-mandment was taken to refer not to ordinary stealing but to the kidnapping of human beings. This unintuitive reading could shed light on a deeper principle, one that finds in the Ten Com-mandments the origin not simply of our ideas about property, but of liberty itself—and of the connection between the two.

This kind of elaboration of the Ten Commandments may be very helpful in our day, when oppressive regimes routinely flout the individual's property and freedom. I will argue, however, that all ten of the commandments similarly represent broader, foundational principles of enduring relevance. Every com-mandment represents a whole world of value, an awakening of the redemptive spirit in its own area of life.

The second point has to do with the debate over the histori-cal origins of the text. I sidestep the whole question of how and when the Ten Commandments came into our possession, and who wrote them. Again, some readers will find this difficult. If the text was given by God on the mountaintop, some will argue, its authority is divine and therefore overrides all consid-eration of whatever we mortals might think it means; instead we should be thinking only about how to apply its laws. If, on the other hand, its origin is human, it is not in itself an obliga-tory text and should be treated, at best, like an ancient philo-sophical work, akin to Plato or Confucius, or at worst, like an ancient legal work, akin to the Pharaonic or Babylonian codes.

My project, however, is at heart more philosophical than

theological or historical. What is known about the text's history is enough to convince me that it warrants serious attention regardless of how it came into our hands. We know, with a great measure of certainty, that by the end of the first millennium B.C.E.—what Christians see as the time of Jesus and Jews see as the end of the Second Temple period before the great exile—the Ten Commandments were understood by the Jews as the core not only of faith but of moral wisdom as well. At the time of Jesus, they were recited daily as a centerpiece of the Jewish worship service in the Temple in Jerusalem.[10] Throughout the ages, they continued to be a major symbol for Jews and Christians alike, a symbol of righteousness distilled into a few short lines etched in stone. If the text is divine, this does not absolve us of the duty to understand it carefully, creatively, critically. If it is man-made, its status through the millennia is alone enough to impel us to try to understand how, why, or whether the Ten Commandments are important to us, and why they were so central to the thinking of our forebears. My claim is that they are indeed of great importance, that they are worthy of revival in the hearts and minds of Western people—and thus the burden is on me to show it, regardless of whether they reveal the hand of God, man, or a combination of the two.

The third and final point has to do with the traditions I draw on to illustrate these principles. Although any number of traditions have made their way into this book, I pay special attention to the Ten Commandments' context as part of the Old Testament as a whole, and to the ancient Jewish interpretations that followed.

There are a number of reasons for this. First, I think that if we are to shake ourselves loose of the awe or skepticism that tends to prevent an open reading of the biblical text, it is helpful to look at the Ten Commandments independently from their

Christian interpretations. The commandments predate the rise of Christianity, perhaps by a thousand years, and have sat at the core of all the great monotheistic faiths that today claim the commitment of a large portion of the human race. The Jewish tradition—especially midrash, or rabbinic allegory—is a sea of philosophical commentary on the biblical texts, one that is most helpful precisely where creative interpretation is needed. Understanding the Ten Commandments requires a good deal of creative interpretation, and an excellent way to get us thinking is by introducing ourselves to a very different tradition of biblical interpretation.

The rabbinic tradition is worthy of special attention for another reason. Classical Christianity focused its teachings on, more than anything else, the moral and religious life of the individual. The Jewish teachings, broadly speaking, added a dimension we may call political. According to tradition, the Israelites who emerged from the revelation at Mount Sinai were not just a faith community but a political one as well, destined to reconquer their ancestral homeland at the hands of Joshua, to establish a monarchy there under David and Solomon, and to live for half a millennium under their own sovereign rule before facing destruction at the hands of the Assyrians and Babylonians. It was during this long period of national rise and decline— stretching from around 1200 to 586 B.C.E.—that the great majority of the Bible was composed. When, late in the sixth century B.C.E., a group of Judeans returned to the land under the leadership of Ezra and Nehemiah, they founded not just a spiritual community, with its priests and scholars and a new Temple, but also a political one, a second commonwealth, including kings and soldiers and legislators. It was during this period that the Ten Commandments were interpreted and placed at the center of the Temple service.

By the time the second Jewish commonwealth was destroyed by the Romans in 70 c.e., sending the Jewish people into many centuries of exile, the basic foundations of what would be called "Judaism," or the rabbinic tradition, had been laid. Much of Judaism owes itself to a national, sovereign tradition that grew and developed over a thousand years before the Jewish communities took the exilic form they would retain for two thousand more. While the classic texts of rabbinic literature, the Mishna and Talmud, were composed several centuries after the exile had begun, they reflected the profoundly political nature that characterized the origins of their people: They dealt not only with virtue and the challenges of remaining morally and spiritually upright but also with law and society, economics and war, and much of what we call public affairs—how cultures, nations, and civilizations may survive and thrive.

So when Jewish tradition came to speak of the Ten Commandments, beginning in the Hebrew Bible and through the ages, it looked at them not just as a basis for righteousness but also as the cornerstone of a good society. Looking at the Ten Commandments in this way can give them new meaning for Western life today. For while their origin lies in what can be called a religious tradition, their meaning extends far beyond the most obvious religious categories—Catholic or Protestant, Jewish or Christian or Muslim, religious or secular, conservative or liberal. The Ten Commandments should be looked at as an engine that continues to drive the West at its deepest levels, a key to understanding who all of us are, and why we have acquired many of our most basic beliefs about society, nationhood, and our place in this world.

At the same time, I do not ignore the powerful messages that really are directed at each of us as individuals—as spiritual, moral, and rational beings. Indeed, a close reading of these principles reveals how difficult it is to separate public and private at all. In a democratic society, there always has to be some distinction made: The essence of liberty is the affirmation of every person's right to think, believe, and behave differently from everybody else. At the same time, however, the "public" is made of individuals and ultimately will come to reflect their innermost longings, beliefs, perceptions, and habits. One cannot promote truthfulness in public life, for example, if we as individuals are not personally sensitive to truth and falsehood in our own lives. This applies on some level to all regimes; it is triply true in a democracy, where leaders are replaced when they fail to speak to people's ideals.

It is for this reason that the Ten Commandments are written no more for princes and presidents than for every private person. In the original Hebrew grammar, each appears in the second-person singular: *You,* the individual, shall not murder or steal. Every one of its precepts goes straight to our hearts as thinking, acting, private people.

The ancient rabbis emphasized this point when they taught that when God revealed himself at Sinai, every Israelite was greeted by a ministering angel who put a crown on his head.[11] The Ten Commandments are not merely revelation but also coronation—the establishment of every person as a responsible sovereign in his own world, who has the power to represent the moral vision on earth, but who as a result must take ultimate, cosmic responsibility for his own life, and for the values and morals that underlie each and every action he takes.

We can make a good society, but only if we insist on being good people, and if we raise our children to be good people as well. We know it is possible, because in some cases we have risen above the barbaric basin from which the West emerged—rampant murder and theft being examples where Western societies

have worked hard to stamp them out and teach their wrongfulness. And yet beyond such exceptions, it is extremely hard for
most people to cling to firm principles of right and wrong to the
point of sacrificing for their sake and teaching their children to
do the same.

Against the storm of rapidly shifting cultural winds, and the
debilitating sense of impermanence that characterizes human
life today, the Ten Commandments stand as a beacon of principle for each and every one of us. In a world that sometimes looks
like it's sailing into a hurricane, they are also a beacon of hope.

1

Redemption

I am the Lord your God who took you out of Egypt, from the house of slaves.

Imagine you are a ten-year-old child, living in Europe in the middle of the last century. Your father disappeared when you were a baby, sent off to war like so many fathers. All you know of him are stories you've heard from your brothers and sisters, or maybe a photo or two in an album. He is a stark presence in your childhood, sometimes painful and sometimes revered, but always missing.

But then the war reaches your own country. Enemy forces overrun your town, and your community is plunged into darkness and fear. You and your family are transferred to a prison camp where you suffer intense deprivations of hunger and cold and forced labor, every day and night for long months—just a child, enduring the horrors of war, dreaming of being saved.

And then one night, you are awakened by gunfire and confusion. Guards and prisoners fall dead, sirens blare, and quickly it turns out that partisan forces hiding in the nearby forest have engineered a daring escape from the camp. For weeks you are led through snowy woods, struggling with the elements but free from your captors, until finally you reach an encampment where you are given food, clothing, rest, and medical attention. On the third day, the rebel commander finally makes his appearance, a tall and imposing figure sporting a uniform and beret, inspiring both awe and fear. He takes your hand, looks you in the eye—and suddenly you recognize him. "I am your father," he says. "I took you out of prison."

This is something like what the Israelites must have felt when hearing the dramatic opening of the Ten Commandments. Born into unbearable slavery in Egypt, they had been taught all their lives that one day God would fulfill his promise to their father Abraham and lead them to freedom. Now a leader had appeared, Moses by name, claiming that God had sent him to take the Israelites out of slavery, but such an escape required the miraculous devastation of Egypt and an unfathomable journey into the wilderness of Sinai. The Israelites had followed, not because they knew what was coming (they didn't), but because anything was better than where they had been. For three days now they had encamped at a mysterious mountain, watching in terror as storm clouds gathered and supernatural sounds and sights grew ever more intense. And yet none of this prepared them for the revelation of the First Commandment. God was here after all. He had a name. He had saved them.

Many of us have a hard time with God. Throughout our lives we hear contradictory messages about who or what he is and what he wants from us, and we're forced to choose among countless teachings, theories, and accounts of him in order to define our own faith. He is, we are told, a pristine and perfect being, a loving father, a violent ruler, the Unmoved Mover, the entirety of everything, or even a dead relic, a fiction that has led countless people astray. He has been commercialized, dehumanized, metaphorized, turned into a philosophical proposition, an idea or hypothesis, an immoral mythological beast whose proper place is the same dustbin that holds Apollo and Thor. As religious people we have developed thousands of denominations, Jewish and Catholic and Protestant and Muslim streams, each with its own theology and practices. As secular people we have scrutinized God as either a literary character who changes drastically over the course of the Bible, or an amalgam of unconnected textual traditions with no coherent personality or meaning to him. If God is dead, as Nietzsche said, it is because we have beaten him to death by endless redefinition.

But beyond the problem of knowing who God is, we often carry emotional baggage that makes him hard to focus on. According to some of our traditions, the Almighty is so awesome as to render us mortals worthless and irreparably sinful, robbing us of any hope for existential self-confidence or a decent spiritual life.

When I was in fifth grade, I had an ex-marine for a teacher, a man who instilled fear and reverence in every child. In woodshop, he taught us to make household items the way they made them in the eighteenth century. The Colonial Spoon Rack—the words still make me shiver—consisted of two pieces of wood: a larger one as the backing of the rack, and a small, thin piece with holes in it where you put the spoons. It was this smaller piece that I kept failing at; I'd misalign the holes, or screw up the little slots you cut in the wood to make the spoons slide into them. This went on for days, and when I brought it to him on the third or fourth try, this giant of a man looked at my piece of wood in cool disdain, saw that one of the slots was a little crooked, and said, "Do it again." It seems petty now, but at the time I felt like my world had collapsed, that while all the other kids somehow managed to finish the job and go play kickball,

I would likely spend the rest of my days drilling holes, cutting slots, and failing.

Many of us have been taught to feel the same way when we hear the word "God": infinitesimal and unworthy and condemned. To think about him seriously means either plunging into despair or rejecting him, feeling not inspiration but resentment for being reminded of our inadequacy.

All these issues make it hard enough to approach the First Commandment with a fresh eye and an open mind. Add to it the fact that this text appears in the thick of the Old Testament, a vast and complex ancient work to which we have little direct access (usually we read it through the eyes of later Jewish and Christian interpreters) and more than a little discomfort—especially with the description of God.

We want to find God as a perfect and sublime being, something pure and antithetical to us flawed mortals. But in the Old Testament we instead find a God who is exceedingly human. He is creative, impassioned, demanding, irascible, loving, vindictive, wrathful, deeply engaged in our world. He has high expectations for his greatest creation, man, and reacts in frustration, anger, and disappointment when they are not met. Adam and Eve eat the forbidden fruit, and God banishes them from Eden. Cain murders his brother Abel, so God exiles him from human society. A wretched world of thievery and slavery emerges, and he brings down a flood to destroy all and begin again. In Babel, the greatest nation on earth attempts to challenge their Creator with a tower to the heavens, and he disperses them and confounds their tongues. Sodom and Gomorrah, two particularly iniquitous cities, are reduced to brimstone. And so on.

God is human also in a more positive sense: Through all his anger, he continues to believe in the potential of humanity, preserving the race through unique and beloved individuals: Adam and Eve, Enoch, Noah, Abraham, Isaac. Eventually Abraham's grandson Jacob, or Israel, is chosen to found a "great nation," a people that will benefit from a special relationship with the Divine, who will be protected and guided, who will serve as a "light unto nations."[1] This is a God who hears the cries of Israel's descendants in bondage, who destroys their enemies with plagues, who vents his emotions through his prophets, who is deeply concerned with everything that happens on earth.

We cannot read the Ten Commandments without coming to terms with this God, the God of ancient Israel, the too-human God of the First Commandment. Nothing would be easier than to dance around "the God issue," to use the multiplicity of definitions and the psychological burdens as an excuse to describe the Ten Commandments solely in secular terms for a secularized twenty-first century. The First Commandment's phrasing forecloses that option. Like the child in the woods, like the Israelites on Mount Sinai, we do not have the luxury of distance, of treating these words as some kind of metaphor, of avoiding the presence of God. *I am the Lord your God who took you out of Egypt, from the house of slaves* is not a proposition to be debated, or a command to be accepted under duress. It is a bold introduction to the Divine, a revelation of a relationship each of us may have with him.

The First Commandment introduces us to the God of Israel— a God whose eyes we recognize but whom we do not yet really know.

After the initial shock of the First Commandment had worn off, we may guess that the Children of Israel were filled with questions. Who is this God who addresses us in the first person? What does it mean for him to be "our" God, as the text insists? And why is his role in the exodus from Egypt the only thing about him worth putting into the First Commandment? To answer these is to get to the bottom of what the First Commandment asks of us.

A description of God is first of all a description of an ideal to guide our lives. If he seems too human, too imperfect, it is because this is the God we humans are meant to emulate.

Unlike the gods of ancient Greece, and unlike the ephemeral god ideas of the East, God in the Bible is neither arbitrary nor abstract, but *righteous*—which is another way of saying that we are meant to see his behavior as a model for our own. The Bible describes man as God-like, having been created, as God puts it, "in our image, after our likeness," and becoming even more God-like after Adam and Eve eat the fruit of the tree of knowledge of good and evil, when the Lord begins to fear that man might "become like one of us." Man is commanded to "walk in his ways"; Enoch is depicted as having "walked with God"; while Moses is said to have spoken with God "face-to-face."[2]

Earlier I hinted that the word "commandment" might not be such a good translation of the Hebrew *davar,* which means something like "utterance" or "pronouncement," and nowhere is that felt more acutely than in the First Commandment, the only one that is not phrased as a command. But despite this, there is a normative statement being made, an assertion of God that has implications for our self-understanding as human beings. The pronouns here are crucial: "I am the Lord *your* God": not a dry theological statement but a vibrant moral one; the listener is as deeply implicated as is the speaker. To have a God means to embrace his example.

But to say he is an ideal does not move us any closer to knowing what, exactly, he is meant to represent. We need to learn who this God is, and the only way to do so is to look at what he did before he uttered the First Commandment—to read it, in other words, in its literary context. We need to go back to the very beginning, to the Creation of the universe in Genesis, where God makes his first appearance.

I've always read the Creation story with a feeling that it is not just a story but an introduction to God, that everything we need to know about him is encapsulated in it. It is here, after all, that we first encounter the relationship between God and the universe—that is, between the ideal we are supposed to emulate and the reality to which we are supposed to apply it. The first and third days of Creation offer a good example of this:

> In the beginning God created the heavens and the earth. Now the earth was unformed and void, and darkness was across the depths, and the spirit of God hovered over the waters. And God said, "Let there be light," and there was light. And God saw that the light was good, and God separated the light from the darkness. And God called the light day, and the darkness he called night, and it was evening, and it was morning, a single day . . .
>
> And God gathered the waters that were below the heavens into one place, that the dry places be revealed, and it was so. And God called the dry places "land," and the gathered waters he called "sea," and God saw that it was good. And God said, "Let the land be full of grass, plants that create more plants, fruit trees that bear fruit each of its kind, which have the seeds in them to plant in the ground," and it was so. And the land produced grass, plants that create more plants, trees bearing fruit with seeds in them, each of its kind, and God saw that it was good. And it was evening, and it was morning, the third day. (Genesis 1:1–13)

Two things become clear about God here. First, he *creates*: As though effortlessly, he introduces the basic elements of our life-giving world and acts to change things according to his design. Second, he *judges*: He draws conclusions about the value of what has been done, and observes that it is "good." This combination of creation and judgment is the essence of what God is throughout the Hebrew Bible—a powerful synthesis that has reverberated through the generations and continues to resonate in our own lives.

To create is to intervene in the world and change it according to our design and will. Anytime we see something in our world that is different from what we want to see, and we change it, we are "creating" in the biblical sense. Most of us think of creativity as bringing into being something that was not there before: a work of art, a handicraft, a business or building or book. This view of creation is limited, because it prejudices our judgment as to what kinds of change are or are not "creative," when in fact what is most interesting here is the idea that God can change things at all.

In most of the ancient world, the prevailing belief was that neither gods nor men could change the basic functioning of the universe, that there was a certain primordial reality that everyone needed to adapt himself to. In the Bible we have the opposite. God creates the universe, and he does not stop there. His continued interventions include also catastrophic acts of destruction—the tower of Babel, Sodom and Gomorrah, Egypt under Pharaoh. God continues to impose his will, and indeed much of the biblical narrative is dedicated to his interventions. Every word he utters, every punishment he metes out, every act of redemption is another act of creation, for he is acting in freedom, imposing his will, changing things. One need think only of the flood, when God, having seen the depth of human corruption, "repented" at having created the world and sought to begin again. He is an inventor, forever tinkering with his imperfect work. God "re-creates the universe each and every day," says the Talmud.[3]

When we change things, we re-create the universe just as God does. A changed world is a new one, even when the change is small. One of our most important discoveries in early childhood is that the world is not a given, but that we can affect it: A baby pushes buttons on a toy, causing a light to flash and music to play; a toddler builds a tower of blocks; an older child invites her friends over and avoids an afternoon alone; a teenager changes his attitude toward schoolwork and begins getting better grades. All these minor successes give us a rush of the effectiveness of our will—something especially cherished by children who are so used to having the world and its rules presented to them as unchangeable.

We often forget how easily we may be agents of change. We no longer live in a world where the crucial choices of spouses, careers, and religious commitments are dictated by our parents and communities. Our lives are our own to a degree unimaginable just a few centuries ago, and even as we grow older, we are free to make both major and minor changes in the contours of our lives. Some of these, such as embarking on a new career, marriage and divorce, or religious conversion, entail not only promise but also enormous risk and pain. But as major acts of change, they reaffirm the infinite possibilities of which every one of us is capable. In a sense, every time we exercise our will in recrafting our lives, we imitate God in re-creating the universe.

Our modern, democratic world could never have sprung from a civilization that did not believe in change the way the Bible, and pretty much no one else in the ancient world, did. Modernity, if nothing else, is the unleashing of the individual's creative will, through political institutions that protect our right to make choices, and through the cultural reverence for the individual as a source of change. This is most obvious in economics and business, where all growth begins with the creative entrepreneur who seeks to provide new goods and services that people will want to pay for. But it is no less central to democratic politics, where every new candidate must prove his ability to change things, even in societies where people are generally happy and prosperous. This is also the assumption behind the vast self-help industry: You do not have to accept things as they are, we are told. You can change anything in your life.

We should not be too quick, however, to praise change for its own sake. The creative will includes the potential for making things worse or for hurting those who are weaker than we are in our effort to get ahead. The world as we receive it is full of things that are as they are for good reason and should not be changed; traditions often contain wisdom that the compulsive reformer lacks. To take the point to its extreme, the most murderous regimes of the twentieth century all started out as movements for change, as an effort to reinvent the world in light of their leaders' new designs.

When man exercises his creative will on the world, in other words, he can do great evil as well as great good. For this reason, he requires the second aspect of God in the story of Creation: He must also be a judge.

To judge is to evaluate reality in light of an ideal—to assess the "is" in light of the "ought." When God judges the universe to be "good," he is saying that it could have been otherwise, that there is always a better and a worse way to do things. In doing so, he also affirms the human obligation to judge the world in light of a moral ideal of which it frequently falls short, and to make sure that our interventions are actually good ones. If creativity means change, judgment means deliberation. In human society, this is most strikingly exemplified in the figure of the judge in a court of law, who is tasked with arbitrating disputes, freeing the innocent, and convicting criminals—that is, of determining, carefully and definitively, how life should be lived in light of a conception of the good represented in the laws of the land.

It is difficult to overestimate the role of the judge in the Hebrew Bible. In the modern era, we tend to look at judges as a professional class, to whom the responsibility of adjudicating legal matters is delegated, separate from questions of morality. In the biblical view, however, no such separation exists. Everyone is potentially a judge. In the legal passages of the Torah, the number of admonitions and prescriptions aimed at judges far exceeds those for political leaders. And when the rules governing priests or kings are addressed, these figures are invariably addressed in the third person ("the high priest shall do such and such"), whereas statements about how to be a good judge appear in the second person ("Do not pervert justice; do not favor the poor, nor give favor to the rich"). Moses, we find, spends the great majority of his days in the desert not in prayer, study, strategy, or speeches, but rather in judgment, adjudicating the day-to-day disputes and petty crimes of ordinary Israelites—an occupation so important that he is reluctant to delegate it to anyone until the burden grows so great as to threaten his own health. From the time of Joshua's conquest of the Promised Land until the advent of the monarchy centuries later in the book of Samuel, the Israelites live under the rule of "judges"—an extremely unusual title for rulers in the ancient Near East—who appear to emerge organically as judicial, moral, and military leaders. And the reign of King Solomon, depicted as the pinnacle of the Israelite commonwealth, is known above all else not for the king's grand public works, nor for his considerable military achievements, but for his wisdom in judgment.

The Bible's preoccupation with judges reflects its belief that God himself is a judge, and that we should be as well. To be a judge means not only developing opinions about how things ought to be, but developing *good* opinions, grounded as deep as possible in an understanding of both what is and what can be. Though we tend to think of judgment as something cold and dispassionate, in truth it begins with a passionate urge to identify good and evil in our world, to find out what we can do about it, and to go beyond ourselves and take responsibility, at least with our minds, for what happens to others.

So often we fail to be judges precisely because we lack this sort of moral passion. We send our children off to school, accepting its policies, contents, and standards as givens, breathing a sigh of relief when our kids get good grades and avoid trouble but never asking whether our schools are really educating them, morally and intellectually, to their fullest. We watch the news about our country's ills without so much as wondering what we could be doing about it, or whether we have a duty to learn more about questions of economics, public policy, and foreign relations on which informed political action must be based. We hear the cries of a child or wife next door and do not ask ourselves whether there is a horrible string of abuses taking place, a crime to which we may be lending a hand if we do not act.

In such cases, our "lapse of judgment" begins with a kind of laziness, an intellectual absence from the world. It is only when we habitually think about our world as something that we not only can but must understand, a place where we have a duty to be mentally and morally *present,* only when we habitually ask whether the school, the government, or our neighbors are doing right and undertake to learn enough about them to make an informed assessment of our own—only then have we internalized the call to judgment implicit in the First Commandment. Our opinions are our most precious moral asset, and by developing the habits of opinion making, we imitate God with our minds just as we imitate him in our actions by pushing for a changed world.

By presenting God as a deeply opinionated personality, the Bible is teaching us the importance of the restless moral mind, a mind that constantly seeks to understand and appraise. This restlessness is absolutely central to the biblical ideal, so central that on more than one occasion we find the greatest heroes challenging even God's own judgment, invoking higher ideals in an attempt to influence God's decisions—as when Abraham challenges God over his intention to wipe out Sodom and Gomorrah ("Shall the Judge of all the world," he asks, "not do justice?" [Genesis 18:25]), or when Moses takes God to task for threatening to destroy the Israelites for the sin of the Golden Calf and convinces him to withhold his wrath.[4] The assumption in these stories is not that God is perfect and everything he does or says is by definition right, but that just as he is the supreme judge, so too are we obligated to judge right and wrong as he does—and therefore to question even the actions of God when they look wrong to us.

Later on the rabbinic tradition took this a step further, suggesting that moral judgment is so central to the biblical worldview that it is embedded in the founding act of Creation, that at its deepest level it is inseparable from God's creativity. "When any judge judges truthfully, even for a moment," the rabbis taught, "it is as though he were a partner to the Holy One in the creation of the universe."[5] Our capacity to judge good and evil is similar to our creative capacity, in that it starts with the belief that the world should not be accepted as is, and that we have a responsibility to make it better.

Yet judgment is different in its dynamic experience from the creative will. Here we muster not just our courage but also our intellect, imagination, and moral instinct to understand how things really ought to be; here we assume a position of humility rather than presumption, of patience in action and impatience in thought, because we are searching for a right answer. We start out assuming that we do not already have the answer, but that neither do we have the luxury of abandoning the search, for moral understanding is attainable nonetheless.

These two aspects of the God of Creation—his creative intervention in the universe and his judgment of right from wrong—combine into an exceptionally potent synthesis that is the heart of what the First Commandment is about: the principle of redemption.

Creativity without judgment is change and power for their own sake. In the best case it leads to indifference to others and addiction to the thrill of willfulness; in the worst case, to coherent, methodical evil. Judgment without creation, however, is static and passive, incapable of combating evil of any kind. Like two benign ingredients that react massively when combined, the combination of creativity and judgment yields something beyond both of them, something that sets the Hebrew Bible apart from anything else the ancient world produced, something capable of inspiring an entire world. On some level, redemption *is* the God of the First Commandment. When we accept redemption as an ideal for human behavior, we make him *our* God, regardless of whatever we may "believe" in terms of our faith.

If we consider God's behavior throughout the early books of the Bible, and the way he is spoken of by the prophets in the later books as well, we discover that redemption is the central defining feature of God's character. Where he exhibits emotions such as love and anger, these are always translated into righteous action rather than detached amusement, contemplative repose, or arbitrary willfulness. Everywhere that God reveals himself to us, it is for the purpose of improving the world—either by advising the patriarchs whose importance is bound up in the nations they will sire, or by chastising kings and leaders for their failure to make their nations good, or by intervening directly and miraculously to ensure the salvation of good people.

God always is moved to act, and he is always "right," not by definition but by intention, meaning that in every case there exists a standard of right and wrong against which he is held accountable. God, however, is not that standard: He is, rather, an ideal example of someone living up to that standard. This is a crucial distinction, one whose failure to be grasped has caused endless confusion among theologians. If God's will were good by definition, we would have a hard time understanding Abraham's haggling with him over Sodom and Gomorrah, or Moses' successful attempts to protect the Israelites from his anger. Our goal would not be to imitate him but to carry out his orders, blindly and in good faith—which is precisely what many interpretations of the biblical religion have demanded.[6] God is not the ultimate Commander but the ultimate Redeemer, an archetype, a model to inspire us.

God is not the Bible's only exemplar of the redemptive spirit, however. A very specific type of human hero also is constantly on display. What all the Old Testament's patriarchs, judges, and kings have in common is the idea that worldly deliverance comes from human intervention: from Noah, who builds an ark and saves the living world from destruction; to Abraham, who leaves civilization to found a new people and a new faith; to Moses, who leads this people out of bondage to freedom; to heroines like the judge Deborah, who leads the tribes in war; Yael who kills the evil King Sisera; and Esther, who becomes queen of Persia and saves her people from the murderous Haman; to righteous kings like David and Josiah; to tragic figures like Samson. Even when someone is explicitly known not for valor but for wisdom—someone like King Solomon—it turns out that such wisdom is found first of all in his righteous action rather than theoretical or legal mastery.

Not only bold leaders are revered. The Bible is filled with prophets, as well—men and women who carry a message from God, who have heard his words through a revelatory experience that is the product, apparently, of extensive training and devotion. But here too we find nothing like Buddha's call to self-detachment, or the Greek gods' whimsical one-upmanship, but rather a consistent message enjoining leaders and peoples to correct the ills of their world. Isaiah and Amos, Nathan and Ezekiel, Jeremiah and Jonah—all of them called upon individuals or peoples to correct their ways, to repent from sin, and to build a life on this earth under a vision of the good.

What the prophets share with the kings and judges is that all of them are engaged in a lifelong effort to imitate God as a redeemer, whether through actions or words. Indeed, in *The Guide for the Perplexed,* perhaps the most important work of rabbinic theology in the medieval period, Moses Maimonides asserts that bold, redemptive acts and prophetic words are really two sides of the same coin. The redemptive act is, in his view, a form of prophecy, for it is imbued with what the Bible calls the "spirit of God":

> The first degree of prophecy consists in the divine assistance which is given to a person, and induces and encourages him to do something good and grand, e.g., to deliver a congregation of

good men from the hands of evildoers; to save one noble person, or to bring happiness to a large number of people; he finds in himself the cause that moves and urges him to this deed. This degree of divine influence is called "the spirit of the Lord." . . . All the judges of Israel possessed this degree. . . . This faculty was always possessed by Moses from the time he had attained the age of manhood; it moved him to slay the Egyptian, and to prevent evil from the two men that quarreled; it was so strong that, after he had fled from Egypt out of fear, and arrived in Midian, a trembling stranger, he could not restrain himself from interfering when he saw wrong being done; he could not bear it.[7]

•　•　•

The declaration *I am the Lord your God,* in other words, proclaims the centrality of redemption—as an ideal and as a mandate for our lives. That this is the real meaning behind the First Commandment becomes even clearer when we read the second half of the verse: *who took you out of Egypt, from the house of slaves.*

What should be obvious here is that the exodus from Egypt is, simply, the central story of redemption in the entire Bible. The whole story takes up the better part of five biblical books, Exodus through Joshua, and may be the most stirring catharsis the ancient world has to offer. God is given one shot, as it were, to describe himself in the First Commandment, and of all the possible self-introductions, he chose this one.

In the exodus story, two redemptions are described: God's intervention to save Israel from slavery and to lead them to freedom, and the Israelites' own efforts to save themselves.

That God is above all an exemplar of the redemptive spirit seems so overwhelmingly evident from the story of the exodus that it seems almost as though this, rather than the creation of the universe, is his crowning achievement in the whole Bible. God here is the ultimate redeemer. He "hears Israel's cries" as they suffer in slavery; he appears before Moses in the burning bush and instructs him on how to act; he brings the plagues upon Egypt; he parts the Red Sea as the Israelites are being chased by Pharaoh's army; he leads them to Sinai where they receive the two tablets; he guides them through the desert where they learn the fundamentals of nationhood, from government to warfare to worship; and he takes them on a path to ultimate victory and freedom. Indeed, gratitude to God for the exodus and the journey to the Promised Land constitutes the central theme of Judaism's three major festivals, and whose retelling occupies the entirety of the traditional Passover night celebration.

Yet in all this divine succor, man is anything but passive; indeed, what makes the exodus story so crucial for understanding the First Commandment is not so much God's interventions as those of so many individuals whose heroic efforts make the difference between success and failure.

At the center is, of course, Moses, who must repeatedly overcome impossible conditions—his origins as a newborn male of Israel decreed to die by Pharaoh's order, his exile in the desert after killing an Egyptian who was beating an Israelite slave to death, his speech impediment that made him an unlikely leader, and above all, the infuriating reluctance of the Israelites to be saved.

But there are many other individuals who undertake bold, redemptive acts. We have Jethro, a Midianite desert-king who takes Moses in during the latter's early exile from Egypt, during which time he is exposed to the burning bush and the entire idea of the exodus is presented to him, and who later becomes Moses' father-in-law and personal adviser in the desert, where

he successfully promotes what were arguably the most important governmental reforms in ancient Israel's history. Women
play a conspicuous role in the exodus as well: Whether it is the
Israelite midwives Shifra and Pua, who risk their lives to save
the Israelite babies; or Jochebed, who hides her newborn child,
Moses, avoiding detection by the murderous Egyptian authorities; or the daughter of Pharaoh, who takes Moses in and raises
him despite his evident Israelite origins; or Moses' big sister,
Miriam, who stands watch as the baby floats down the river in a
basket, and then initiates the plan by which Jochebed will serve
as wet nurse to Pharaoh's daughter, hiding the fact that she is the
baby's true mother.

Indeed, so central is the role of the human redeemer throughout the exodus epic that the rabbinic tradition emphasized the
role of redemptive individuals even where the original text
seems to be stressing God's actions rather than man's. In the
parting of the Red Sea, God saves Israel in the most dramatic
fashion. With Pharaoh's chariots barreling down against them,
the slave-mass of Israelites find themselves pinned against the
banks of the sapphire sea with only a pillar of smoke between
them and the pursuing hordes. God tells Moses to put forth his
staff, and the sea parts, creating walls of raging waters on either
side with a dry seabed path offering an unthinkable escape.

In the rabbinic retelling, however, the sea does not part immediately. Rather, it is Nachshon, son of Aminadav, chief of the
tribe of Judah, who must literally take the plunge, wading into
the seething brine in an act of apparent lunacy (slaves in Egypt,
we may presume, were not expert swimmers). Only when the
waters reached his nose, the rabbis tell us, did they part.[8]

The implications of this legend are clear: God may offer
opportunities for miraculous salvation; but only when man
plays his own role as redeemer, through a courageous act of

righteous initiative, will he make the transition from slave to human being and fulfill the mandate of the First Commandment. The tribe of Judah, of course, is a powerful symbol: It is this tribe's patriarch, Judah son of Jacob, who displays consistent and effective leadership in the book of Genesis, saving his brother Joseph from certain death after the brothers cast him into a pit, showing humility and responsibility after his affair with his daughter-in-law Tamar, and playing a decisive role twenty years later in reuniting the brothers after Joseph has separated from them in Egypt. It is from his loins that the kings of Israel, including David, Solomon, and the future Messiah, are destined to emerge. As chief of the tribe of Judah during Moses' time, Nachshon is the heir to this legacy, and it is no surprise that for centuries thereafter, the figure of Nachshon came to symbolize daring and redemptive deeds.

But if this is right, then the First Commandment really is not about God at all. An infinite number of things may be said about the infinite God, the God of the philosophers and theologians, the God who is omnipotent and omniscient and all-encompassing, the God who may be studied and dissected forever. But none of these are the message of the First Commandment.

It is, rather, a message about who we can be, about what every one of us, to some degree, is capable of. What the First Commandment teaches us is that just as God is at heart a redeemer, so too are we, each of us, potential redeemers. Deep inside, we all possess the capacity for creation and judgment, the ability to understand our world, to imagine it better, and to act in its improvement, even in directions where humanity has never gone. We can indeed re-create ourselves each and every day, and re-create our world as well, each of us playing a unique role in, and experiencing our own version of, the trek through the desert and into the Promised Land.

Many of us are resistant to the redemptive calling. Life, we tell ourselves, is hard enough as it is—caring for children and a spouse and parents and our health and our homes and our finances and our careers—without having to worry about other people's troubles.

Yet both the Bible and the rabbinic tradition that followed always insisted that no matter how hard life becomes, we never have the luxury of abandoning the redemptive perspective. Though the Old Testament offers a long list of rules and regulations, many of which no longer speak to us, the central message of the Ten Commandments seems to be that God's word is one that ordinary people can follow if we only set our minds to it. "The Torah was not given to the ministering angels," the rabbis taught.[9] According to rabbinic tradition, Mount Sinai was neither the highest nor the lowest mountain in the region, but a medium-sized one, symbolizing the average person to whom the Ten Commandments were addressed.[10]

The power of the Ten Commandments, in other words, derives not from their impossibly high standards but from the insistence that real human beings, with all their faults and failings, can improve themselves and the world around them.

The jarring truth is that the revelation of God in the First Commandment is, above all, a revelation about ourselves. When the child in the forest looks into the eyes of his partisan father, he recognizes them not just because of the old photos he has seen, but mainly because they are *his own eyes*. In discovering that the redeemer is his father, the child learns about who he himself is, about what he is ultimately capable of being, a lesson he will carry with him for the rest of his life, using his father's example as a measure for his own behavior.

In hearing the First Commandment, we recognize God not just because of the old stories about Abraham and Moses, or because of our commitments to one religious faith system or another. We recognize him because his eyes are our own.

The First Commandment raises more questions than it answers. What does it actually mean to be a "redeemer"? How do we instill in ourselves the redemptive spirit without sacrificing who we really are? How do we tell good from evil? And how does the ideal of redemption apply to our world—to our relationships with family, friends, community, and beyond?

As we shall see in the chapters that follow, it is one thing to recognize this redemptive potential in each of us, quite another to understand it thoroughly, to put it into practice in a meaningful and consistent way. The First Commandment sets the tone, making the boldest possible statement about who God is and what kind of example he sets for us. As such, it lays the groundwork for the entire Ten Commandments, in which the redemptive spirit is explored and elaborated on and applied to every significant area of our lives—morality, integrity, the self, wisdom, life, love, wealth, community, and inner peace.

Yet the redemptive spirit is not itself to be taken for granted. Profound forces are at work today seeking to undermine our belief in one or more of its component parts. We are told that there is no point in worldly or political action, or that the individual self is an illusion, that we have no right to judge right from wrong, or simply that our careers and hobbies are more important than our inner character or the communities around us. There are competing beliefs about "character" as well, some of which push toward a kind of servility to authority or fashion or the workplace, while others place self-expression, rather than improvement, above everything. One by one, a great many of the traditional building blocks of the redemptive spirit have come under brutal critique, and the results have been a steady erosion of our will and ability to struggle for a better world.

Of all these, however, none has been more profound, or potentially more dangerous, than the attack on the concept of moral truth—that there is such a thing as a "better" world at all. To understand what is at stake requires a close look at the Second Commandment, and its prohibition of idolatry.

2

Morality and Loneliness

You shall have no other gods besides me. You shall not make for yourself a carved idol, or any likeness of any thing that is in heaven above, or that is in the earth below, or that is in the water under the earth. You shall not bow down to them, nor serve them. For I the Lord your God am a jealous god, punishing the iniquity of the fathers upon the children unto the third and fourth generations of those that hate me, but showing mercy to thousands of generations of those that love me, and keep my commandments.

There is probably nothing in the Old Testament more alien to modern readers than its relentless assault on idol worship. Across the long arc of the biblical text, in its stories, laws, psalms, aphorisms, and prophetic speeches, there resonates the theme of the evils of idolatry and the need to rid the world of its charms. Kings are judged by God principally on their success in getting rid of the "high places," "Asherot," and "Baalim" sites of idolatrous service. Nations are taken to task for their worship of false gods. Prophets describe idolatry as a betrayal of God, so awful as to merit the destruction of the Israelite kingdoms and the expulsion of the Chosen People from the Promised Land.

What's so bad about idolatry? If the Ten Commandments contain the inner core of the biblical teaching, and they are ultimately about helping us become good people and build a good society, what difference does it make how and what one worships? What does faith have to do with morals?

In the view of the Second Commandment, the answer is: Everything. The Bible's assault on idolatry is derived from its broader concern for morality, a powerful idea that lies at the bedrock of the entire biblical approach to life.

The ancient world was full of gods that represented the most glaring goods and evils that man faced—nature, the power of the state, death. Proper behavior meant pleasing these gods, mainly through obeisance, flattery, and careful conduct. In the words of one scholar describing ancient Egypt, "The ideal picture is that of a correct man, who wisely avoids impulse and fits himself by word and deed into the administrative and social systems. . . . No moral concepts like good and bad come into discussion here." In Mesopotamia, too, the measure of a man's goodness was his obedience to authority, especially the authority of the god-ruler.[1] Good behavior, in other words, was derived not from any higher idea of right and wrong but from whatever the powers of the world dictated.

At the heart of the Bible's rejection of idolatry rests a simple claim: There exists an independent moral measure, a standard for right and wrong that is above our own wills and whims, and beyond the natural and human powers we encounter around us. Just as there is one God of Israel, who is not of this world and cannot be seen, so is there also one moral truth that cannot be seen—it is on a different plane from the worldly goods of power, beauty, and riches. Idolatrous gods, on the other hand, are rooted in our own experience and are invented by people; they are in principle multiple guides, implying a relativism of morality and a dependence on human authority to tell us what to do. To worship them, in the biblical view, is to deny not only faith but goodness as well.

For this reason, throughout the Bible we find a direct link made between idolatry and immorality. Idolatrous practice is repeatedly called "abomination" (*toevah*), a term also used to describe the worst moral deviations. The first person described as owning idols is Jacob's uncle Laban, whose principal role in the story is to deal dishonestly with Jacob, tricking him into working seven years for Rachel's hand in marriage, only to switch the bride with her sister Leah at the last minute, forcing him to work another seven years for his beloved.

Many of the later biblical stories, as well, are devoted to the connection between idolatry and immorality, where the assumption is that the real problem with idols is that they turn us into bad people. After the destruction of one of the two Israelite kingdoms, the northern kingdom of Israel, at the hands of the Assyrians in the eighth century B.C.E., the remaining southern kingdom of Judea struggles alone through a period of decline that is both theological and moral. The worst of their leaders is the evil King Menasseh, the son of Hezekiah, who institutes a vast array of idolatrous practices, from altars to the Baal to ritual worship of the sun and moon, to soothsaying and divination, to sacrificing his own son to the gods. As the text in II Kings is quick to point out, however, Menasseh's practices are not a harmless deviation from the monotheistic norm, but the necessary precursor to intolerable moral decay. "And Menasseh also shed so much innocent blood, until he had filled Jerusalem with it from one end to the other" (II Kings 21:16).

The rabbinic tradition, which emerged after most of the idols had turned to dust, recognized the importance of the Second Commandment for the whole idea of morality. In the view of one sage, to reject it was tantamount to rejecting all Ten Commandments; another described idolatry as a rejection of the whole Bible. In a third passage, the rabbis declared that "whoever repudiates idolatry is called a Jew." And in one case, a fellow named Micah, depicted in the book of Judges as having built a temple around a statue of silver, was retroactively absolved of his sin by the rabbis. "Why was Micah not counted among the wicked?" they asked. "Because he offered his bread to travelers."[2] By discounting Micah's actual idol worship on account of his generosity, the rabbis were essentially saying that his commitment to a moral standard showed he was innocent of the worst parts of the crime.

What is an idol?

An idol is anything that we focus on and worship with all our might, bending ourselves to its will. It can be a person, a body of nature such as the sun or moon, or something we produce ourselves—a statue, an institution, a job, a flag, or an idea. What all these have in common is that they distract us from God—that is, they take our minds off the basic idea of right and wrong that underlies the redemptive ideal.

The Second Commandment's main aim is to warn us against all those forces in life that absorb our attention, make moral choices feel easier than they are, and distract us from being good people. It is phrased in a way that made the most sense at the time: People would carve images of their gods; the ban on graven images is a ban on worship of anything other than God himself, since God has no image. And because these gods were perceived as powerful, God of the Second Commandment had to flex his own muscles as well, declaring himself to be "jealous" and willing to punish his enemies "unto the third and fourth generations."

But beneath all this posturing, the central message of the Second Commandment has little to do with God's jealousy or punishments. Any symbol we carve for ourselves carries the risk of distracting us from the redemptive ideal, from the idea of a better world.

We no longer worship idols the way people did during the time of the Bible. But idolatry, in the most important sense of the term, has not disappeared. If anything, it has taken new forms, forms that make it an integral part of our modern world, forms that make the Second Commandment every bit as urgent today as it was when Moses first proclaimed it to the Israelites. We are still, many of us, idolaters in one way or another, even if we believe in God.

Of all the stories in the Bible, the most important one for understanding the Second Commandment is that of the Golden Calf, which appears in Exodus shortly after the Ten Commandments are given. The Golden Calf is the Bible's archetypical case of idolatry, and we should not be surprised to discover that both Jewish and Christian commentators have overwhelmingly seen it as some kind of paradigm for the problem of evil considered more broadly. "Every generation," the rabbis taught, "contains within it an ounce of the Golden Calf."[3]

Immediately upon receiving the Ten Commandments, Moses faces an impossible moral challenge. He is still up on the mountain, having just been given the two tablets and a long list of additional commandments concerning rituals, civil laws, and the Sabbath, when suddenly God says to him, "Go, get you down, for your people, which you brought up out of the land of Egypt, have become corrupt. . . . They have made them a molten calf, and have worshipped it, and have sacrificed to it, and said, 'This is your god, O Israel, that brought you up out of Egypt'" (Exodus 32:7–8). As he descends the mountain, Moses sees the Golden Calf and the wild dancing and celebration that the Israelites are holding for the new god they have made.

No person on earth has ever felt as alone as Moses did at that moment. The Ten Commandments did not come with a user's manual. God may have told Moses that idolatry was evil and could not be tolerated, but he says nothing about how it was to be overcome, or what to do if Moses returns to Israel only to find that the Ten Commandments no longer have an audience. God, for his part, is so angry about the calf that he tells Moses he wants to kill all the Israelites and build a new nation out of Moses—a threat that Moses successfully talks him out of. God's solution is unbearably extreme, but on the other hand the people are no longer with Moses. He needs an answer, and fast.

The commitment to moral truth means sometimes consigning ourselves to a loneliness that has no parallel. All of us reach moments in life when we are forced to make intense moral decisions, when the choice of action is ours, the consequences infinite, and time limited. A father or mother must decide whether to listen to the doctors pressing for a risky operation on their child or to those who caution restraint; a manager whose budget has been cut must decide whom to fire; a commander must decide whether to send his soldiers into a dangerous battle. The moral decision may be the most painful moment in our lives.

There are two easy ways out of any moral question, both of which make the loneliness disappear in an instant. One is to detach ourselves, concluding that there is no true answer, that life is absurd and ultimately our decisions don't matter all that much, and that no dilemma justifies the kind of anguish we put ourselves through. The other is to shift responsibility onto someone else—a pastor or rabbi, a group of friends or advisers or revered teachers, an ancient text—and to conclude that if these dictate one course and not another, it is good enough for us. In either case, often we reach an answer we can "live with," not because we know deep down that we are right, but because we no longer have to feel the searing loneliness of Moses descending the mountain.

The commitment to moral truth means recognizing this loneliness, not as something to be feared and avoided, but as a healthy indicator of our belief in two seemingly contradictory things: That there is a right answer; and that nobody, not even God, can give it to us on a platter. That while right and wrong are outside us, waiting to be discovered, the authority and responsibility to render moral judgments reside entirely in ourselves; that if and when we are one day held to account for our decisions, there will be no philosophers or teachers or preachers to hide behind as we face judgment.

We can hardly imagine what must have gone through Moses' mind during those crucial minutes. He held in his hands the very teachings of God, the revelation of which had been the entire purpose of leaving the slavery of Egypt. Yet he now faced a nation no longer ready to receive them, a nation that had slid back into the idolatrous ways of the Egyptians, to the bacchanalia and the gold and silver, to the whirlwind of depravity that they were supposed to have left behind, to spiritual enslavement. The tablets he held were, at once, both infinite in value and worthless. What was he to do?

At that crucial moment, the rabbis teach us, the tablets began to feel heavy in Moses' hands.

• • •

But while Moses was suffering the loneliness of the moral choice, the Israelites were rejoicing in the communal warmth of its abdication.

Moses had been on the mountain too long. His people had suffered the horrors of slavery, and had been through the twin trials of the escape from Egypt and the journey into the forbidding wilderness. But now they faced a different sort of trial: the trial of waiting, waiting for their leader to return, waiting for someone who had disappeared into the darkness more than a month ago, with no sign of ever coming back. The people were showing signs of impatience, perhaps even rebellion. The leaders of the tribes approached Moses' brother, Aaron, with a plan.

> And when the people saw that Moses delayed to come down from the mountain, the people gathered themselves to Aaron and said to him, "Up, make us a god, which shall go before us; as for this man Moses, who brought us up out of Egypt, we know not what is become of him."
>
> And Aaron said to them, "Break off the golden earrings, which are in the ears of your wives, of your sons, and of your daughters, and bring them to me." And all the people broke off the golden earrings which were in their ears, and brought them to Aaron. And he received the gold at their hand, and fashioned it with a graving tool and made a molten calf, and they said, "This is your god, O Israel, that brought you up out of Egypt." (Exodus 32:1–4)

Usually the Bible portrays sinners in unequivocal terms, but here it goes out of its way to show us the sin from the perspective of the sinner, to show us how reasonable the whole affair seemed at the time.

Indeed, the Golden Calf was the perfect solution to an acute human problem. Human beings want and need symbols to rally around; after a month of waiting for a leader who might never return, the calf gave them the concreteness, the presence, the focus of worship that humans inevitably need in order to withstand their trials. The Israelites, for all their freedom, still faced a long trek through the desert, and then would have to conquer hostile lands in order to found their state. All this seemed far beyond their abilities, and what is leadership if not giving people the symbols, words, and figures to rally around in order to withstand hardship?

For any other people at any other time, the Golden Calf might well have been a very good answer. This was far from the worst of the idols that the Israelites would encounter among the cultures around them. There was only one calf, so the theological problem of multiple gods had been sidestepped. We do not know of any particularly egregious practices associated with it. As religion, the calf was far more "progressive" than what they had left behind in Egypt or what they would encounter in the Promised Land.

The problem with the calf, rather, was how different it was from God. The Israelites abandoned an invisible deity for a visible one, a God that was beyond their control and imagination for one they had invented and could now parade through their camp, a sublime being for a lump of gold. In this change alone, they had already abandoned not only God but morality as well.

The Golden Calf represents all the forces of life that distract us from the lonely morality that Moses faced on the mountain, from the invisible morality of the invisible God. Life has its own logic: It is filled with attractions and distractions that convince us, each in its own way, that we really do not need a higher sense of right and wrong to guide us. Animals instinctively do what they need to in order to survive and thrive. But morality is an attempt to raise man above the level of animals, to give humanity a life that is somehow higher, better. In exploring the nature of idolatry, the Bible focuses on three main problems, three forces that have enough good in them to convince us that they deserve our allegiance. All three of these converge in the Golden Calf.

They are: power, beauty, and the works of our hands.

Idolatry first emerged as a way of explaining the mysteries of the world. Man looked about himself and found too much that was beyond explanation: the sun, moon, and stars; the changing of the seasons; the roar of the seas; fire and thunder and rain. These were explained as being either gods or controlled by gods. And then, in an effort to bring some sense of control to man, it was asserted that people, or at least some people, could influence the decisions of these gods through sacrifices, temples, and other rituals.

Idolatry, in other words, begins as a way of dealing with the powers of the universe. This is especially evident in Greek mythology: Helios controlled the sun, Poseidon the oceans, Zeus the sky, Dionysus the fruits of the vine, Eros the passions. These gods usually had temples dedicated to their worship, and they were hungry for humans to declare their loyalty through ritual service.

In this context, we can easily understand the inclination to idolatry. It is born of fear, of an existential reality in which every individual may live or die according to forces beyond his control. Much like someone who changes his diet or takes medication because he heard it might reduce the risk of contracting some awful disease, people back then did not claim to have mastered the heavens when they appealed to their gods. They were just doing their best to stay alive.

According to the rabbinic tradition, it was Abraham who first discovered the power-logic of idolatry. As legend has it, Abraham is sent off by his father to meet King Nimrod, the Mesopotamian tyrant, who challenges Abraham to a debate:

> [Nimrod said to Abraham]: Let us worship the fire. Abraham said to him: If so, let us worship the water, which puts out fire.
>
> Nimrod answered him: Then let us worship the water. [Abraham] said to him: If so, then let us worship the clouds, which carry the water.
>
> [Nimrod] answered: So let us worship the clouds. [Abraham] said to him: If so, let us worship the wind, which disperses the clouds.
>
> [Nimrod] answered: So let us worship the wind. [Abraham] said to him: If so, let us worship man, who breathes the wind.
>
> [Nimrod] said to him: This is idle chatter! I will worship the fire after all—and I will throw you into it. Let the God whom you worship come and save you![4]

With every argument, Abraham takes the power-logic of idolatry to a next step, and the king is forced to go along: Water is more powerful than fire, clouds more than water, wind more than clouds. When Abraham reaches the fourth step, he reveals his real point: When morality is dictated by power, ultimately it is man's own power that is really behind it all. The worship of power will always come down to the worship of men who possess it. To worship power is to be a slave to others.[5]

The king cannot stand having the lie revealed, for it is this very lie upon which his own life is based, as an idol-king in an ancient land. He throws Abraham into the furnace—itself a symbol of human power, the very place where gods are forged. Yet in the end Abraham miraculously survives, because even in his darkest moment, he refuses to let go of the belief that power is not, can never be, the measure of all things.

Much of our world is still dominated by tyrants and power-hungry rulers who, like Nimrod, bend their citizens to their will with the threat of force. In free societies, however, the temptation of power worship is felt most keenly in the workplace, where servility and the reduction of the individual to the role of a soulless cog have become so widely accepted as to be seen by many people as the cornerstone of the employer-employee relationship, the very engine of economic growth. For many bosses, it is not the employee's job to worry about whether the way people are treated is right or wrong, about whether corners are cut to save money at the expense of safety, about whether the advertisements are misleading customers or reports are misleading shareholders. The employee, we are told, is not paid to think.

Such a logic frequently puts people in the position where in order to succeed they have to distort their judgments of right and wrong to the point where they subordinate their moral sense to the advancement of the company—and to their own advancement within the company. We all know people like this, people who will lie, spy, or actively damage the reputation of others in order to get ahead. Or we may even do these things ourselves, convinced that these are the "rules of the game," that our first obligation is to ourselves and the families we are supporting, and that we need to do whatever it takes to care for our own.

Why do we let this happen to us? Because we are afraid—afraid of failing to impress our "superiors," afraid of wrecking our chances for a comfortable life, afraid of losing our jobs, and with them both our self-worth and our financial security. The same fear that gripped the ancient farmers who prayed to the rain gods for their sustenance grips us as well.

But as we all know, fear is often exceptionally hard to overcome, if only for the simple reason that many things really are worth fearing, and overcoming means first of all knowing how to tell the difference between real and false dangers, and how to adopt a healthy attitude toward the real ones. Power is a fact of life. Our fears about making a living, about war, about personal safety, or about getting fired are all often legitimate, because life is not an illusion but the essence of who we are. To cut ourselves off completely from fear requires a detachment from the most important things, a refusal to consider important the basic elements of life—sustenance, health, security, and safety—a detachment that itself is inimical to goodness. Moreover, we all know power can often be a good thing: One cannot effect change without power (by definition), and when the good are powerless, the good they can do is extremely limited.

At the same time, the fear of power, the pursuit of power, the exercise of power all have the intense capacity to convince us that there is no truth other than power itself. Taken too far, it makes genuine moral judgment impossible. It is the worship not of God but of men.

Defeating idolatry means being stronger than fear, stronger than the powers that threaten our prosperity, stronger than all those people who will look down on us for clinging to our conscience. It means not ignoring these threats but placing a strict limit on their ability to affect our judgment. It means never losing our acute moral sense, never allowing fear to define who we really are, never allowing ourselves to become enslaved—even at the risk of losing our jobs, our public standing, or our closest relationships. Defeating the power-logic of idolatry, in other words, is the hardest thing in the world.

Yet even if we succeed in overcoming all this, there are other aspects of the Golden Calf that blind us to right and wrong. The calf was also immensely beautiful, a rich work of pure gold that stood out stunningly against the bleak wilderness of Sinai. The Bible next warns us about the enticements of the beautiful things of this world.

Should one kiss with one's eyes closed?

Lovers may debate this to no end, but there is a question here more profound than romance: what role we give visual data in our perception of truth. For a kiss is no less an experience than an action, and we seek truth in this experience—the truth of another's love. Some cannot experience the truth of the kiss without seeing a lover's eyes; others find seeing as somehow distracting from truth, an imposition of stimulus that can distort the experience by drowning out other senses.

There is of course reason on both sides. Sight is our most powerful sense, containing the most information, guiding our every move. At the same time, we will distrust it when it might interfere with the true perception of experience. When smelling a wine, searching for a gas leak, checking if the milk has gone bad, or listening to a work of music, we often close our eyes to focus intently on the scent or sound.

This duality of sight—at once revelatory and distracting—appears in the Hebrew Bible in full force. Like the religions of the East, the Bible distrusts the senses, taking the view that they inevitably threaten in their sheer intensity the very existence of a moral plane in the human conscience. Yet unlike those systems of belief, the Bible never takes such distrust to the extreme of rejection or declaration that the world itself is illusory. We are human, and our lives are nurtured by stimuli of the spirit, including beauty. We draw upon the aesthetic but are never to worship it; on the contrary, we recognize its source in life, and in the Creator who gave life.

For this reason, the Bible never rejects outright either beauty or the senses. God proves his presence to Israel through visible signs and wonders. Moses discovers God through the sight of a burning bush; God leads the Israelites through the desert with a pillar of fire; they are healed in the desert by looking at the copper snake held by Moses; they are reminded of God's commandments by a thread of blue in the corners of their garments. The rabbinic tradition, too, often affirmed the inner truth that beauty entails. "Three things deepen a man's understanding," the rabbis taught. "A beautiful home, a beautiful wife, and beautiful clothes." The rabbis cautioned us never to describe ourselves as unattractive, and always to take advantage of the beauty of this world.[6]

On the other hand, the biblical and rabbinic traditions understood that people are often mesmerized by beauty, that they look for the divine in it, and that this is one of the major challenges of the idols—that in their beauty they convince us of their truth. "The decisive moment in the erection of an idol," writes the French philosopher Jean-Luc Marion, "stems . . . from its investment as gazeable, as that which will fill a gaze. . . . The first intention aims at the divine, and the gaze strains itself to see the divine."[7] For this reason, idols in the Bible are frequently called "gods of silver and gods of gold," emphasizing their beauty. One of the most ready sources of our moral downfall is our willingness to subordinate our moral sense to the beauty of the world. "Do not stray after your hearts and after your eyes, which you go whoring after," we are instructed. "So that you shall remember, and perform all my commandments, and you shall be holy for your God" (Numbers 15:39–40). We often "go whoring" after the sights of our eyes, which entice us not merely to appreciate beauty but also to worship it.

The overcoming of beauty is found at the center of Jewish ritual worship. On the holiest day of the year, Yom Kippur,

Jews stand before the judgment of God and pray for atonement for sins. In the ancient Temple service, the high priest would, on this day only, enter the Holy of Holies and utter the divine name. But before doing so, he would shed his garments of gold, which served him the rest of the year, and put on clothes entirely of white. The rabbis interpreted this as a direct response to the problem of idolatry:

> Rabbi Simon said in the name of Rabbi Yehoshua: Why does the high priest not enter the Holy of Holies in his garments of gold? . . . To avoid feeding arguments to Satan, who [in trying to get God to punish Israel] might say, "Yesterday they worshipped gods of gold, and today they want to serve you in garments of gold?"[8]

By setting strict limits to the employment of beauty in the service of God, the Bible teaches us to recognize that beauty, while important and true and amazing, is ultimately deceitful if we allow it to displace our moral perspective, if it becomes an idol. The garments of white serve as a powerful reminder that we have fallen, in the past, to the sway of beauty, and that we should limit it to its proper place when addressing the ultimate questions of our lives.

For many centuries, Western civilization has struggled with the relationship between beauty and morality. For Plato, beauty was identical to the good. One must therefore learn to appreciate the beauty of nature, he taught, as a first step toward understanding moral truth. Catholic theology affirmed this approach: Augustine called beauty "but the fragmentary solace allowed us in a life condemned to misery" and suggested that the human body was so utterly beautiful and balanced that "in the creation of the human body God put form before function." Throughout the Renaissance and into the modern period, beauty, understood as the imitation of nature, was seen as approaching the heights of the human experience. Keats famously wrote that " 'beauty is truth, truth beauty'—that is all ye know on earth, and all ye need to know."

Yet most of us know there is something wrong with this equation. We examine the specimens of fashion in magazines or the emaciated models on the runways of Paris or New York; we notice that almost every news reporter, advertising figure, pop star, or politician is better looking than average, skinnier than average, better dressed than average; we are shown endless images of beautiful people and cars and homes and vacation spots aimed at getting us to spend our money a certain way—yet we know there is nothing guaranteeing that these people or things are any more honest, kind, wise, or dependable than our less comely friends at work or synagogue or school. Life would be so much easier if we could judge a man's character entirely by the aesthetics of his face. But as with power, the linkage of beauty and truth is little more than the abdication of the harder moral questions in favor of what nature, and those who command it, lead us to believe.

We are right to feel ambivalent about the West's heritage of beauty. On the one hand, it has led us to understand the profound connection between nature and life, to appreciate the importance of a glowing, healthy body, to enjoy our world and its beautiful things to an extent otherwise impossible. Artistic beauty is indeed an imitation of nature, and nature is indeed often beautiful. Yet nature is not a god, but is God's creation. And what sounds here like a mere theological issue is pointedly a moral one: For to see nature as a product of God's creation rather than an ultimate truth is no different from seeing the power of others as a limited, if undeniable, force. The most beautiful society is not necessarily the best one, even if the best ones are likely to have their share of beauty in them.

We may wonder if Moses didn't hesitate, just for a moment, at the sight of the Golden Calf, a stunningly beautiful symbol of the Egyptian civilization he had left behind. Who wouldn't?

Beyond power and beauty, there is a third idolatrous factor, more insidious than the other two precisely because it comes from inside us and makes us feel almost like God himself. It is the force of *creation*—the inevitable appeal of the works of our own hands.

Creation, as we have seen, is an essential part of the redemptive spirit. But there is something about the creative process that can be perversely addictive. We create, and we are deeply attracted to what we have made. We see it as an affirmation of our worth, a validation of our uniqueness. We fall in love with our creations—and as a result, we identify too strongly with the houses we build, the music we write, the businesses we establish, or even the children we bring into this world. Instead of cultivating independent moral selves, we escape into our creations and wind up corrupting our world instead of improving it.

The Second Commandment warns us of the allure of our own creations. *You shall not make for yourself a carved idol*: Our idols are, first of all, things we make for ourselves. Perhaps the most common descriptions of them in the Bible are "works of wood and stone" and "works of your hands." "Cursed be the man who makes any carved or molten idol, an abomination to the Lord, the work of the hands of a craftsman, and sets it up in secret" (Deuteronomy 27:15). The prophet Jeremiah did everything in his power to convince Israelites of the falseness of gods fashioned by human hands:

For the customs of the people are vanity: A tree out of the forest is cut down, the work of the hands of the workman, with the axe. They deck it with silver and with gold; they fasten it with nails and with hammers, that it move not. They are like a rigid post, and they cannot speak; they must be carried, because they cannot walk. Be not afraid of them; for they cannot do evil, neither is it in them to do good. (Jeremiah 10:3–5)

The Bible's main response is to point out the fallacy, even the stupidity, of attributing divinity to things we have made. Isaiah berates the makers of idols, who take cedar, pine, and oak, grow and strengthen the wood, then put it to contradictory purposes that belie the worth of their endeavor:

Half of it he burns in the fire; with this half of it he eats meat; he roasts the roast, and is satisfied: Indeed he warms himself and says, "Aha, I am warm, I have seen the fire." And of the rest of it he makes a god, his carved idol. He falls down to it, and worships it, and prays to it, and says, "Deliver me, for you are my god." ... A deceived heart has turned him aside, that he cannot deliver his soul, nor say, Is there not a lie in my right hand? (Isaiah 44:16–20)

Isaiah's frustration here is not so much with the multiplicity of gods as with the inanity of worshipping our own creations. "The idols are . . . the work of men's hands," we read in Psalms. "They have mouths but cannot speak; eyes but cannot see; they have ears but cannot hear, noses but cannot smell, hands but cannot feel, legs but cannot walk; their throats utter not a word. Those who make them, or trust in them, shall become like them" (Psalms 115:4–8).

The direct result of worshipping our own creations, we learn, is that we risk becoming like them. Just as they are blind, deaf, and dumb, so too does our self-subordination to them limit our own judgment of right and wrong, giving us little to say to the world, rendering us incapable of seeing and hearing the realities around us. Earlier we saw that to say that God is "ours" means internalizing the redemptive principle that he represents; now we see that the same is true for the idols we produce: Whatever we make becomes our moral guide, a symbol of our inner truth. But if our moral guide is itself our own creation, then we are caught in a loop of self-affirmation, worshipping whatever we already think or feel, rather than searching for truth outside ourselves. We worship ourselves.

Modern culture pushes us to judge ourselves solely according to the works of our hands. The wealth and status we accumulate, the families we build, or the artistic works we produce all become idols when our basic self-assessment is bound up in them, when we subordinate all our principles and judgments to their success. But as we know too well, bad people can build successful businesses, raise successful kids, and make successful movies. The message of the Second Commandment is that everything we create can become an idol, and an honest look at our lives will reveal that many of us fall into the trap of worshipping the works of our hands every day.

How many of us have allowed ourselves to deceive other people in trying to protect our property, our homes, or our businesses?

How many of us have ignored the struggles of the passerby— an old man who needs a ride, a mother taking a heavy stroller down the stairs—because we were too protective of our time, too committed to achievement to stop and look at the opportunities for doing good that life gives us?

How many of us have, in trying to ensure the success of our children, encouraged them to lie on a college application, not caring that the example we set for them may be far worse for their moral character than any advantage they may gain from getting into the college of their choice?

How many of us have turned our backs on our friends when they faced a financial or personal crisis?

When we worship the works of our hands, we become enslaved to our own goals. Time and people become "resources" to be most effectively channeled toward our aims. Human interactions become instruments for our advancement: A meal becomes a meeting, a smile becomes a "massage" for someone's ego. We meet someone, evaluate his worth to our goal-driven lives, and when he does not measure up, we become neglectful and indifferent, justifying our behavior on the grounds that we have only so much time in the day, and a phone call returned to someone irrelevant means a more "important" phone call is left unreturned.

In worshipping the Golden Calf, the Israelites fell into the trap of worshipping their own creations. The people commissioned a god to be made, and then they bowed down to it. Nothing makes us feel more powerful, more beautiful, more divine, than the works of our hands.

We do not know how much of this was going through Moses' mind when he decided to smash the tablets bearing the Ten Commandments.

In doing so, Moses was not just teaching the Israelites a lesson. He was also fulfilling an inner need, responding to the loneliness of the moral decision with an act of self-redemption that was no less important than what he did for his people.

At that moment, Moses transformed himself from a bearer of

God's words to a perfectly free moral individual, from a disciple into a redeemer. One moment he was a symbol, a man carrying the Ten Commandments like a burden for his taskmaster, like a flag for the people to rally around, like a monument to God's one truth. The next moment, the tablets lay in ruins, and Moses stood alone, symbolizing nothing beyond himself. A mere man, having done an unthinkable act, representing the truth and loneliness of the moral decision that is entirely of ourselves. At that moment, the spell of the Golden Calf was broken, and all Israel's eyes were now on him.

The Ten Commandments and the Golden Calf cannot reside in the same world. Moses smashed the tablets because in the shadow of the Golden Calf, they too had become another symbol, another potential focus of worship. Even if he could persuade the Israelites to abandon the calf and accept his leadership, they would do it not as a free people committed to higher morals but as a bleating flock in search of another shepherd. It was in a sense an artistic act, expressing in the most resounding way the incompatibility of Israel's new idol with the moral message of God. It was also a political act, reasserting Moses' reign that had deteriorated completely in his absence. But above all it was an act of morality, for in destroying the tablets, he made room for a moral vision that is beyond symbols, a morality that is accessible to every individual but is above him, a morality that is invisible just like God. In destroying the symbol of the Ten Commandments, he was upholding their contents in the most stunning way. "Sometimes," the sages said about Moses' act, "one must destroy the Torah in order to establish it."[9]

Nothing frees us more than smashing our idols. And sometimes our idols are not just the Golden Calf, but also the two tablets themselves.

• • •

What emerges from all this is that morality according to the Old Testament is very different from what many people think it is. Our culture supplies us with an endless stream of righteous people, who make their morality into a calling card, parading their wholesome families, their spotless records, and their ability to formulate clear moral teachings. Some of them we see on television, stellar examples of the same idolatrous forces that the Bible seeks to uproot. Others live next door to us, hiding their sins behind a cloud of public uprightness and a vibrant, self-affirming moral glow.

It is enough to make anyone who knows better never want to hear the word "morality" again, to conclude that there is nothing so appalling as the very assertion that there is some kind of righteousness higher than the simple art of living one's life.

For many of us, the temptation to do without morality comes not from a principled rejection of the good but from a rebellion on the part of sensitive people who, having seen how subtle, complex, and painful life really is, cannot stand the facile outrage of the preacher or the ideologue, of the self-righteous neighbor for whom the answers to life's hardest questions seem to be always at hand, always formulated in clean, chlorinated sentences. Inevitably we discover that for these people, as well, life is never as easy as they make it seem, that they too must struggle with the distortions of power, beauty, and the works of their hands—a permanent struggle from which they do not always emerge victorious; indeed, to which they often seem oblivious.

In the Old Testament, morality is not a formula, with a clear yes or no that emerges in every situation. It is more of a disposition, an attitude toward life in which the easiest answers are frequently the wrong ones, in which real people grapple with unexpected situations, looking for guidance wherever they may find it. By telling us not to make graven images, the Second Commandment gives us a first step toward instilling in ourselves the moral attitude. If you can see it, smell it, feel it, hear it, become thrilled by its beauty or its power, if you fear it or have made it yourself and it gives you a rush of belonging, of facile yet stirring hope—it is probably an idol, and the truth lies somewhere beyond, as yet undiscovered.

As soon as we have internalized the moral attitude, we naturally begin to look at ourselves, to examine our moral and intellectual habits, to hunt down our inner idolatries. We want to uproot all those lies we have harbored, have told ourselves and others, have lived. We quickly find out that the immediate application of the Second Commandment translates into an unflinching quest for honesty, truth, and personal integrity. For this, however, we need the Third Commandment.

3

Our Lies Destroy Us

You shall not invoke the name of the Lord your God in vain. For the Lord shall not hold blameless one who invokes his name in vain.

The first and last time I had a job in sales was the summer of 1988. I was nineteen years old and found myself in one of the hardest of hard-sell fields. Of all the things you can sell, nothing combines evocative dreams with affordable pricing like time-share condominiums—or, as we called it euphemistically, "vacation ownership."

The idea was straightforward. For $8,000, you received a deed that entitled you to one week of every year in a gorgeous New England vacation spot with world-class skiing in winter and rolling, majestic green mountains and forests in summer and fall. You owned this week of vacation for the rest of your life and could even pass it on to your children. And to make the package even sweeter, the resort was part of an international network, and every year you could trade your week for a similar week at hundreds of other resorts around the world.

My job was to sell this. We sent out invitations to thousands of people, who would come to our sales center to hear a three-hour presentation, at the end of which they would receive a "television" or a "computer," even if they didn't buy. For three hours, we subjected them to a comprehensive experience aimed at manipulating their senses, exciting their imagination, tricking them into divulging their financial status, and ultimately getting them to buy something they had no intention of buying when they first showed up. To make sure we could sell the resort in the most convincing way, we were each treated to an overnight visit at the resort, which inevitably made us believers. And to ease our consciences, the sales manager emphasized how important this product would be in the lives of our customers, and how careful we would be to follow the requirements of state laws protecting them from fraud.

"You may lie about everything," the sales manager told us on the first day, "except the product."

And lie we did. Under the framework of being honest about the "product," we became masters of manipulation. Very few of us started the job with real sales experience, but many of us had traveled abroad, and in slow hours we traded stories about places we'd been to and then incorporated our friends' adventures into our pitch as if they had been our own. By summer's end, all of us had been on luxurious trips to Cancún and Aruba, Tel Aviv and Milan, Scotland and Australia.

The manager also taught us all the tricks of breaking down a skeptical customer's resistance to buying. The first half hour was spent "warming up," sharing our personal experiences and asking questions about theirs to build their trust, lowering their guard in every way possible, getting them to say things that would later be used against them—such as how much they could afford to spend on vacations. We became our customers' best friends, showing them how they were doing irreparable harm to their financial well-being by continuing to pay for those increasingly expensive trips, offering projections about how within ten years a vacation would be about as affordable as a Lamborghini. Later, after they had been impressed by the photographs of our resort and blown away by the video about the network, we would start talking about our low monthly payments. Then, at a carefully chosen moment, we would bring in the sales manager, who would slash the price by 30 percent before their eyes, just for them, but only if they signed now. Under the blistering pressure of the slickest sales stratagems, enough of the customers signed on to make it the most profitable summer of my life.

Was there anything wrong with this? On one level, everything in the company seemed on the up-and-up. Certainly this was not the worst kind of salesmanship—there are plenty of people out there who intentionally deceive, if not lie outright, about what they are selling. Anyone who has ever been lied to by a salesman knows how awful it feels to have been knowingly sold a bad used car. But we were honest about the product, and we convinced ourselves that this was good enough to keep a clear conscience. Given truthful information, we reasoned, mature adults can make a decision, even if it is a bad one. Ultimately they, not the salesperson, are responsible for what they buy. Aren't they?

Yet on another level, a human level, looking back there was something deeply troubling about what we were doing.

We were not just selling a product. We were representing ourselves to other people in a way that was deliberately false, a phony version of our lives, thoughts, feelings, and beliefs all crafted for the sole purpose of making the sale. In order to extract their checkbooks from their pockets, we created an environment, a context, and a narrative all geared toward convincing them that their previous financial decisions had been wrong, when in fact we had no idea who they were and what they had been through; that the international vacation network would open the door to the most luxurious experiences imaginable, when in fact none of us owned the time-share or had used the network. Our projections about what vacations would one day cost were transparently preposterous, and the manager was not slashing the price at the end because both he and the client had worked in the fire department or served in Korea, but because it was part of an act. And when we got to the end of the session, our prey would finally discover that the "computer" or "television" was a mere shadow of what the word implied, junk electronics just functional enough to avoid a lawsuit. Even if we were technically truthful about the "product," we were deceiving them almost every moment we spent with them.

But the real question was not so much what we were doing to our customers. It was: What we were doing to ourselves?

The Third Commandment prohibits making false oaths, and in the process establishes personal integrity as a core value of the redemptive society. In the ancient world, people swore in the names of their gods whenever they wanted to prove their sincerity. To break an oath was to shatter one's name as a fundamentally reliable person—and to risk the wrath of not only man but also of all the mysterious forces in the universe.

Although every society is committed to honesty on some level, few of our ancient texts devote so much energy to it as the Old Testament. "You shall distance yourself from lying words," we read in Exodus 23:7, suggesting that deception is not just a simple question of truth and falsehood, but something spacious, that you can be closer to or farther from. We learn of prohibitions on false weights and measures, which merchants use to defraud their customers; on unexpectedly delaying wages to employees;

on taking unfair advantage of someone's extenuating circumstances, such as lending to the poor at interest or taking a poor person's clothing as collateral on a loan; on clandestinely adjusting the boundaries between your field and your neighbor's; on slander and perjury and fraud. And in the famous passage in Leviticus that begins, "You shall be holy, for I am holy, the Lord your God," we are told, among the list of behaviors that constitute holiness, "You shall not steal, nor deal falsely, nor lie to one another. And you shall not swear by my name falsely, neither shall you profane the name of your God; I am the Lord" (Leviticus 19:11–12). Here personal integrity is directly juxtaposed with false oaths: It is in a context of lying and cheating one another that false oaths become possible, and with them the collapse of society as a whole.

So terrible, indeed, are the consequences of dishonesty that the prophet Jeremiah attributed the obliteration of Judea and the destruction of Jerusalem—in short, the end of God's kingdom on earth—to the prevalence of lying:

> Oh, that I were in the wilderness, in a lodging place of wayfaring men, that I might leave my people, and go from them! . . . For they bend their tongues, their bow of falsehood: But they are not valiant for the truth upon the earth; for they proceed from evil to evil, and they know me not, says the Lord. Take heed everyone of his neighbor, and trust not in any brother: For every brother acts deceitfully, and every neighbor goes about with slanders. And they deceive everyone his neighbor, and do not speak the truth. . . . Therefore so says the Lord of Hosts, behold I will smelt them, and try them. (Jeremiah 9:1–6)

Taking its cue from the Bible, the rabbinic tradition held a similar disdain for deceivers. We are told, echoing Jeremiah, that Jerusalem was destroyed because of liars, that communities where lying is prevalent are cut off from the divine Presence, that lying is akin to idolatry, that liars will be punished the way Sodom and Gomorrah were, that "the Holy One hates" the liar.[1] The rabbinic legal discourses contain extensive prohibitions against improper business practice, fraud, and "theft of consciousness" (*gneivat da'at*), which refers to misleading another in commerce, such as faulty advertising. We are taught that when we die and are called upon to account for our lives, the first question we are asked is not one of belief or the fulfillment of religious ritual, but of our honesty in commerce; that the central sin for which God destroyed the earth at the time of the flood was dishonesty in day-to-day affairs; that defrauding another is worse than outright theft, for you assault the person's trust and not just his property. And just as employers are expected to treat their workers fairly and pay them on time, so does the employee have a solemn obligation to work diligently and efficiently for his wages, even at the expense of ritual duties. Rabbi Yohanan, for example, prohibited a schoolteacher from fasting on one of the holy fast days if it made him underperform at work—the sin of defrauding one's employer being far greater than that of breaking the fast.[2]

Probably the most extreme story of honesty the rabbis offered is that of Rabbi Safra. He had something he wanted to sell, and a man appeared in his home to ask about it. Rabbi Safra, however, was in the middle of saying his prayers—specifically, the shema prayer, when one takes upon oneself the yoke of righteous behavior—and was therefore unable to speak. The man offered a price; then, mistaking the rabbi's silence for refusal, he raised it. When the rabbi finished his prayers, he told the man he would take the lower price, since "for that price I had decided to give it to you."[3] We see just how far the rabbis thought that integrity was supposed to go: In a case where no court of law would ever have ruled against him, nor even was it likely the buyer would have known he had bargained under false pretenses, the rabbi insisted on concluding the deal according to unfavorable terms because of his initial, silent agreement.

Integrity, we learn, is not limited to honest words: Here it is silence that inadvertently misled the customer, and only the truth of the rabbi's inner intentions that would have been betrayed had he accepted the higher offer. Integrity is portrayed as a commitment to honestly representing our inner thoughts, even where no one will know otherwise. And such integrity is seen as a core principle upon which all other morals rest. "If one is honest in his dealings and people esteem him," the rabbis taught, "it is accounted to him as though he had fulfilled the whole Torah."[4]

Looking at the world around us, it is easy to come to the conclusion that honesty is a myth.

The problem is not just in sales, where nine times out of ten the professionals we meet have fashioned a façade every bit as false and shallow as the one I was encouraged to make for myself in selling time-shares. The problem is vast and wide, covering everything from politics to law to management, and even to the relationships we develop with family and friends. A culture of manipulation has taken over our lives, seeping into every human interaction, undermining our sense of self, enslaving us to our machinations, draining our souls. We exploit others for our gain, wrapping ourselves in a spiritual cloak that covers our fears and weaknesses, our eccentricities and true longings, creating a saccharine presentation tailored to our goals. We work on our lines, sharpen our act, dress the part, and unleash our falsified selves on others, caressing their egos and coddling their sensibilities, fashioning a fantasy so compelling that we can no longer tell what is real and what is fake. So many people are not as they seem, are using us to get whatever it is they desire, and so often we find ourselves doing exactly the same to others that we begin to question whether integrity is possible at all. We want to yell out to others, or even to ourselves, "Is there a real person back there?"

Part of the problem is that lying is itself an ambiguous issue. We all know that there are lies, and there are lies. Any reasonable person with healthy moral instincts will tell you that there are cases when falsehood or deception is unavoidable, times when to fully divulge all our thoughts, feelings, or the facts at our disposal is ill-advised or needlessly harmful to others. Philosophers cite the extreme case of a killer coming to your home where his intended victim has taken refuge. When the killer asks you if he's there, would you not lie to save a life? But falsehood is justified in everyday situations as well. Often the damage done by hurting someone's feelings, betraying a promise to keep a secret that can be kept only by lying, revealing an intimate fact that is nobody's business, or trying to tell someone (such as a young child) something he cannot understand, far outweighs any damage done to ourselves or others through the lie. As the rabbis taught, you do not have to tell a groom on his wedding day what you really think about his new bride.[5] "None of us could live with an habitual truth-teller," Mark Twain wrote, "but thank goodness none of us has to."

The fact that there are exceptions to the rule, however, often blurs our understanding of how bad most lies and manipulations really are. The Third Commandment does not say "You shall not lie" but *You shall not invoke the name of the Lord your God in vain*—meaning the key issue is not so much the technical accuracy of a word as the substantive truthfulness of our souls, our ability to act truthfully and represent ourselves honestly to others. Our lives are filled with countless opportunities to distort, endless places where, as with my summer job, we can find creative justifications for deceit, to the point that in practice the concept of integrity risks becoming a hollow shell, a farce that only adds hypocrisy to our sins. Almost every liar, if he is willing to admit he lied at all, can tell to you why it was okay.

The Third Commandment is telling us that honesty is not a farce, that there is a powerful conception of integrity that all of us long for, a vision of human honesty that the Bible insists is crucial for us to live good lives.

To flesh this out, the Bible focuses on two specific kinds of truth telling that go beyond the simple idea of saying true things and representing yourself honestly. Taken together, the biblical stories tell us a great deal about what integrity really means, why it is crucial—and why it is possible, despite the churning brine of manipulation that constantly threatens to take us under.

The first is the keeping of promises. How many of us generally pride ourselves on our honesty but consistently fail to meet our express commitments—making a phone call, paying a bill, or showing up to meetings on time? What about greater commitments, such as the honoring of contracts or bonds of friendship? The fact is that oaths in the ancient world were rarely about things that happened or were happening—they were mainly about things that would happen in the future, commitments to protect, to avenge, to defend, even to the point of death. From the perspective of the Third Commandment, integrity is not just about showing our true face in the present. A more difficult kind of integrity is found in the words we speak about the future.

Jacob, the grandson of Abraham and last of the patriarchs of

Israel, was dying. Having lived most of his life in the Promised Land of Canaan, he and his sons had escaped the famine of his homeland and relocated to Egypt, where he now faced the end of his days, far from both his origins and his offspring's promised future. On his deathbed, he called for his son Joseph, who had become the grand vizier of Egypt, and asked him to swear that when Jacob died, he would be buried not in Egypt but in the land that God promised to Abraham and that would one day be the eternal homeland for Jacob's descendants, the Israelites.

The text details the logistic and political difficulties Joseph had to overcome in fulfilling this oath: As second-in-command in Egypt and himself of foreign origin, Joseph had to receive special permission from Pharaoh to make the trip, which was to include an extended military procession, a "very great company" including "both chariots and horsemen" that would both mark the occasion and protect the dignitaries from attack. When Joseph himself grew old and neared his death, he similarly made his brothers swear that he too would be buried in the Promised Land—a promise that would be kept only in the time of Moses and Joshua, centuries later, when the Israelites leaving Egypt took Joseph's embalmed body with them across the perilous desert.[6]

Promise keeping is central in the story of the Israelite conquest of Canaan in the book of Joshua as well. Having entered the land with a vast army and a divine directive to destroy all its inhabitants, and having done so already at the cities of Jericho and Ai, the Israelites under Joshua instilled fear in the Canaanite peoples. To save their own lives, the terrified Gibeonites sent representatives to Joshua. Knowing that Joshua had no intention of letting any of the Canaanites live, they disguised themselves as members of a faraway tribe, exhausted and famished from an extended journey. In this way, they succeeded in tricking Joshua and the Israelite princes into forging an alliance with their people.

When the ruse was discovered, the prevailing opinion among the Israelites favored reducing the four cities of the Gibeonites to rubble. But Joshua and the princes stayed their hand, "for we have sworn to them in the name of the Lord, God of Israel; now we may not touch them" (Joshua 9:19). To Joshua, the promise made to the Gibeonites had to be kept even though it was made under false pretenses, even though all the Israelites pressed for it to be broken, even though it meant violating God's own commandment to vanquish all the local peoples.

Of course, the paradigmatic biblical promise keeper is God himself, who forges an "eternal covenant" with the descendants of Abraham, one that he will honor regardless of how often or egregiously the Israelites fail to keep their end of the deal. It is God who promises the land in the first place, and the whole exodus story is about how God kept his promise, taking Israel out of Egypt, through the desert, and ultimately back to the land of Abraham. In Deuteronomy, we read with horror the catalog of punishments God intends to lay on the Israelites when they falter, from famine and infighting to invasion from without, to the confiscation of their lands, property, and children, and ultimately their exile in foreign lands. Yet even in their desuetude, when they "remain, tiny in numbers, among the nations," God awaits their repentance, explicitly mentioning the promise he made to their forefathers. "And from there you will ask for the Lord your God, and you will find him ... for the Lord your God is a merciful God, who will neither abandon you nor destroy you; he will not forget the covenant of your fathers, which he swore to them" (Deuteronomy 4:27–31).

Elsewhere God invokes his commitment to earlier promises

as a warning to the Israelites not to become arrogant in the face of their military victories:

> When the Lord your God scatters your enemies from before you, do not say in your heart, "it is because of my righteousness that the Lord brought me to inherit this land, and because of the iniquity of these nations that God drives them away." It is not because of your righteousness that you come to inherit this land, but because indeed of the iniquity of those nations that the Lord your God drives away, *and in order to keep the word that the Lord your God swore to Abraham, Isaac, and Jacob.* (Deuteronomy 9:4–5; emphasis added)

Indeed, as we saw earlier, there is at least one case where God's indictment of Israel is so harsh that he is tempted to forget this covenant, threatening to destroy the children of Israel due to their backsliding—and he needs Moses to invoke the promise in order to quell the Lord's anger. Thus we see immediately after the incident of the Golden Calf:

> And the Lord said to Moses: "I have seen this people, and it is a stiff-necked people. Now leave me, and my anger will burn at them, and I will destroy them; and I will make of you a great nation instead."
>
> And Moses beseeched before the Lord his God, and he said: "Why shall the Lord be angry at your people, that you took out of Egypt, with great power and a mighty hand? . . . Return from your anger, and restrain the evil on your people. Remember Abraham, Isaac, and Israel your servants, to whom you swore, saying to them, 'I shall multiply your seed like the stars in heaven, and all this land that I have spoken of, I shall give to your offspring, and they shall inherit it forever.'" And the Lord

repented from the evil which he had spoken of doing to his people. (Exodus 32:9–14)

Nothing can defuse God's anger like the prospect of failing to keep his promises.

The fulfillment of promises thus represents a powerful statement about the nature of integrity, for it requires far more than just telling the truth in the present. To maintain integrity in the biblical view requires the rigorous, almost fanatical fulfillment of our promises over time, which often requires patience, toil, and willingness to endure a high cost to make sure that one's word is kept.[7]

No less important than keeping our promises, however, is our honesty regarding things that happened in the past. The willingness to admit fault is possibly the highest measure of integrity in the biblical vision, for it is here that we have the most to lose by telling the truth.

Indeed, the biblical stories suggest that it is this single virtue that distinguishes those who are worthy to reign over God's Chosen People from those who are not. Earlier we saw that Judah, son of Jacob, is the symbol of kingship; he is the forefather of David, Solomon, and the future Messiah; it is he who earns the blessing of Jacob that "the scepter shall not depart from Judah" (Genesis 49:10). In the stories about Judah we see a man capable of asserting himself before Jacob, Joseph, and his other brothers, a leader showing both wise judgment and moral responsibility. Yet the most important insight into Judah's character is found in the one story in which he appears as his own man, apart from his brothers and father.

After the death of his two older sons, Judah promises his former daughter-in-law Tamar that she will be allowed to marry his last son, Shelah, as soon as the latter comes of age. When he fails to fulfill his promise, Tamar resolves to avenge her honor. Disguising herself as a prostitute, she seduces Judah along the highway. Judah has left her his signet ring, his cloak, and his staff as a deposit against payment,[8] but the prostitute disappears into the night, taking his effects with her, and cannot be found.

Three months pass and it emerges that Tamar is pregnant. Judah lays a death sentence upon her—"Take her out and let her be burned!"—for having turned to prostitution. Tamar then plays her hand:

> She sent word to her father-in-law, saying: "To the man who owns these things, I am with child." And she said, "Do you recognize these? To whom do this ring, this cloak, and this staff belong?"
>
> And Judah recognized them, and he said, "She is more righteous than I! For it is I who did not give her to Shelah my son." (Genesis 38:25–26)

According to rabbinic teaching, it was this single act of integrity on Judah's part, more than any of his other deeds, that earned him the title of father of Israel's greatest kings.[9] This is, indeed, a reasonable reading of the Judah story: Because of the centrality of King David and King Solomon, direct descendants of Judah later on in the Bible, we may reasonably presume that much of what we read about Judah carries with it a literary presaging of the concept of kingship and righteous rule, and if there is a single story about his virtue, we may assume it is meant to resonate with meaning for kingship more broadly.

That this is in fact the Bible's intention becomes clear in the story of Israel's first king, Saul, depicted in I Samuel. Saul, who is not a descendant of Judah, has been commanded by God to vanquish the evil Amalek nation in its entirety—not only all the fighting men, but also women, children, and even livestock. Saul fights and defeats the Amalekites, yet he falls short of the commandment's absolute, radical nature and spares the best sheep and cattle, as well as the life of the Amalekite King Agag. Upon learning of this, the prophet Samuel confronts Saul for his failure to live up to the demands of his job, and there ensues one of the most bizarre exchanges in the entire Bible, one that is worth quoting at length:

> And Samuel came to Saul, and Saul said, "Blessed are you to the Lord—I have fulfilled the word of the Lord."
>
> And Samuel said, "So what is this voice of the sheep in my ears, and the voice of the cattle that I hear?"
>
> And Saul said, "They were taken from the Amalekites; the people desired the best of the sheep and cattle, to offer as a sacrifice to the Lord your God; the rest we destroyed. . . ."
>
> And Samuel said, "Though you may be as a small child in your own eyes, you were made the chief of all the tribes of Israel, and the Lord anointed you king over Israel. And the Lord sent you on a mission, and said to you, 'Go and destroy the sinful Amalek, and fight them until they are utterly consumed.' So why did you not listen to the voice of the Lord, but instead leapt upon the spoils, and thus did evil in the eyes of the Lord?"
>
> And Saul said, "But I did fulfill the word of the Lord! I went on the mission that the Lord sent me on, and I captured Agag the king of Amalek, and I destroyed Amalek. And the people took sheep and cattle from the spoils, the very best of the devoted property, to sacrifice to the Lord your God at Gilgal."
>
> And Samuel said, "Has the Lord as great delight in burnt offerings and sacrifices, as in obeying the voice of the Lord? Behold, to obey is better than sacrifice, and to hearken than

the fat of rams. For rebellion is like the sin of witchcraft, and stubbornness is like idolatry and teraphim. Because you have rejected the word of the Lord, he has also rejected you from being king."

And Saul said to Samuel, "I have sinned. For I have transgressed the commandment of the Lord, and your words as well; for I feared the people, and obeyed their voice. Now therefore, I pray you, pardon my sin, and turn again with me, and I will bow down to the Lord."

And Samuel said to Saul, "I will not return with you: For you have rejected the word of the Lord, and the Lord has rejected you from being king over Israel." And as Samuel turned to leave, he laid hold of the corner of his robe, and it tore. And Samuel said to him, "The Lord has torn the kingdom of Israel from you this day, and has given it to a neighbor of yours, who is better than you. And also the Eternal One of Israel will not lie nor change his mind, for he is not a man, that he should change his mind." (I Samuel 15:13–29)

On the face of it, Saul is stripped of the monarchy simply because of his failure to fulfill God's commandment down to its most extreme letter. Yet a more careful reading leads us elsewhere. There are plenty of instances where kings fail to live up to God's will but do not thereby lose their right to reign; it is not clear why the failure to butcher Amalekite sheep would in itself justify the end of a dynasty. Moreover, the length and complexity of this dialogue seem to suggest that there is more going on here than Saul's simple failure to follow orders; when God makes a decision, we rarely get to hear the extended pleas of those who are judged unfavorably. Finally, Samuel's summation, that "the Eternal One of Israel will not lie nor change his mind, for he is not a man, that he should change his mind," makes little sense if the only problem with Saul were his failure to fulfill God's command.

The real problem with Saul is not his failure to follow orders but his failure to admit fault. We get the picture of a cowardly dissembler, who insists he did God's bidding when he manifestly did not, and who hems and haws and admits he is wrong only when he stands to lose everything. It is to this inability to speak courageously and truthfully that Samuel responds when he speaks of a God who does not lie or change his mind—for it is Saul's dishonesty, more than his disobedience, that has kindled Samuel's ire. We get the feeling that if Saul had confessed right away, he might have kept his crown.

Saul, in other words, is the anti-Judah, a man who could never say, "She is more righteous than I!" He is to be replaced with David, the worthy descendant of Judah, who proves capable of admitting fault when confronted with his own misdeeds. When, in II Samuel, he falls in love with Bathsheba, wife of Uriah the Hittite, David orchestrates the latter's battlefield death so that he can take Bathsheba for his own. In an exchange clearly meant to parallel Samuel's confrontation with Saul, David is visited by the prophet Nathan, who accuses him of both murder and of taking another man's wife by force. At the end of the prophet's lengthy indictment, David says simply, "I have sinned before the Lord" (II Samuel 12:30). Nathan responds to David's swift contrition by commuting his death sentence, and David remains king over Israel, enduring unending strife in his country as punishment for his sin, but retaining his kingship and, ultimately, the legacy of Israel's most glorious monarch.

Admitting fault is the most important form of integrity, even a prerequisite for kingship, because it does not just limit the kinds of manipulations we can do to others; it positively shatters our façades. We try to project an image of being good, reliable people; when we admit fault, we risk severely hurting our reputation. But someone who cannot admit his mistakes is, at best, willing to sacrifice the truth in order to save his self-image; at worst, he has failed even to recognize in his own mind that what he did was wrong and has thereby traded his inner moral self for a self-image that is ultimately fake and will, when put to the test, crumble.

Behind all these biblical stories lies a single vision of honesty that goes far beyond simple information passed on to others. Integrity, the biblical tradition teaches, is about how we represent ourselves in the world—whether I can be, as the rabbis taught, someone "whose inside is like his outside."[10] Rabbi Safra's refusal to take a higher price than the one he had silently accepted came from a desire that his dealings in business reflect his true feelings and intentions, even when this hurt him financially and no one would ever have known about it. Joshua's protection of the Gibeonites flew in the face of all his political interests and showed how much he was willing to sacrifice in order to stay true to his word. The willingness of both Judah and King David to admit their guilt attests to their refusal to maintain a façade when confronted with their wrongdoing. In all these cases, we see that a person of integrity intuitively struggles to make his words and actions reflect his inner reality. And if this inner truth does not look so pretty, it is still infinitely better to own up than to cover up.

Integrity means, in other words, rejecting falsehood and manipulation as a way of dealing with others. In business, it means not only never lying about "the product," but also refusing to hide important information from a potential customer and not misleading about who we are, or what our experiences in life have been, anything that may influence the other's decision. In politics, it means full disclosure of a candidate's dealings, health, beliefs, and policy intentions—at least anything that can conceivably be important in a voter's choice. In journalism, it means sticking to a narrative we really believe to be true, even if it makes the story less interesting. At work, it means never misleading our employers about our qualifications, how we spend our time during work hours, what we have accomplished, or whether we really were sick that day. And in personal relationships, it means not only keeping our word to our friends and spouses and children, but also having the courage to confront them with the things that bother us, even at the risk of conflict or separation.

Every time we encounter another human being, we are not just advancing a product, service, cause, or candidate. We are representing ourselves in the life of another. We are showing up for duty in the interpersonal world. We cannot hide behind the directives of our bosses, the deceitful habits of our peers, or our own fears of rejection or loneliness to excuse our actions. Our integrity rests on the permanent prioritization of our own truthfulness: not just in the present, but especially over time; in keeping our promises and admitting our mistakes, and not just in our words, but in everything that is left unsaid as well.

Why is this so important?

A functioning society requires, first of all, the constant reliance of people on one another. We seldom appreciate the extent of our interdependence: From carpooling with our friends to working in exchange for wages to purchasing food for our families, we place ourselves at the mercy of our neighbors, honor laws we hope will be enforced, and depend on leaders to protect us from external enemies.

Yet every act of reliance depends to some degree on trust, which in turn depends on the trustworthiness of others, and the greater the trust placed, the greater the integrity required to sustain it. Whereas it is true that in the absence of trust we can make do with the apparatus of fear—fear of lawsuits, of arrest and prosecution, or of public humiliation and social sanction for duplicitous behavior—to keep people honest, there is no question that such a society is far less fruitful, efficient, enjoyable, and morally heightened than one where human relations include a powerful degree of genuine mutual reliability. "One of the most important lessons we can learn from an examination of economic life," writes Francis Fukuyama, "is that a nation's well-being, as well as its ability to compete, is conditioned by a single, pervasive cultural characteristic: The level of trust inherent in the society."[11]

But there are deeper issues at stake than just social efficiency. Honesty is the key to true connections of friendship with other people, friendship that lies at the core of the Bible's redemptive vision.

Our relations with strangers begin with a self-protective mistrust—that's why we do not share the truths of our intimate lives or finances with people who are not our closest friends. Deep down, however, part of us cannot stand the unfairness of a life where success depends on the ability to fabricate, where lying is so powerfully rewarded that all our other skills, virtues, and inbred talents seem to be dwarfed by it. And yet despite how wrong it is, with each successive deceit employed against us we become increasingly jaded; we start using the same tools that are used against us; we discover the addictive power of calculation and maneuvering in dealing with others, carving out for ourselves ever-smaller circles of real honesty, safe places among close friends or family where we can be open and truthful—until, at last, even these give way, and we find we have given ourselves over completely to the manipulative principle, because there is no one left before whom we feel we may be completely honest.

To overcome this requires a leap of faith—faith in ourselves. It begins with clinging to our own honesty no matter how much the world disappoints us, with adamantly refusing to become lost behind our masks. Through the Third Commandment's prohibition on false oaths, the Bible asserts that there is room in this world for genuine, reliable, true communication between people, a crack in the shell of mutual duplicity, the possibility of bridging the unfathomable gap between souls. Invoking the Lord's name in an oath means stepping outside the rumbling flow of talk and deception that marks our daily lives and putting not just our words but our existential reality, our very being, behind what we convey to others. It is placing a strict limit on manipulation, showing the world that there will always be room for truth on this earth, a sacred place that, if we try hard enough, can expand to include our entire lives.

Honesty is more than a lofty moral ideal. It is first of all a mental habit, a habit of constantly checking our words against truth and our deeds against our words, a habit that is ingrained at an early age and must be continually reinforced as we grow older. Every time we lie, break a promise, or cover up our past, we chip away at the habits of integrity, and undertake bad habits, not just of the lips but of the mind as well.

Over time, in other words, our lies become who we are. Stories, once embellished, become fact in our minds, if for no reason other than that we discover that the more we believe our lies, the better we are at telling them. Habits are like a gravitational field, which makes us feel like we're going straight when in fact we're orbiting around a planet that warps the very space we travel through. And the worst of these are habits of falsehood, because while a habitual smoker can know he is increasing his risk of heart disease with every puff, a habitual liar loses the ability to know when he is lying. For him, truth, instead of being a permanent fixture outside him against which he needs to compare his words and actions, becomes a fluid and rapidly shifting imaginative backdrop that changes according to his rhetorical needs, that supports his self-image at every turn rather than forcing him to confront his failures, that comforts him rather than challenging him.

Our lies, in other words, are idols we make with our hands. "Those who make them, or trust in them, shall become like them."

Whenever we encounter a person of genuine integrity, we sense that there is something within, a kind of presence that is missing in people we know to be dishonest, disreputable, or shallow—a developed inner self that strikes us in every interaction as secure and healthy and bold and true. This kind of self attracts us, for we see in it strength, constancy, and courage, and we intuit that we might be better off learning from, and being led by, people such as these. That our trust might not be in vain.

What are the origins and contours of such an inner self? To attempt an answer is to uncover the deepest foundations of the redemptive spirit. In the Ten Commandments, we do indeed encounter a powerful doctrine of the inner self that is the source of integrity, and of other virtues as well, such as initiative, responsibility, and love. This approach provides the Archimedean point for the creation of a very different world from the one that would have prevailed without it.

We turn now to look for this redemptive self—and find it in a most unlikely place.

4

The Redemptive Self

*Remember the Sabbath day, to sanctify it. Six days you
shall labor, and complete all your work. But the seventh
will be a Sabbath for the Lord your God. You shall do no
work: Neither you, nor your son or your daughter, your
man-servant or your maid-servant, your beasts or your
stranger in your gates. For in six days the Lord made the
heavens, the earth, and the sea, and all that is in them,
and he rested on the seventh day. For this reason did the
Lord bless the seventh day and sanctify it.*

There is nothing so self-evident, it seems, as the need for a
day of rest. Few biblical ideals have become so thoroughly
universalized as the Sabbath, which was either adapted or rein-
vented by cultures all over the world: from Christianity, which
established Sunday as the "Lord's day," to Buddhism, which created the weekly *uposatha* for the "cleansing of the defiled mind."
Modern life would be hard to imagine without our weekends.

Because it seems so reasonable, we often overlook how bizarre
the Fourth Commandment really is. We are told not just to give
ourselves time off from work, but to commemorate the seventh

day of Creation, when God, having completed the universe, rested. But as to the questions of why God would rest, despite having neither a body nor the propensity to get tired; why such rest should be "holy" rather than just "good" like the rest of Creation; and why such grand subjects as God and Creation need to be brought into what looks like nothing more than a smart social policy—to these the Bible offers no answers.

The questions deepen when we look at a second version of the Ten Commandments, appearing in Deuteronomy, which in most cases is identical to the version in Exodus. There, the Fourth Commandment is given a wholly different justification: The Sabbath is to be observed in commemoration of the exodus from Egypt, an event that was anything but restful. And the Bible seems to raise the stakes of the Sabbath at every turn: The prophet Ezekiel claimed that the Israelites' failure to keep the Sabbath ultimately led to the destruction of Jerusalem.[1] The prescribed penalty for Sabbath violation is death, putting it on a par with murder and idolatry. On the other hand, keeping the Sabbath is described in the Fourth Commandment as nothing less than an imitation of God—one of only three places in the entire Pentateuch where such imitation is spoken of (the others being far more general statements, that you should "walk in his ways" and that "You shall be holy, for I, the Lord your God, am holy" [Deuteronomy 28:9; Leviticus 19:2]). The Fourth Commandment takes up more space than any other of the Ten Commandments—four full verses, suggesting that it might be far more central to the entire redemptive project than it looks at first.

The first step in understanding the Fourth Commandment is to ask what our biblical text would have looked like if God had not rested. Without the seventh day of Creation, the universe would have originated with an endlessly energetic God, one who creates worlds without end. We would have an opening statement about our existence in which Creator and Creation were inextricably bound up in each other. There would be no universe without God's creating it—but also no God who was not busy creating. Our initial image of God, in other words, would be of someone in a permanent state of redemptive action with no independent being of his own.

Through the story of the seventh day, we learn that God separated himself from his works and carved out a place to invest in himself, to *be*. God "blessed the Seventh Day, and sanctified it, for on it he desisted from all the work that God created to do" (Genesis 2:3). He set aside the seventh day as holy, because it was on that day that he began to really live.

This is what we are told to imitate. And so, we are quickly propelled to the conclusion that the purpose of the Sabbath is the discovery of ourselves, of our existence separate from our own acts of creation. We do not merely commemorate God's rest but also imitate it—and in the process, we too establish ourselves as independent beings, standing apart from our works, genuinely alive.

In the Fourth Commandment, in other words, we are introduced to the biblical affirmation of the self—one of the most powerful ideas in the entire Old Testament, which sets it apart from many of the other religious traditions of antiquity and down to our own day. It is here that we begin to understand what makes the Ten Commandments unique and enduringly relevant. It is here that we first encounter the biblical approach not just to our own inner selves, but also to much of the world around us—to love, family, community, and so much else of what is yet to follow.

In their effort to fashion a day of rest for an entire people, the rabbis articulated no fewer than thirty-nine categories of labor that were to be forbidden on the Sabbath. These include most major forms of industry and especially agriculture, including planting, plowing, and reaping, as well as cooking, construction, and kindling of fire. Most of these prohibitions are not written explicitly in the Bible; the rabbis understood them to stem from an oral tradition that dated all the way to Moses, and that they constituted the true meaning of "You shall do no work."[2]

The list of banned activities, however, also includes a few things that do not seem very labor intensive—such as writing, squeezing a sponge, or carrying objects outdoors—and the result is that people who live according to rabbinic law often end up asking themselves what all this inconvenience really has to do with resting. My teacher, the theologian Joseph Isaac Lifshitz, offered an analysis of the laws of banned labor on the Sabbath, where he showed that the categories of forbidden labor were derived not from any consideration of how tiresome they are, but from their creative nature. Indeed, according to the Talmud the categories of forbidden work reflect those actions involved in the assembly of, and religious worship in, the Tabernacle that the Israelites carried with them in the desert—meaning that they are symbolic of creative endeavor rather than labor per se.

Lifshitz concludes that "You shall do no work" is precisely intended to bring creativity to a halt. Work prohibited on the Sabbath, he writes, "can best be understood as a deliberate act of productive creative activity—that which combines the will to create with the actual and lasting improvement of one's world." It is, in other words, about redemptive acts. "In the Creation story, the Sabbath is the moment of silence which imparts perfection and wholeness to what has come before." By keeping the Sabbath, he writes, "man learns to recognize the consequence of his creation, to renew his appreciation for the sublime, and to adjust his designs accordingly."[3]

The point, in other words, is to clarify something that is so often misunderstood in our intensely creative Western lives, something I already touched on in the context of idolatry but with the Fourth Commandment now takes center stage. Our creations, while so central to our lives, are not the essence of who we are. Behind our careers, families, and wealth, there is an inner reality, a mysterious, sublime, indefinable yet palpable self that must be deepened and cultivated if we are to be truly good, moral, redemptive beings. It is this rich inner self that keeps our redemptive drive honest, that keeps at bay the potentially obsessive urge to change and conquer and achieve without regard for what is good, that allows us to balance creativity with judgment. It is the source of our inner peace in a world that places a premium on impatient, restless advancement. It is our internal compass; but it is also the source of our inner fire.

The aim of the Sabbath is to spend one day each week diverting the bulk of our energies away from creation and toward recognizing, exploring, and ultimately sanctifying the inner self. One rabbinic legend relates that whereas all the other commandments were given by God to the Israelites "in public," only the Sabbath was given "in private"—aimed at the individual, separated from his role in the world. Another describes the Sabbath as a time when God and the individual dwell in each other's solitary company, "as king and his queen."[4] Of all the Ten Commandments, only the Sabbath is truly intimate and personal, addressing the core of what each of us can be.

It was with this in mind that the rabbis interpreted the Sabbath first of all as a day of leisure. Building on the call of Isaiah that we should "make the Sabbath a delight" (Isaiah 58:13), the rabbis envisioned a day when each of us not merely rests, but *enjoys*. The Sabbath, we are told, should be celebrated with "food, drink, and a clean garment." The thirteenth-century mystical text the *Zohar* elaborates on this, declaring that each person "should prepare for himself a pleasant spot to recline, furnished with embroidered pillows and beddings from all those available in his house. . . . The house should be prepared with multiple vessels for the needs of the Sabbath, and an attractive place to recline should be readied for every member of the household." We are to be comfortable, to rest, even to sleep. "Sleeping on the Sabbath," one rabbinic teaching goes, "is a delight."[5]

Sabbath begins, in other words, as a kind of vacation. With a sense of relief we arrive at a day when we can feel like human beings—take a shower, have a good meal, put on clean clothes, breathe deeply, and get some sleep. We are, so many of us, driven achievers with little time for simple pleasures, for anything resembling the celebration of the self, such that even when we finally reach the weekend, we spend it achieving other things: catching up on emails or laundry or repairs in the home, fulfilling social obligations, crossing things off the list. We spend half our time achieving, the other half noticing how much we have failed to achieve, such that the idea of setting aside time for our own pleasure, for bringing the enterprise of our lives to a grinding halt for an entire day each week, seems nearly impossible.

This predicament has become extreme in our own time, yet the challenge of rest was well known to the rabbis, who instituted a long series of regulations above and beyond the thirty-nine categories of "work," for the purpose of ensuring effective attention to the self, even for those of us who have forgotten how. Perhaps the most interesting of these is the law of *muk-tzeh,* which prohibits even moving objects that are associated with prohibited activities on the Sabbath. Here is Maimonides on the subject:

> The sages prohibited carrying certain objects on the Sabbath, as one carries them during the rest of the week. Why did they

institute this ban? . . . So it will not be an ordinary day in his eyes, such that he will pick things up and fix things and move them around from one corner to another, from one house to another, or bury the stones in the yard, and so on. . . . The result will be that it is not at all the Sabbath, for he has ignored the central aim written in the Torah: "That he may rest."[6]

To ensure the qualitative leisure of the Sabbath, it was not enough to prohibit labor; people who are busy and worried all week would find ways to stay busy and worried in spite of all those forms of banned labor. So the rabbis enacted a more extreme set of regulations whose purpose was solely pedagogical. Our physical world is filled with objects that we associate with our creative endeavor and weekly toil: a keyboard, a screwdriver, a saucepan, a shovel—all these things that are so central to life during the week become "marginal" (the literal meaning of *muktzeh*) and are to be left alone, not to be moved around during the day, in an effort to drive home the importance of leisure.

But to what end? There is a purpose to the Sabbath deeper than just attending to our bodies or escaping the pressures of work, and it is here that we learn why the Sabbath is so central and its presentation in the Bible so deeply connected with sanctity and the divine realm.

In rabbinic thought, the Sabbath was meant not only for rest but also for the assertion and celebration of the self through spiritual growth. An extra soul is given to the individual on the Sabbath, the rabbis teach; a special light shines from his face.[7] It is of course a day of prayer, when the individual must stand alone before the Creator and express his love. But even more than prayer, the Sabbath is meant for the spiritual enterprise of the individual, the exploration of the deepest truths of life. This is embodied in the concept of Torah study.

• • •

Torah study is one of the least understood aspects of traditional Judaism, in part because it means different things to different people. Yet its centrality to the Sabbath is a key to understanding what exactly we mean by investment in the self, and to the kind of deepening and growth to which the Bible seems to be referring.

Technically, it refers to the study, individually, with a partner, or in a class, of what is in effect an ocean of traditional literature, beginning with the Bible and continuing through thousands of years of rabbinic thought, parables, and legal discourse. These works were written with the aim of exploring the truth of God as passed down through a tradition that is anything but monolithic, a tradition of endless debates and inner contention, of conflict about many of the most basic elements of Jewish faith and practice, from the question of how literally to read the six days of Creation, all the way to the nuances of *muktzeh*—all of this is Torah. Neither is the study of Torah confined to texts; it is first about the way life is to be lived, and as such, includes exposure to good and wise people, watching how they live their lives and questioning them about it. This was understood by the rabbis to be a crucial form of Torah study as well.

Torah study, in other words, is the Jewish tradition's answer to all the important questions of life. "Turn it over and over again," the rabbis taught, "everything is in it." The Talmud, which is the most comprehensive collection of classical rabbinic statements, allows itself no restriction on subject matter, covering everything from the minutiae of law to the foundations of politics, economics, and the family. One rabbinic story takes this to a comical extreme. The rabbi known as Rav was headed for the bathroom, when he discovered one of his students following him there. When asked why, the student replied, "This is Torah, and I must learn it." The same night, as the rabbi lay in bed with his wife, he found the student hiding under the bed. "This is Torah," the student pleaded, "and I must learn it."[8]

While the range of subjects covered by Torah study is nearly universal, as an activity the study of Torah is deeply individual. One is told to study, but the choice of whether to study the stories of Abraham, the book of Proverbs, laws of the Sabbath, or the tales of the rabbis—that is for each of us to decide for ourselves. And though everyone can benefit from the wisdom of others, the rabbis told us to "find yourself a rabbi." A teacher is required, but the choice of a teacher is up to the individual, who alone knows his own interests and instincts, strengths and weaknesses. Nor is there a prescribed pace of study—one student may focus on a single page of the Talmud for six months, another will attempt to cover as much ground as possible. And the deepest secrets of the Divine, we are told, cannot be learned even from a teacher; they can be understood only by the individual struggling on his own.[9] Although it is rarely phrased as such, Torah study is the affirmation of individual exploration in the most profound way.

Such an exploration is seen by the rabbinic tradition not as a luxury but as a fundamental element of the self. The study of Torah should be a fixture of our daily lives, we are told, even more than earning a living. According to one tradition, whether one set fixed time for the study of Torah is one of the questions each person is asked when he dies and reaches heaven. According to Maimonides, the duty to set aside a fixed period each day for the study of Torah is incumbent upon every Jew, "whether poor or rich, healthy or ailing, young or old and feeble. Even a man so poor that he is maintained by charity or goes begging from door to door, as also a man with a wife and children to support, is under the obligation to set aside a fixed period during the day and night for the study of the Torah. . . . Until what period in life is one obligated to study Torah? Until the day of one's death."[10]

For our purposes, therefore, the study of Torah means two things, both of which are crucial to understanding its central role on the Sabbath. First, it is the personal, individualized exploration of the most important questions of life. Second, it is a life habit, a continuous investment in the spirit of which every person is capable, indeed which is part of what makes us human.

This is why the rabbis taught that "the Sabbath was given only for the study of the Torah." The highest aim of the Sabbath is our spiritual advancement, through whatever means we need to find our deepest truths. Although traditional Jews today usually restrict their studies to authoritative texts, the ancient rabbis went much further, seeking wisdom wherever it could be found. It is told of Rabbi Yohanan ben Zakai, the greatest of the rabbis and leader of the Jews during the Great Revolt against the Romans in 66–73 C.E., that his explorations went well beyond studying texts, to include "constellations and calculations, the sayings of launderers and the sayings of fox-keepers, the conversation of demons and the conversation of palm-trees, the conversation of the ministering angels, the great things and the little things."[11]

The affirmation of the self on the Sabbath, we come to understand, means not just resting our bodies, nor even resting our minds either. It means freeing our spirits and investing in them according to our unique tastes, dispositions, and talents—by indulging in those late-night conversations we thought were a thing of the past, reading literature, walking through the woods alone with our thoughts, studying philosophy, meditating, analyzing poetry with a friend, attending a moving and enlightening lecture, or spending time with people we consider wise.

In the Fourth Commandment, we carve out time to nurture our body and soul, ensuring that against the raging waters of ordinary life, there is what Abraham Joshua Heschel called an "island of stillness." "The island is the seventh day, the Sabbath," he wrote, "a day of detachment from things, instruments, and practical affairs, as well as of attachment to the spirit."[12]

In the biblical stories, the most common symbol of the developed individual is the shepherd. As opposed to the farmer or hunter, the shepherd spends his days tending his flock, roaming freely through the mountains. He need not pray for the rain to come on time, nor does he have to search endlessly for prey in the field. He is independent in every way, finding both food and clothing in the meat and wool produced by his sheep. No less important, he has *time*—time to count the stars, to consider the works of creation, to internalize the dynamic of life.

We should not be surprised, therefore, to discover that the most stirring individuals in the Bible are shepherds: the patriarch Abraham, founder of the Israelites, who has enough of a sense of his own being to discover God's voice in a world where he is unknown; his grandson Jacob, who overcomes the menace of his elder brother, Esau, and gives birth to twelve shepherd sons, who become the forefathers of the twelve tribes of Israel; Moses, the prophet of prophets and leader of the Israelites out of captivity and into the unknown wilderness; and David, who founds the most revered Israelite dynasty, establishes Jerusalem as its capital city, and conceives the wondrous Temple there as a testament to God's greatness.

It is no coincidence, then, that the Talmudic sage who taught us the most about the self was a shepherd. Rabbi Akiva was illiterate until the age of forty, tending the flocks of others and living in poverty, when he suddenly discovered the study of Torah as the key to advancing his own inner spirit. According to the legend, he was standing at the mouth of a well and asked someone why a certain stone had been hollowed out. When told that it was because of water that had been falling on it every day, and that such wisdom can be found in a verse in the Bible, he replied, "Is my mind harder than this stone?" He immediately began an intensive course of study, beginning with the alphabet and continuing for decades, until he had mastered the biblical and rabbinic teachings.[13]

Rabbi Akiva's unique success flowed from a boundless determination, itself a reflection of his belief in the inner self which, when rich and confident, is capable of incredible achievement. "Anyone whose own spirit is comfortable with itself," he said, "that is a good omen; and if his own spirit is not comfortable— it is a bad omen." The world turns on the deeds of "comfortable spirits," of hearty shepherd-individuals who have the strength to change the course of their own lives and those of others. Rabbi Akiva saw the redemptive individual as an imitation of the divine. "A special love was given man," he said, "for it was made known to him that he was created in the image of God." By affirming our redemptive selves, we affirm our own godliness.[14]

Rabbi Akiva was not alone in emphasizing the independent, creative inner self as the key to redemption. "You find that every person is called by three names," one rabbinic saying goes. "One that his father and mother call him by; one that people generally call him; one that he gives himself. The most important of all of these is the one he gives himself." In another, the rabbis praised God for making each individual unique: Whereas when men make coins from a stamp, they all come out the same, God in his greatness made human beings from the stamp of Adam, and every one came out different. But perhaps the most famous statement about the self was made by Hillel the Elder, the first of the great rabbinic sages, four generations before Akiva, described by tradition as the founder of rabbinic Judaism.[15] It appears in *Ethics of the Fathers,* the premier collection of rabbinic philosophy:

> If I am not for myself, who will be for me? And if I am for myself alone, what am I? And if not now, when?[16]

In the first part of the statement, Hillel seems to be justifying investment in the self on pragmatic grounds: Without it, one will eventually be abandoned by others. Our attraction to strong, robust people is a fact about human nature. Like God, we are inclined to help those who help themselves. And while we believe it our duty to protect the helpless, it is also the case that as soon as we discover that someone is apathetic or lazy, that he lacks not just the means but the basic self-respect or inner strength required to emerge from his plight, we lose a great deal of our zeal to assist. Self-affirmation, it turns out, is the first step toward gaining the respect of the world around us.

Yet the connection between the self and others is not limited to the help we receive; as the second part of Hillel's statement suggests, there is something in the redemptive self that makes it necessary to reach out in order to fulfill one's own being. As strongly as the biblical current pushes us toward the saline shores of the self, there is also a powerful undertow, pulling us back out again, to the sea of humanity and interpersonal life.

The Bible has no patience for the hermit. When God first creates Adam, he swiftly concludes that "it is not good for man to be alone" (Genesis 2:18) and immediately sets about fashioning a companion for him, trying first to mate him with all the animals of creation, and finally concluding that only another human, a woman fashioned from his very flesh, would resolve the acute, infinite problem of loneliness. The Bible sees something deeply wrong in a self that does not include others, that does not love or help or draw inspiration from them. The Bible is a social text, oftentimes a political text, telling stories not of the lone mystic but of striking, socially minded individuals who found a nation, of kings who rule over them, of prophets whose inner meditations are of little interest compared with their warnings and yearnings about the future of society.

The most extreme of these figures was the prophet Elijah, whose story appears in I Kings 19:1–16. Frustrated by his failure to influence the souls of his people, terrorized by the threats on his life by Queen Jezebel, Elijah makes his way through the harsh wilderness, traveling all the way to Mount Sinai, seeking as Moses did the truth of God. When he arrives, he fasts for forty days and forty nights—recalling Moses' forty days without food or water on the mountain. In his own mind he is another Moses, returning to the same holy place to seek an ultimate encounter with the Divine. Yet unlike Moses, who led an entire nation to the mountain, Elijah goes there all alone, not leading the people but escaping them. God finally speaks to Elijah as he sleeps in a cave on the mountain, and the conversation does not go as planned:

What are you doing here, Elijah?

In English, these words may be read as either a simple question or an impatient critique. In Hebrew, however, there is no ambiguity—*ma lecha po eliyahu* is a dismissive, almost nasty query, as a father might ask of a son whom he finds wandering among the brothels.

There is something wrong, we learn, with abandoning the

world of men and seeking ultimate truths alone. "I have been very zealous on behalf of the Lord God of hosts," Elijah tries to explain, "but the children of Israel have forsaken your covenant, thrown down your altars, and slain your prophets with the sword; and I only, am left; and they seek my life, to take it away." Elijah appeals in every direction: *I am here for you; I am here for them; I am here for myself.* His plea suggests that the search for the deepest truth is a matter of overwhelming importance not just for himself but for all and everyone. In a way, God grants his wish:

> And he [the Lord] said, "Go out and stand upon the mountain before the Lord." And behold, the Lord passed by: And a great and strong wind rent the mountains, and broke the rocks in pieces before the Lord; but the Lord was not in the wind. And after the wind, an earthquake; but the Lord was not in the earthquake. And after the earthquake, a fire; but the Lord was not in the fire. And after the fire, a still, small voice.

Elijah's efforts to understand the truth of God are answered in two distinct, almost contradictory ways: There is definitely an inner being, an essence to the divine, an ultimate truth that is captured in the "still, small voice." Yet at the same time, Elijah learns much more about what God is not than what he is. He is not all the fire, the storm, the earthquake that he brings into the world, but rather is to be found in the quiet that follows, in the Sabbaths of the world—an absence that is nonetheless a deeper presence, a silence that is detectable but understandable only through the vast effects of his action.

But then, just at the moment when Elijah has come as close as possible to encountering the ultimate truth, we are reminded how problematic is his quest when it comes to exclude the outside world. God asks again, "What are you doing here, Elijah?" When Elijah responds with the same speech as before, God has had enough of the interview and sends him away, back to the world of men. "Go, return on your way to the wilderness, toward Damascus. When you arrive, anoint Hazael to be king over Aram; and Jehu son of Nimshi shall you anoint king over Israel." Elijah had rejected society and wanted to be alone, driving himself so deeply into himself that he sought refuge in the wilderness, hoping that God would accept him in his solitude. *I only, am left.* But he was wrong, and God now rejects his request even as he reveals himself, telling Elijah to go back to the world.

In the biblical view, the most profound truths are found by the individual in his own solitude; yet the developed self is of such a nature that it inevitably reverberates back outward again. According to the kabbalistic teaching, God created the universe because his infinite self could no longer be contained in him alone—it needed to push outward, to create a universe, and ultimately to create others like him, creators in his own image. And God's solution for man's loneliness is not just to create more men, but to fashion for him a woman—stressing the role that companionship plays not only in personal fulfillment but in reproduction, in creating still more creators. The self that seeks only its own pleasure, only wisdom or meditative truth, is on the wrong track.

This is the key to understanding how the affirmation of the self embodied in the Sabbath is not the same as selfishness—and even implies a thorough rejection of it. The most obvious objection to a worldview that praises and honors the self is that it encourages greed and the willful disregard for others. The problems connected with the absolute worship of the self are manifold, but let it suffice to say that nothing could be further from the biblical ideal than affirming the self at the expense of humanity. It was, after all, the same Hillel the Elder who, when asked to boil the entire Torah down to a single sentence, replied: "That which is hateful to yourself, do not do to your neighbor. That is the whole Torah. The rest is commentary—now go and study." And it was the same Rabbi Akiva who declared that the verse in Leviticus 19:18, "And you shall love your neighbor as yourself," was nothing less than "the great principle of the Torah."[17]

Affirmation of the self and concern for others are not contradictory forces; there is no obvious tension between them. "Selfish" and "selfless" appear to be part of a coherent whole, a single conception of the self that naturally wants to expand and embrace the other, seeks him out and fights for his interest, glows outward and loves the other deeply without sacrificing anything—a bush that burns but is not consumed.

To understand how this works, let us step outside the biblical discussion for a moment, to look at one of the most primal forms of interpersonal relation, and the most basic act of human affection: the physical caress.

When you caress a child or a lover, what do you feel? Whether it is to heal someone's hurt, a spontaneous act of affection, or a prelude to deeper intimacy, the caress comprises two different feelings. One of them can be called "selfless": We hope to make the other person feel good and are satisfied when our caress is well received, when the other is calmed and relieved or excited and energized by our hand. But there is another feeling as well. We also enjoy the caress itself, the physical act of touching someone we love. In some sense, this may be called "selfish," because it is our own simple pleasure, like that of a child at play. We receive even as we give.

Most people would agree that if all you care about is your own pleasure in the caress, there is something deeply wrong.

Someone who caresses another without concern for the latter's feelings is either a young child or shackled by childish motives, and will end up hurting many people in the long run. But this still leaves two different ways for mature adults to relate to the caress: Either it should be purely selfless—the same caress we would give a stranger in distress—or it should be a combination, a creative merging, of the two. The pivotal question, then, is this: Is the ideal caress one in which we only give but do not receive? Or does our own pleasure have a decisive stake in the meaning of the caress? How we answer may dictate the course of everything we do in relating to others, in how we understand love, and how we give of ourselves to the world.

Western culture tells us many conflicting things about how we should relate to ourselves. On the one hand, there is a powerful theme, derived from classical Christian thought, that teaches us to dedicate our lives and thoughts solely to others. Words like "selflessness" and "self-sacrifice" carry an extremely positive connotation; we should strive to overcome our natural, childish drives toward fun, greed, and pleasure, for the benefit of others. Eastern religions too call upon us to dissolve our egos, to erase the self in favor of all existence. But the emergence of the field of psychology in the last century has shown us that absolute self-sacrifice or self-dissolution can be profoundly harmful: If we deem ourselves unworthy of pleasure and satisfaction and health, we end up crippling our souls and bodies, to the point that we cannot help anyone else. A healthy life requires, at a minimum, taking care of both ourselves and others: We may work hard and prosper, but we should also put our wealth to good causes. We may take care of our physical and mental health, but we should also volunteer our energies to help those in need.

But the question of the caress takes the issue to a deeper level. From the perspective of the Fourth Commandment, "selfishness" and "selflessness" are not separate and compartmentalized. They do not in fact appear to be competing at all—if anything, they can be mutually supportive. The pleasure I receive and the pleasure I give work together, creating something greater than both. It is possible to indulge our pleasure and give to others, not just concurrently, but in a single, unified way, a way that spins out into another level of love, that is beyond the self and the other. "Love your neighbor as yourself" is a great principle of the Torah, because of its more profound, *literal* meaning. The self expands to include the other, and the pleasures of both are one.

Nowhere is this more obvious than in sexuality. Sex is the source of so much conflict and inner turmoil largely because we are so vulnerable to the distorting questions of selflessness and selfishness. Naked before another, dependent on another's affection, we must overcome so many barriers, past traumas and guilt, questions of giving and receiving and our self-worth. One person may worry that she is giving too much, but then, awash in self-loathing, worries that maybe she has no right to the "selfishness" that receiving entails. Another is selfish as a child, seeking only his own gratification and ignoring the reality of another.

All these are overcome only when both partners accept that the pleasure of union must come with a union of pleasure, that it is right to please another even as we enjoy ourselves, that if anything, the enjoyment of giving and receiving merge together in the souls of both partners, creating the most powerful and gratifying of human experiences, and expressing the genuineness of love for another and ourselves at the same time. For this reason, while those doctrines advocating extreme selflessness usually undercut sexuality as well, in Jewish tradition sex is seen as a supreme expression of both love and the sanctified self. So we discover that the Holy Temple in Jerusalem, where man and

God met in the most intimate way, was adorned with sexual imagery. And when a wife and her husband lie in bed together, the mystics taught, the Holy One is there with them.[18]

Sexuality is the caress taken to its physical extreme. Yet we can see this kind of self-expansion to include the other in many areas of our lives. Any shared experience has the potential to both affirm and join the self with another. This, indeed, is the model of redemptive action as envisioned in the Ten Commandments: It begins with the powerful, healthy, expansive self, who sees another person's being as, in some sense, an extension of his own—and therefore deserving of the same protection, the same love, and the same concern for his well-being. And the greater your own self, the greater you will want the other to be as well.

For the redemptive spirit, to "love your neighbor as yourself" is to love him very much indeed.

But this is not the only kind of love people talk about. Only when we appreciate the self as the true source of love may we fully realize what is wrong with "universal love," the belief that one should love all human beings equally.

All true love begins in the self, and is of the self, and aims itself at real, true human selves beginning with those around us. We give a gift to someone—a music album we enjoyed in our youth, a gold necklace—not because we want to impose a universal vision of goodness on her, but because we have thought of her, have asked ourselves what it is that she, in her individuality, would enjoy, that would successfully express our love for her, that would bring her closer to us. The most successful gifts reflect a sensitive consideration of the individual and come from the peculiar excesses and flourishings of the giver.

Universal love, by contrast, is an abstract belief rather than a true expression of the self. It requires deliberately ignoring the particularities of individuals, in favor of what they have in common with all humanity. It is the antiseptic experience of the hospital, where all spirits are reduced to their common physicality, where the very light is pure, cold white rather than fiery sun-yellow, which fills us with dread at the thought of undifferentiated love, because although all humans are worthy of fundamental respect and rights, we scarcely love them at all when we love them for their humanity alone.

Do you feel loved when someone gives you a gift that is identical to the gift he gives everyone else? When on your birthday your closest friend gives you a standard gift of cash—as opposed to other gifts you received, tailored by real people to suit your particular wants, needs, or passions? Certainly, those of us who have been through a grueling medical emergency feel unbounded gratitude for the medical personnel who cared for us. There is some form of love there—but it is a distilled, abstracted love, a love that, to maintain its professional effectiveness, must forbid truly personal attachments. There may be no profession more noble than medicine, but how can the doctor's concern for a patient compare with the knowing generosity of the lover?

Unlike universal love, redemptive love cannot exist in the abstract, but requires timely action toward real people. This is the meaning of the third part of Hillel's statement—*if not now, when?*—which suggests an urgency in our push to expand beyond ourselves. Like any living being, given the right kinds of investment the redemptive self grows and expands, looking to care for and nurture the real people we encounter. If the inner soul is made of fire, then our spiritual Sabbaths—our hobbies, our reading, our time alone or with friends—are fuel and oxygen, stoking our spiritual coals. We grow through these experiences; we become more human, more diverse, more sensitive to nuance, more wise. And the richer our inner being, the more natural it feels to include others in our love.

We are propelled outward: both toward our immediate family and friends, and also toward communal and political involvement. Just as our family and friends are our own, so too do we look to make our religious groups, our communal organizations, and our nations a part of ourselves.

This gives us some insight into the unique character of the biblical prophets. On the one hand, the Bible describes them as traveling in bands, engaging mostly in their own religiosity, perhaps through meditation and mystical experience; on the other hand, the prophetic words are redolent with public urgency—their messages are to kings and priests and the people, calling upon them not just to return to God as a spiritual calling, but above all to change their behavior and policies. For this the prophets take extraordinary risks with their own freedom and lives, spitting in the face of corrupt kings in an ancient world that had little tolerance for this sort of thing. They saw the people as their own extended selves, and there is nothing so natural as to risk yourself to save yourself.

But political action is only the outermost reach of the redemptive self. The urgency to expand finds its first voice in the active love of those who are closest to us. Fire spreads outward from the source—we seek the betterment, the health and happiness, and the inner well-being of our spouses, our children, and our friends. It is for this reason that the Sabbath, for all the investment in the individual it suggests, is also a time for nurturing our families, for taking responsibility for their physical and spiritual needs, for spending time with those we love. In our own Sabbath pleasure, we seek the Sabbath pleasure of our own.

All this helps us understand why the second version of the Ten

Commandments cites the exodus in describing the Sabbath. If the Sabbath represents the affirmation, emancipation, elevation, and expansion of the self, the escape from Egypt was all about the affirmation, emancipation, elevation, and self-expansion of the Israelite slaves.

Here is the text of the Fourth Commandment as it appears in Deuteronomy:

> Keep the Sabbath day, to sanctify it, as the Lord your God commanded you. Six days you shall labor, and complete all your work. But the seventh day will be a Sabbath for the Lord your God. You shall not do any work: Neither you, nor your son or your daughter, nor your man-servant or your maid-servant, your ox or your ass or any of your beasts, nor your stranger in your gates; that your man-servant and your maid-servant may rest as you do. And you shall remember that you were a slave in the land of Egypt, and the Lord your God took you out of there, with a strong hand and an outstretched arm. For this reason did the Lord your God command you to make the Sabbath day. (Deuteronomy 5:12–15)

Beginning with the words, "that your man-servant and your maid-servant may rest as you do," the entire text goes into waters uncharted in the first version in Exodus. It first doubles back to reemphasize one's servants and the importance of recognizing that they deserve to "rest as you do." To justify this, each of us is to remember our own past servitude, the horror and degradation of having our individuality taken from us, our freedom denied, our very selves treated as instruments for someone else's goals. The phrasing of "you shall remember" (*v'zacharta*) is pointedly in the singular: The exodus is a personal memory, one that every Israelite harbors in his soul. Finally, we are told that

115

"for this reason" did God command the Sabbath—a deliberate echo of the "for this reason" in the first version, which is about God's rest on the seventh day of Creation. The first time, it was about being alive, independent of our creations; the second time, it is about our emancipation.

These two justifications are in fact one. To be is to be free.

Modern life poses unprecedented challenges to the redemptive self, who struggles to maintain his independence and identity in the face of infinite pressures. Having earned the freedom to chart our own course, we find ourselves thrown by that very freedom into a highly competitive world. We are told to excel, to invest unbounded energy in advancement, to sharpen our marketable skills, to build our contacts. Every person we meet, we are told, is a potential client or employee; every minute is to be channeled toward goals we have set for ourselves. Our role models are inevitably those who have subordinated their whole lives to such goals.

The Fourth Commandment stands against these forces, providing room for the development of rich inner lives for each of us. Although the Sabbath is just one day a week, its importance stretches well beyond its hours. Throughout the week we find endless opportunities for personal growth—to read, to undertake hobbies, to spend time with our loved ones. Through the Sabbath we learn to take advantage of these opportunities and to create new ones, setting aside our goals and building our souls. In our recreation we find not only respite but also the keys to our love.

Where does such love begin? The first and most primal relationship we have, in which the self is inextricably enmeshed with another person, is our connection with our parents. Having established the self as both affirmed and expansive, the Fourth Commandment leads us logically into the Fifth, where the meaning of parenthood is explored, for us as both parents and children. Honoring one's parents, we quickly discover, is not as simple as it seems.

5

Wisdom of the Heart

Honor your father and your mother, that you may lengthen your days on the land which the Lord your God has given you.

The Bible offers very little elaboration on the Fifth Commandment. Other than a vague promise of "lengthening your days," we hear almost nothing about how we are supposed to honor our parents, when, or even why. Those few biblical stories that do talk about parents and their children usually focus more on rebellion than honor, and they are equivocal. Some, like that of Abraham who abandoned his father's home and religion to start something new in the hills of Canaan, are inspirational. Others, like that of King David's son Absalom, who challenged his father's rule and hurled ancient Israel into a bloody civil war, are wretched. Looking at the Bible alone, the Fifth Commandment remains something of a mystery.

The rabbis, on the other hand, had plenty to say on the subject, illuminating the Fifth Commandment with aphorisms and stories. "A person who has food in his home," they taught, "but does not give honor, food, and sustenance to his father and mother, is viewed by God as someone who engaged in murder all his life." We learn of people who went to extreme lengths to honor their parents. Rabbi Eliezer tells of a certain Dama, son of Netina, a Roman officer living in the coastal city of Ashkelon, who passed up a business offer that would have earned him six hundred thousand gold dinars because he was unwilling to disturb his sleeping father, under whose pillow lay the key to the safe where he kept his precious gems. When asked how far the commandment to honor one's father should be taken, Rabbi Eliezer answered: "Even if he throws a bag of gold dinars into the sea before your eyes, you should not chastise him."

Rabbi Tarfon, another sage of the time, was renowned for going far beyond the call of duty to help his aging mother. Once, when her shoe strap tore as they were walking in public, he put his hands under her foot and let her walk on them all the way home, until she reached her bed. But when she, troubled by her son's fawning, asked the rabbis to tell her son not to honor her so much, they answered that "even if he were to do this a million times, he would still not fulfill half the duty prescribed by the Torah."[1]

Such examples give us at least a partial picture of how the rabbis understood the Fifth Commandment. We honor our parents through boundless acts of love and caring, which begin with the understanding that they are not just authority figures of our past, but also living human beings with sensitivities and foibles like anyone else. We shower them with public displays of respect and deference: The Talmud teaches us "not to stand in his [one's father's] place, not to sit in his place, not to contradict him or defeat him in argument . . . to give him food and drink, clothing and shelter, to escort him as he enters and exits the home."[2] No less important, we also take responsibility for their well-being as they age, seeing that they are provided for, physically and financially, and that they enjoy companionship and care from the children they raised.

But the extremity of the rabbis' traditions, while showing us how seriously they took the commandment, does not go beyond the hows and into the whys—why honoring our parents is important in the first place, so important as to make it one of the Ten Commandments. For this, we will have to dig deeper.

We remember.

I remember my mother's insatiable embrace, my father's calming caress, my mother's operatic singing, my father's temper, my mother's hysteria, my father's restraint, my mother's dark glasses and black flowing hair done up sixties-style, my father's moral purity to a fault, my mother's refusal to care what the neighbors were doing or saying, my father's sharp and dry wit, old-world jokes, and Russian hat, my mother's terror at the idea of my playing softball after school ("there is nothing *soft* about that ball!"), my father's refusal to buy me swim fins ("first you learn to swim like a person, then you can swim like a fish"), my mother's penchant for avocado and endless piano études, my father's commitment of time playing catch or teaching me chess, my mother's mental illness, my father's efforts to protect me from it, the incessant screaming between them as I tried to sleep and pounded on the wall dividing our bedrooms to try to quiet them, my mother's deterioration after we moved out, my father's efforts to rebuild his life with a teenage child under his wing, my rejection of her and embrace of him. We look at old snapshots, some in albums and others in unfaded memory, and all the emotions come back, the smells of our parents' clothing, the feeling of being in their presence—even when our parents have hurt us, even when we cannot admit to ourselves that, deep down, we continue to love them.

We are full of unique memories of our parents, every one associated with the intense emotions of the child, amplified in our reliving them, memories that do not always lead to respecting them, indeed often lead to painful anger, to feeling sorry for the child who was us, to hatred for the flaws they saddled us with, maybe even a satisfaction in knowing there is someone to blame for our failures besides ourselves.

But there are also the good things—so many good things that as soon as we open ourselves to them, we are overridden with gratitude for the sacrifices they made, for the instincts and talents and education and skills they gave us, for an attitude of hope and determination they passed on to us, for just being there for us.

So many memories. What purpose do they serve?

Memory is the anchor of our souls. It is the thing we hold on to, the proof that there is a reality to who we are that is grounded in the past, in the experiences of our childhood—experiences that begin with mother and father. Our memories are *us,* and our parents are at the core of them.

We can never overstate our parents' influence on who we are. Sometimes it seems like our whole lives are nothing but a long series of decisions taken in their light, either imitating their teachings and examples, or consciously rejecting them. For every hug received, every pearl of wisdom imparted, every struggle undertaken on our behalf, every hour spent in their company, there is a reprimand resented, a falsehood, a betrayal, a bad decision, an abandonment, an act of violence—and all these are stored in our souls, burning in us, acting within us, replicated in our behavior to others.

So if the Fourth Commandment taught us about self-discovery as the key to the redemptive spirit, then one of the first things we learn about ourselves is how deeply we have been branded by the stamp of our parents. This does not mean we cannot act on our own—such hardwiring is no different from inborn talents and personality traits, which we spend our lives either celebrating or ignoring or overcoming. The difference is that our parents are also people, and this creates an obligation to see them as a first focus of our love, of an irrational commitment that nothing can ever break.

If you cannot honor your parents, you cannot honor yourself. If you cannot love them, you cannot love your own soul.

Yet the Fifth Commandment has still more to say. A careful look at the biblical passages shows that we are to honor our parents not just out of loyalty or gratitude, but because of something very specific they have given us.

It is a kind of wisdom, something no books or teachers can replace, something that almost all parents gives their children, to one degree or another: the basic instincts about how to be good. The real point of the Fifth Commandment is to honor our parents first of all for the good they have imbued in us— for the good they *are* inside us. Before we know anything about ethics or laws or abstract moral theories, our parents teach us intuitions about how to behave, patterns of honesty and curiosity and caring for others. This is the kind of wisdom we need throughout our lives, an inner moral compass without which the redemptive spirit is forever at a loss.

To understand what this really means, we must first take a brief look at the meaning of "wisdom" as it was understood by the ancient Israelites. There is a reason why our parents, and only they, deserve mention in the Fifth Commandment.

According to modern scholarship, most of the Bible was put into writing somewhere toward the middle of the first millennium B.C.E., around the time when other civilizations around the world also began articulating their views about wisdom. In China, India, Persia, and Greece, different teachings about wisdom emerged, teachings that would eventually express themselves in Buddhist, Hindu, Zoroastrian, and Greek philosophy. The Buddhists taught that wisdom was to be found in meditation, detachment from worldly concerns, and adherence to the abstract realm of the All; the Greeks found wisdom in the study of the nature of things and the employment of reason to draw true conclusions. The Israelites too developed an approach to wisdom, but theirs was very different.

The biblical figure most directly associated with wisdom is King Solomon, who reigned in the second half of the tenth century B.C.E. In the first book of Kings, we learn that soon after Solomon's ascent to the throne, God appears to him in a dream and asks him what is his wish. Solomon passes up on the more obvious gifts of riches and power, and instead asks for one thing only: wisdom. God is pleased, and immediately grants his request:

> Because you have asked this thing, and have not asked for yourself long life; neither have you asked riches for yourself, nor have you asked the life of your enemies, but have asked for yourself understanding to discern judgment: Behold, I have done according to your words. Lo, I have given you a wise and an understanding heart so that there has been none like you before you, nor after you shall any arise like you. (I Kings 3:11–12)

As the story progresses, we are told that "Solomon's wisdom excelled the wisdom of all the children of the east country, and all the wisdom of Egypt. For he was wiser than all men.... And there came of all people to hear the wisdom of Solomon, from all kings of the earth, who had heard of his wisdom" (I Kings 5:10–14).

Solomon's life takes up about half of I Kings and a large section of II Chronicles. Yet of all the accounts of his wars, wives, and wiles, there is only one story presented as an explicit example of his wisdom, and we should take it as deeply indicative of the Bible's overall view of what wisdom really means.

Soon after the night of his dream, two prostitutes come before King Solomon asking that he settle their dispute. The two, who live in the same brothel, each gave birth within a span of a few days. One of the babies has died, and one of the women now claims that the other took her own living child and replaced it with her dead one in the middle of the night; the second insists that hers is the living child. After hearing each side and considering the problem, the king makes a shocking pronouncement:

> And the king said, "Bring me a sword." And they brought a sword before the king. And the king said, "Divide the living child in two, and give half to the one, and half to the other."
>
> Then spoke the woman whose child was the living one to the king, for her love was enkindled toward her son, and she said, "O my lord, give her the living child, but do not slay it." But the other said, "Let it be neither mine nor yours, but divide it."
>
> Then the king answered and said, "Give her the living child, and do not slay it: She is its mother." And all Israel heard of the judgment that the king had judged; and they feared the king, for they saw that the wisdom of God was in him, to do judgment. So King Solomon was king over all Israel. (I Kings 3:24–28)

We may leave aside the apparent cruelty of Solomon's famous trick, for the story is meant to teach us something about his wisdom. Solomon faced one of the most excruciating cases imaginable: A wrong decision would leave a woman without her beloved child, and a child who would never know his own mother and would instead be raised by a deeply unscrupulous woman. To render his judgment, Solomon required a profound sensitivity to the connection between a woman and her baby, as well as for the overwhelming envy that would bring the guilty woman to prefer the child's death over his return to his mother.

It was this acute sense of how people work, and his extraordinary means for employing it in judgment, that showed the nation that Solomon had the "wisdom of God" and established his reign.

Wisdom is not, as Aristotle taught, knowing the causal relationship between events; it is not, as Plato taught, the knowledge of the ideal forms of things. It is not scientific knowledge or philosophy, metaphysics or meditation or technical excellence. What Solomon's story teaches us is that true wisdom is *human* wisdom: knowing the inner workings of the heart, and being able to tell right from wrong in a human world.

A crucial turn of phrase in Solomon's story sharpens the point. Solomon asks God not for a brilliant mind but for an "understanding heart"—and this is what God explicitly grants him. Later too we are told that "God gave Solomon very much wisdom and understanding, and greatness of heart like the sand that is on the seashore" (I Kings 5:9). Throughout the Bible, the seat of our wisdom is in the heart—which is also the seat of our passion, our mercy, and our redemptive fire.

Indeed, while there is no consistent word in the Bible for "brain" or "mind," the word "heart" (*lev*) appears countless times in speaking of the spirit, moral insight, and wisdom. Later, in the time of the Talmudic sages, when the influence of rationalist Greek philosophy was already felt, one rabbi actually proposed that the source of wisdom was in the head; but a second, Rabbi Yehoshua, quickly overruled him, declaring that it was "in the heart" and offering a flurry of biblical sources to prove his point.[3]

To say that wisdom is in the heart is to say that the deliberative, abstract thinker, the plodding researcher, and the quickly calculating mathematician are all far from being wise in and of themselves. The mind processes and accumulates information; the heart uses knowledge to respond to reality and react with the power of sentiment and judgment. By focusing on the heart, the Bible is suggesting that true wisdom is not in our thoughts, ideas, or beliefs, but in our intuitive responses to human realities.

We often think of morality as a system of rules: There are things you should do (help others, save lives, respect property) and things you shouldn't do (lie, steal, murder). In the modern era, an entire field of ethical philosophy has emerged with the sole purpose of deriving correct rules of behavior from philosophical assumptions grounded in reason—mostly without taking into account the inner qualities of character that make a person not just follow rules but also do the right thing without needing them. In the biblical view, moral rules may be useful in preserving social order, or as a shorthand for describing good behavior; but they are meant to reflect something deeper. It is our intuitive grasp of other people, our inner sense of right and wrong, and our reflexive acts to help others that are the only wisdom really worth having.

"All rivers go to the sea," the rabbis taught, "and all of a man's wisdom is in his heart."[4]

Where does such wisdom come from?

It comes, first of all, from our parents. For all they give us in terms of food, clothing, and shelter, none of these shape our souls as much as the thousands of moments when a parent teaches a child how to be good to others. While other moral teachers, whether historical figures like Socrates or the professors and preachers of today, engage our minds with doctrines and rules, and may inspire or scare us with the rewards or punishments in this life or the next, all these teachings are shallow and fleeting compared with parental wisdom. The former can be cast off like a dirty garment, others as easily donned in their place. Our parents, on the other hand, carve their teachings indelibly in our hearts.

They do this in three ways. The most important is moral conditioning, training our reflexive responses to human situations more than our conscious thoughts about them. We are not born knowing how to act when someone affronts us, shows us kindness, lies to us, or needs our help. We need to be trained, training our parents undertake as the first task of active parenting. No matter how many sermons we hear about right and wrong, none of these have the impact of rewards, punishments, and judgments handed down over the years of our childhood. The common expression "Spare the rod, spoil the child" is often taken as an endorsement of the physical punishment of children. Yet it actually comes from a verse in Proverbs—and the original offers a different message:

> He that spares his rod hates his son; but he that loves him chastises him early. (Proverbs 13:24)

By talking about "the rod" and "chastising" together, it is clear that this proverb is not about physical punishment per se, but about discipline in general, as a central component of moral conditioning. The danger being warned against is not "spoiling" the child (that is, causing him to lack discipline), but rather "hating" the child—cruelly allowing him to lack moral reflexes and to suffer greatly as a result. "Chastise your son while there is hope," we read later on, "and let not your soul spare for his crying" (Proverbs 19:18). It is when our kids are young that we may hope to train their moral instincts, and parents have to learn to suffer their tears so that their children will have the wisdom of the heart to be good later on.

Second, our parents give us wisdom through their example. When we are young, we imitate our parents' behavior without even knowing it—not just their patterns of speech, tastes, and interests, but also their basic habits of relating to other people, politeness and consideration, tolerance and urgency.

As we grow older, their example continues to make itself felt at every turn. Many of life's challenges come with the realization that our parents were there long before us: Building a career, enduring pregnancy and childbirth, raising children, maintaining a marriage or coping with divorce, caring for parents, and facing death—all of these can be painfully difficult aspects of adult life, and in every case we look to our parents' example, consciously or unconsciously, for guidance. Their example creates a comfort zone for our behavior: If we have seen them staying up late with a sick child, caring for an ailing parent, returning things that don't belong to them, giving to charity, protecting their family, reflexively helping those in need, we will have a much easier time doing the same.

Of course, this is true for negative examples as well. If our parents deceive or betray their friends, or neglect their families, we become far more comfortable with behaving similarly, no matter how many times they may have told us never to do such things. "A man should never tell his son, 'I will give you something,' and then not give it," the rabbis taught, "for in this way he teaches his son to lie."[5]

The third way our parents give us moral wisdom is through stories. We could call it "narrative parenting," for it refers to the tales they tell us about where we came from, and what we—the expanded "we" that includes our parents and ancestors—had to go through in order to get here. We return, again, to memory.

Throughout the Bible, the Israelites are told to remember the stories that their parents have taught them—especially about the exodus from Egypt:

> When your son asks you in time to come, saying, "What mean the testimonies, and the statutes, and the judgments, which the Lord our God has commanded you?" Then you shall say to your son, "We were the slaves of Pharaoh in Egypt; and the Lord brought us out of Egypt with a mighty hand; and the Lord showed signs and wonders, great and sore, upon Egypt, upon Pharaoh, and upon all his household, before our eyes. And he brought us out from there, that he might bring us in, to give us the land that he swore to our fathers." (Deuteronomy 6:20–23)

What an odd passage. A child asks about the meaning of "testimonies, statutes, and judgments," the long string of moral teachings and ritual obligations his parents have piled on him. The answer begins not with theories about politics and ethics, not with universal truths about peace and justice; neither are we given a vision of reward and punishment, or even a declaration of divine authority—"because God said so." Rather, the answer begins with the story of the exodus. For in the biblical view, it is precisely this story, and stories like it, that serve as a crucial basis for our wisdom of the heart, underlying all the other moral pronouncements in the Bible.

We have already seen the incredible potency of the exodus story. Through the memory of our own enslavement in Egypt, we learn about human suffering, a horrible experience that gives us the fundamental tools for identifying with the suffering of others, and for believing in the possibility of redemption.

But in biblical eyes, the exodus is not just a story about redemption; it is *our* story, a personal memory of what happened to our own ancestors—and, by extension, to us. This is emphasized in the Jewish ceremony on the first night of Passover, the holiday dedicated to celebrating the exodus from Egypt, when we are told that "in every generation, a person should look at himself as if he had come out of Egypt." The Passover service also includes the famous passage about the "four sons," each of whom asks his parents about the holiday in a different way, and each of whom receives a different answer. One of them, the "wicked" son, asks: "What does all this worship mean to you?" The response is brutal:

"To you"—and not "to us." Because he has removed himself from the community, he has denied the fundamentals of faith. So you shall set his teeth on edge and say to him, "For this has God taken me out of Egypt." "Me"—and not him. If he had been there, he would not have been redeemed.

This rebuke is meant to show just how important the first-person perspective is in telling redemption stories that have an impact on our moral sense. We may study the past with the dispassionate eye of the anthropologist, examining critically and scientifically the way traditions influenced other peoples at different points in time. But as soon as we take this kind of distance from our own history, we immediately risk cutting ourselves off from the source of our identity, and from the moral wisdom that has reached us through our parents. Such wisdom is so crucial to our moral fiber that if we do not identify with it, believing in the possibility of redemption with all our hearts because it has happened to us before, then redemption itself risks losing its place in our imagination, and becomes yet another ancient myth. We too "would not have been redeemed."

Of course, the exodus is not the only story worth telling. Each of us carries stories of earlier generations, of a past filled with struggle and challenge, hope and oppression and kindness to others, stories of how one grandparent arrived on our nation's shores in abject poverty and built a successful business from scratch, how another escaped the horrors of war in a far-off country and braved the winter on a long trek to safety, how another endured slavery or overcame an abusive husband or fought in the nation's wars.

In the Fifth Commandment, we learn that our parents have given us, in such stories, an inner platform for our moral fiber. They have given us countless exodus narratives, each offering the lessons of redemption, each one deepening our moral instincts and showing us what we are capable of, if we put our hearts into it.

To reject your parents' teaching is to give up on all of this—and to lay the groundwork for your own apathy, indifference, and systematic wrongdoing toward others.

And so, while other ancient traditions tried to show us how shallow parental wisdom was compared with the great truths of this prophet or that philosopher, the Bible repeatedly draws a direct link between honoring our parents and being good. The prophet Ezekiel assails the Judeans for their misdeeds by first mentioning their failure to fulfill the Fifth Commandment. "Among you they have made light of father and mother; in the midst of you have they dealt by oppression with the stranger; in you they have wronged the fatherless and the widow" (Ezekiel

22:7). And in the book of Proverbs, the failure to uphold parental honor is described as the first step toward evil:

> There is a generation that curse their father, and do not bless their mother. There is a generation that are pure in their own eyes, and yet are not washed from their filthiness. There is a generation, O how lofty are their eyes! And their eyelids are lifted up. There is a generation whose teeth are like swords, and their jaw teeth like knives, to devour the poor from off the earth, and the needy from among men. (Proverbs 30:11–14)

Here again we see a logical progression from dishonoring our parents to being generally bad people. By speaking of a "generation that curse their father, and do not bless their mother," the problem is framed as the cultural rejection of wisdom of the heart. People who ignore the Fifth Commandment naturally become "pure in their own eyes": They have convinced themselves that the moral teachings of their childhood are uneven and arbitrary, and should be dismissed in favor of "pure" ideology and a sweeping universal truth they have discovered on their own.

As a result, such people have nothing but their own self-invented values to guide them, no matter how bad they may really be—the license of the artist painting a picture of morality according to his taste. But because such people no longer are constrained by inbred habits of goodness, no longer rely on their memory to show them what true kindness and sensitivity look like, they inevitably end up deteriorating to the level of beasts, their sharp teeth devouring "the poor from off the earth, and the needy from among men."

Anyone who rejects the memory of his parents loses his inner moorings of right and wrong. He has repudiated his parents' secret wisdom of the heart. He deludes himself into believing that a new ideology or philosophy can replace it. In the end, his lack of inbred instincts makes him insensitive and cruel, outweighing anything he may have gained.

I will never forget an exchange I had with my father when I was in high school. He was a professor in the sciences, and when I started looking at colleges in eleventh grade, I asked him whether there were any schools he would refuse to let me attend. His answer took me by surprise.

"You can go anywhere you want," he said, and then paused. "Except MIT."

When I asked him what was wrong with MIT, he weighed his words carefully. "It's a pressure cooker," he said in his Israeli-accented English. "All the time I hear stories of students killing themselves there."

He was, of course, being unfair about MIT. Many of my friends ended up there and went on to build superb careers in research or industry without any noticeable trauma. But there was a deeper message here, a truth that has guided me at every turn. In a society where excellence is rewarded more than anything else, where the battle to the top knows no bounds, we have to struggle to make room for our own inner balance, our mental and spiritual health, our deepened selves. For my father, MIT epitomized a much broader societal ill, a culture of competitive excellence that distorted the important things in life to the point of endangering the well-being of young people. He wanted to protect me from that. In this sense, he was right.

Then there was the time when, as a child, I asked my father why our backyard was not nearly as lush and green as our neighbor's. "Look at that guy," he said. "Every week, I see him breaking his back on his lawn. Fertilizing, mowing, trimming, planting, he does it all by himself, over and over again. When I come home from work, I have been away from my kids all day. I want to talk to them, ask how their day was, maybe play a game or watch television with them. The lawn can wait."

Sometimes, a whole world of wisdom can be found in a parent's few words.

Yet like the masters of so many ancient schools, many of the teachers I encountered later on had very little respect for the teachings of our parents.

At the age of twenty-one, I was a rabbinic student at a prestigious Manhattan seminary. One of the more extreme rabbis was giving an afternoon talk about our future career paths. Speaking before a full auditorium, he implored us to ignore the advice of our parents, many of whom were telling us not to go into the rabbinate as a career, but instead to become lawyers or doctors or businessmen. He spoke of holiness, of the purity of one's God-given life, of his overwhelming love for the study of Torah. But at a certain point, deep in his sermonizing, he lost control of his rhetoric. "If your mother told you *not to wear underwear*," he asked suddenly, "would you listen to her?"

The old man smiled, for he thought he had given an elegant, New York–style slam-dunk argument against parental wisdom. You have all the answers you need right here, he was saying. Embrace the ocean of goodness and godliness that a life of religious study and teaching offers, trust your mind over your received instincts, and ignore the so-called wisdom of your benighted mothers and fathers.

Over the years I have met many rabbis who were sensitive and sensible people, dedicating their lives to a humane and insightful version of the biblical teaching. He was not one of them. Unlike the Bible, which teaches that there is a fluid consistency between moral truth and our parents' teachings, he unwittingly embraced the single most destructive commonplace of modernity: that our parents' wisdom is arbitrary, obscure, disconnected from what's really right and wrong, and that the greatest truths are found in the simple and sweeping prescriptions of ideology. One can take the Jewish "Torah" and replace it just as easily with Islam's "submission" or Christianity's "faith" or the facile axioms of communism or fascism or the French Revolution: Once you have the truth, he was saying, you no longer need your parents.

The rabbi's mistake should have been readily apparent, however. For, as opposed to the question of our career choices, *nobody's mother was actually telling us not to wear underwear.* The mothers and fathers who cautioned against entering the rabbinate were not advocating some stupid hygienic lapse. Rather, they were giving voice to a whole range of deeper concerns about their kids' career choices, some earned from hard experience, some out of their own religious traditions. Like my father's worries about MIT or excessive gardening, these parents had something deeper to convey. Maybe it was the belief in economic self-sufficiency as a way of avoiding the hard life of poverty and dependence that life as a rabbi brings. Or maybe it was more of a moral argument, that there is something corrupting in such dependence and detachment from ordinary life. Maybe they knew about the many voices in the rabbinic tradition that had opposed the whole idea of a professional rabbinate.

Parents are not always right, but their wisdom is rarely foolish or arbitrary. The rabbi, however, was telling us to ignore the Fifth Commandment.

Our parents' wisdom is the mother of all wisdom, for it is from our mothers and fathers that we get the first tools we need to relate to our human world. They alone give us the background morals we use to interpret our experiences, challenge fashionable beliefs, and judge the claims of political pundits, literary artists, religious leaders, moral philosophers, or anyone else who tries to tell us about right and wrong. The wisdom of our parents forms the first basis of our whole moral dialogue with the world.

All the rabbis' wild descriptions of honoring our parents make sense only in this light. We honor our parents because we celebrate ourselves, and to honor them, to ease their lives and publicly show our respect—these are the expressions of that celebration. For we know that the very best parts of who we are, we owe to them alone.

And just as we received our deepest goodness from our parents, we pass it on to our children. Every moment we spend with them, every casual outing to the mall, every time we help them with their homework, every rule we enforce or question we ask about their friends and romances and plans, every decision we make about their schooling or bit of advice we offer about their careers—in each and every act of parenting, we are passing on our wisdom of the heart.

Bringing children into the world is, for this reason, the ultimate redemptive act. There are good reasons why "Be fruitful and multiply" are the first words God says to man in the Bible. Like God, we are creators of humanity, investing our world with new life, expanding ourselves in love, challenging our beloved creations to live and grow, to develop themselves as sensitive human beings, as vital actors, as savvy redeemers driven by an inner fire, as profound and expansive selves. The Bible repeatedly aims its moral message not just to individuals or leaders, but specifically to parents, who are given the burden of transmitting its deepest truths.

When Moses concluded his farewell address to the Israelites just before they were to cross the Jordan River into the Promised Land, he put the entire moral heritage of the Bible into the context of parenting:

> And Moses made an end of speaking all these words to all Israel. And he said to them, Set your hearts to all the words which I testify among you this day, which you shall command your children to observe to do, all the words of this Torah. For it is not a vain thing for you; because it is your life: And through this you shall lengthen your days on the land, into which you go over the Jordan to possess it. (Deuteronomy 32:45–47)

The promise of "lengthening your days" is not common in the Bible, and when it appears we should take notice, for it is likely a deliberate reference to the Fifth Commandment's own words, *that you may lengthen your days on the land which the Lord your God has given you.* Indeed, wherever this specific reward appears, we find some reference to the unique link between parents and children. Solomon's gift of wisdom is predicated on his following in the footsteps of his father, King David: "And if you will walk in my ways, to keep my statutes and my commandments, as your father David did walk, then I will lengthen your days" (I Kings 3:14). In Deuteronomy we are told that the entire point of the biblical commandments is in order "that you might be in awe of the Lord your God, to keep all his statutes and his commandments, which I command you—you, and your son, and your son's son, all the days of your life, and that your days may be lengthened" (Deuteronomy 6:2).[6]

Malachi was the last of Israel's prophets. He ended his book with his vision of a messianic future when mankind as a whole finally abandons evil—a future, however, that depends entirely on the restoration of the link between parents and children. These are his very last words:

Remember the Torah of Moses my servant, which I commanded him in Horeb for all Israel, both statutes and judgments. Behold, I will send you Elijah, the prophet, before the
coming of the great and dreadful day of the Lord: And he shall
turn the heart of the fathers to the children, and the heart of the
children to their fathers, lest I come and smite the land with a
curse. (Malachi 3:22–24)

Amid the gloom and awe of humanity's final days, we again
see that the key to redemption lies in our "hearts"—parents
embracing their children, and children embracing their parents.
The threat to "smite the land with a curse" is the dramatic opposite of the Fifth Commandment's promise of "lengthening your
days on the land." The future of mankind rides on people's ability to turn their hearts to their parents and children—to ground
their moral instincts in memory, in redemptive wisdom passed
from one generation to the next, and in a love that spreads outward from ourselves, first of all to our most primal of relations
and then beyond, eventually embracing all of mankind.

We are bound to our parents by our memory, which contains
the keys to understanding ourselves, to preserving our deepest
instincts of right and wrong and passing them on to our children.
Memory is a gift, for it shows us who we are, and who we can be.

Yet there is another gift our parents have given us. It is the
gift of life, the brute physical fact of our being. Life is the most
irrational aspect of who we are, the one gift we can never even
contemplate, much less repay. With the gift of life, we leave the
realm of understanding and pass into the deepest mystical folds
of our existence. Memory we can grasp. Life is unthinkable.

For this reason, life gets its own commandment. It is to the
meaning of life that we now turn.

6

The Meaning of Life

You shall not murder.

In my adult life, I have lived in two places where murder was prevalent.

One was in New York City in the early 1990s. This was at the height of the horrific crime wave that devastated America's urban centers, and New York was leading the way. Every single day, six New Yorkers were murdered. This was the peak of a huge mountain of iniquity, of a kind of civilizational collapse, in which women could no longer walk outside at night for fear of being raped and routinely carried mace in their handbags, where many people avoided the subways and put two or three dead bolts on their doors, and whole sectors of the city were taken over by drugs, organized crime, and misery. In my neighborhood, Washington Heights, gunshots were often heard at night.

The other was in Jerusalem a decade later—literally worlds apart. Compared with New York, Jerusalem had no crime to speak of. No multiple locks, no fear of walking alone at night. But there was murder, nonetheless, in the form of terrorist attacks. For several months in 2001, barely a week would go by, often less, before another café would be blown up, or another city bus, over and over again, the heart-wrenching scenes of blood, the sirens, the dreadful wait until the list of victims was published and you would find out if a friend or relative was among them. Hundreds of people were murdered in a span of just a few months, in a city a twelfth the size of New York.

One of them was Gila Kessler. A gorgeous brunette in her late teens, a gymnast with Olympic hopes, sharp and smart and responsible, with a crazy love of life and an unbelievable way with kids. I had hired her countless times as a babysitter including for two full days when my family moved to Jerusalem in the summer of 2001. It was only a few weeks after that when she stood on a broad sidewalk at an intersection leading out of the city, together with many others who, like her, were waiting for their rides home in the suburbs. A suicide bomber ran into the crowd and blew himself up.

Gila was standing under a concrete bus shelter, which collapsed from the impact of the explosion. She died instantly.

I was still in bed the morning I heard about Gila, and I literally writhed with the madness of the news. Part of me mourned, as I would have if she had died from illness. But another part raged, sought revenge, was bewildered by the distortion of humanity required to do such a thing. Over the next week, my political views changed four times a day, and I alternated between depression and desperate rage against the attacker and those who sent him. *Who were these people? Where could I find them?*

Few of us have experienced the murder of a close friend or loved one, and fewer still have ever killed another human being for any reason. For most of us, murder is a faraway thing, far more distant than lying or stealing. We do not think about it too seriously, and live our lives more or less as if we and those we love are completely safe from it.

There is a reason for this. Unless we are directly involved in fighting crime or defending our country, we are usually the beneficiaries of a vast societal apparatus geared at shielding us from murder—from intelligence to the military to law enforcement to the courts to the prisons. Without all these, our world would swiftly deteriorate. Like the animals of the wild, many of us would die prematurely, and those who survived would do so only because they learned to fend off attackers, to become predators instead of prey. Instead, most of us can spend most of our energies building careers, loving, providing, creating, enjoying life. "Pray for the welfare of government," the rabbis taught, "for without it, man would eat his neighbor alive."[1]

Murder is so distant that we have no problem being entertained by it. We watch scary or silly movies where heroes and villains spray bullets into one another's bodies, TV dramas where investigators scour crime scenes and chase killers with wisecracking sobriety, news broadcasts that cover murder trials and genocide in far-off places with the same singsong concern they apply to sports and the weather. We debate the use of force in other countries and the propriety of the death penalty in our own, often mimicking the rehearsed pleas of politicians and pundits who share our well-honed ideological commitments. We reflexively disavow vengeance and retribution, usually without ever having even tasted the searing violation of the murder of someone close to us, without having ever held a gun in our hands pointed at someone who may die according to our decision, someone who may have just killed our friend in battle. We have the luxury of using our reason rather than hot passion.

Indeed, the neutralization of murder as an immediate concern in our lives is probably the greatest success of our civilization.

But it has come with a price. There is no avoiding the fact that the great majority of us are desensitized to murder. It is outside our experience.

Our numbness to the most hideous of evils allows us to live without fear. But it also lets us develop a whole range of political and cultural expressions where human life is belittled, demeaned, or forgotten. Our music and movies and literature condone violence to a radical degree. We embrace romantic political ideologies, thrilled by their simple answers and optimism, without caring about all the historical precedents that show how often they lead to the widespread killing of innocents. We entertain ourselves with flirtations and fantasies of violence, killing, and barbarism, watch *The Sopranos* and boxing and hang posters of Che Guevara on the wall. *Hasta siempre!*

The word "murder" should not inspire just horror-movie fear, bemused curiosity, rote outrage, or self-comforting political enlightenment. It should inspire, first of all, acute revulsion.

Hate the sin and not the sinner, we are told. Maybe that's okay for thieves and swindlers, for liars and Sabbath breakers and idolaters. If we cannot hate a murderer, we have a problem. We have lost something deep in ourselves, a spark of life, a natural and affirmative urge that is connected in its very foundations to the mother's primordial passion in protecting her baby, to the father's reflexive defense of his kin. Anger and hatred, as problematic as they can be in so many situations, nonetheless have their origin in a native desire to cling to life with all our might, and if we try to uproot those emotions completely, if we say that even murder should be framed in clinical and clerical equanimity, then we risk destroying the deepest sources of our humanity as well. In trying to dump out the brutal bathwater in us, we have thrown out the humane, redemptive baby. We have become creatures of detachment down to the core. God help us.

• • •

Maybe our problem is that we don't value life enough.

This may sound overwrought. We are very proud of ourselves as free, modern Westerners, committed to the sanctity of human life. And indeed, the West has two great things to be proud of. One is science, giving us the most rapidly developing, technologically advanced civilization in history. The other is political freedom, bringing emancipation and rights to women, to minorities, to foreigners, and all classes. Taken together, we have created a world where the individual can live longer, can choose his own life and his political leaders, can communicate with others, can get places faster than ever before. We have discovered the radical combination of reason and liberty needed to unleash the unbounded potential of the individual.

But when it comes to the value of life itself, sometimes it feels like we're still waiting for the revolution. From violence in our streets to terror in our skies, from honor killings to organized crime to wartime atrocities to domestic violence, we tolerate murder to a breathtaking degree. Not so long ago, the most enlightened nation in Europe embarked on the most far-reaching plan of genocide in human history, exterminating its innocents by the millions as the world stood by. Today, similar wickedness is repeated elsewhere in the world, in places like Sudan and Rwanda, places where if we really cared we could stop the killing. Our collective Western pride blinds us to our collective failure to stop the worst crimes. Do we really care about life as much as we think?

In the decades that have passed since the Holocaust, a stunned and cowed West has pondered how it was possible. Whole movements of art and philosophy have cropped up to express the sense of being morally dumbstruck that seems to be the only coherent response to the utter failure of modernity. How could

Germany, a nation that produced Goethe and Beethoven and Einstein, do such a thing? And what does it say about us?

There is a simple answer, if we want to hear it. It is not that Germans are so different from Americans or other Western-ers. Nor is the Holocaust to be dismissed as a unique moment of societal insanity, when charismatic conjurers captured the minds of an innocent populace.

The problem, rather, is that life is a different value from reason and freedom. We may preach the wonders of scientific thought and civil rights all we want. But if we don't believe in *life* with all our heart, if we don't celebrate it and defend it with our whole being, if we allow our own cleverness and sophisti-cation to distract us from the threats to the value of life that we entertain every day, then we should never be surprised to find ourselves lacking tools to overcome the brilliant machinations of the mass murderer.

The street killer, the jealous husband who shoots his wife, the troubled teen who gets his hands on an AK-47 and guns down his classmates, the war criminal, or religious fanatic killer—on the face of it, they have almost nothing in common. The word "murderer" includes so wide a range of psychological and cul-tural antecedents as to make it almost meaningless.

What all these share is not their psychology or ideology, but an *absence* of anything to stop them: a profound sense of the preciousness of human life, one powerful enough to overcome the will to kill, whatever its source. What is missing is a deeply ingrained, culturally conditioned, conscientious revulsion to murder, an overwhelming *No* that stays their hand, the most basic moral instinct we can ask for—the instinct to cherish the lives of others. For all these people, murder has become a real option, a deed that can be weighed, considered, justified.

The Sixth Commandment teaches us that where murder is

reviled, civilization begins. And where it is condoned, human-ity is destroyed. Phrased positively, the Sixth Commandment affirms human life as the cornerstone value of civilization.

But what do we mean by human life? Herein lies the trouble.

There are basically two approaches to the primacy of life, and the one you choose can make all the difference in the world. One of them looks at life as an impossible miracle, an unfathomable gift from God, an unchallenged axiom of all our equations. It is precious and holy. The material world is so depraved, this rea-soning goes, it is unthinkable that God of the spirit would imbue our putrid flesh with divinity. For many ancient and modern thinkers, only detachment from the mundane affairs of this world gives us the perspective needed to refrain from destroying it. Killing is the ultimate crime because it means giving your-self over entirely to the forces of the wild, to animal passion. In an ideal world, no one would ever take the life of another. War would cease, and there would be no need for armies or police.

This sounds like an appealing stance, but it contains some serious flaws.

The biggest problem is that it is arbitrary. Miracles brook no reasonable discussion. To describe something as miraculous means there is no possible way to understand it. Because we can-not understand life, we inevitably get caught up in a debate over definitions, without any obvious way out: Do we include human embryos or not? Do we include animals or not? What about a terminal cancer patient easing the end of his life by refusing treatment? Such an approach to life renders its contours cere-bral and assertive instead of intuitive and coherent; we try to describe it without ever feeling like we understand it. And if we cannot understand it, we cannot really make it a part of our inner moral sense, our wisdom of the heart.

By way of comparison, look at the way we relate to the other two great Western values, reason and freedom. We do not speak of them in terms of "sanctity." These are not seen as miraculous, but as very real parts of our lives. Because of this, we can explore them and appreciate them, exercise them every day, intuitively know what promotes or undermines them, develop coherent policies and curricula for our colleges. Because we understand them deeply, we can try to work them into the depth of our instincts and those of our children.

The "sanctity" of life, however, is mainly a negative value. We try to prevent killing and violence, and insist on safety standards for our children. But can we teach them what life *is,* and why it is so important?

A second problem is that such an approach to life often ends up being both unfair and impractical. Again, recourse to the miraculous makes us disregard any contradictions and refuse any exceptions. If life is sacred and unthinkable, then we come to focus on the act of taking life rather than its context: It becomes easy to draw an equivalence between the police officer who guns down an armed assailant and a murderer who stalks and kills a child. But how are we supposed to live, if life is so sacred that we cannot even defend ourselves without being somehow immoral? How can we disdain the basic elements of the material world—flesh, blood, passions, anger—and still say that we affirm life, which is built on these very foundations?

We have, however, inherited another approach to life from the ancients, championed by the Israelites thousands of years ago. The phrasing of the Sixth Commandment gives us a first clue of what we're after. In Hebrew, it reads *lo tirzah*—which I, along with most Jewish and Protestant translators, have rendered *You shall not murder.* The King James version, which was the first authorized English translation of the Hebrew Bible, has the more common "Thou shalt not kill." But in Hebrew, "to kill" is a different verb, just as it is in English. It would have been *lo taharog.*

To say that every time one person "kills" another he has violated the Sixth Commandment, is to make every soldier or police officer, every victim who kills in self-defense, into a kind of murderer—perhaps a permitted one, a tragic one, but cut from the same cloth nonetheless. One can understand where this is coming from: If human life is the ultimate irrational holy thing, then by taking life we are guilty, no matter the circumstances, and no matter the kind of destruction that would be wreaked in human life if all our soldiers and police officers were suddenly to declare their conscientious objection to service. Absolutes are absolutes, and miracles are miracles. There is nothing more important than the purity of the soul—even if the whole of human society collapses under its weight. Better never to put your finger on the trigger and be innocent of shedding blood, even if more blood is shed as a result. Be pure, and avoid damnation.

The Israelites did not believe in this kind of purity. They believed, rather, in the success of human life in the real world. If "Thou shalt not kill" implies the absolute inviolability of biological life, *You shall not murder* implies something else: an affirmation of humanity as such, of *human* existence, body and spirit alive. When someone allows his rage, his ideology, his jealousy, or his poverty to bring him to killing another, he destroys humanity, dehumanizes all of us, and reduces redemption to rubble. But when soldiers and police protect their citizens, enabling them to watch movies, go to work, raise their kids, and sit in coffee shops without the permanent fear of predators or external enemies, they are affirming humanity—even if they are forced to take the lives of those who seek to destroy it.

The murderer, in other words, is the ultimate antihuman, one who, in killing another, has negated the idea of humanity that is the pinnacle and purpose of Creation.

The morning of the sixth day of Creation started much like any other. After spending most of his week making the sun, moon, stars, waters and land and trees and birds and fish, God made cattle and beasts of the field. As in the past, he declared these things to be "good."

But then he tried something new. His final act of Creation was to re-create himself.

> And God said, Let us make mankind in our image, after our likeness. And let him have dominion over the fish of the sea, and over the birds of the air, and over the cattle, and over all the earth. (Genesis 1:26)

This is rather surprising and scarcely elaborated on in the verses that follow—we hear about mankind appearing as both male and female, and what they may and may not eat, but very little about what human life really is made of.

In the second chapter of Genesis, however, we get another account of mankind. Because it returns to the subject of how the world was formed, many scholars see it as a "second Creation story," perhaps an alternate text that has been woven artificially into the narrative. Yet it is clear that this chapter serves a purpose different from the first Creation story. There we learned of man's place relative to the rest of Creation—as the very peak, as the "very good" in contrast to everything else which was merely "good." In the second chapter, we learn what makes man unique.

> These are the generations of the heaven and of the earth when they were created, in the day that the Lord God made the

THE MEANING OF LIFE

earth and the heavens. And no plant of the field was yet in the earth and no herb of the field had yet grown, for the Lord God had not caused it to rain upon the earth, and there was not a man to till the ground. But there went up a mist from the earth, and watered the whole face of the ground. And the Lord God formed man of the dust of the ground, and breathed into his nostrils the breath of life; and man became a living soul. And the Lord God planted a garden eastward in Eden; and there he put the man whom he had formed. (Genesis 2:4–8)

In the run-up to the Garden of Eden story, Creation is reduced to a single day rather than six, suggesting that all existence is of a single kind, willed into being by a single God. Yet this world is at first lifeless, and man is formed not as the end of Creation but as the beginning of life, without whom the living world has no hope. God takes the soil from the primordial moonscape and fashions man, breathing "into his nostrils the breath of life," transforming him from a purely material dust form into "a living soul." No mention is made of Adam's having a preexisting or eternal existence. But his life spirit, the singular gift from God that makes him ready to enter the garden, sets him apart from all Creation. And his body, his material reality, sets him apart from everything divine.

There is no ancient text that affirms human life the way the Old Testament does. When other traditions, such as the Greek philosophers, ancient Christians, or wise teachers of the East, affirm life, inevitably they end up affirming only part of it— usually the life of the "soul" or of "reason," a life completely gutted of our more "animalistic" side. Biology is, in many senses, seen as our enemy.

The Hebrew Bible, by contrast, embraces the totality of man—body and spirit in a single, unbreakable unity that contains in it both the culmination of Creation and the "likeness" of God. Life is *life,* from its lowest material origins to the height of moral and artistic achievement. To celebrate life is to celebrate ourselves as we really are: breathing, thinking, loving, redemptive selves.

Consider the Bible's attitude toward the human body.

Modern culture has serious issues with the body. Sometimes we are told to focus intensely, almost obsessively, on health and fitness—as anyone browsing a bookstore, attempting to dodge the joggers filling our streets in the morning, or watching the procession of pharmaceutical advertisements on television will attest. At the same time, our bodies' appearance has become a permanent source of concern, the bedroom mirror an ebullient oracle of dismay pushing us toward ever-stranger diets and compulsive cosmetic surgery. Beyond the worries about our health and looks, we are also often told that physical pleasures—the natural signals that tell us what is life-affirming and good—are to be distrusted, so we avoid our favorite foods, or are pushed to a Puritan aesthetic that makes us feel guilty about beauty. And when we are not obsessing about our bodies, we are often in denial, abusing them through drugs, alcohol, overeating, or willful neglect. As we age, we often speak of our bodies "betraying us," which makes them sound like a servant or a fickle friend, rather than just who we are. For many of us, the body is a realm of dissatisfaction, alienation, and guilt.

This deep insecurity about physicality goes way back. From its origins in ancient Greece, and well into modern times, a powerful stream of Western thought took a very dim view of our physical existence. According to this teaching, the body is a depraved jumble of feelings, urges, and mindless tissues, whereas who we really are is found in the "soul"—a pure, eternal self, separate from the body and connected with all things that are abstract, truthful, and everlasting. Plato taught that "the philosopher dishonors the body; his soul runs away from the body and desires to be alone and by herself." The Jewish-Greek thinker Philo, a contemporary of Jesus whose teachings influenced Christianity at its earliest stages, described the body as "wicked and a plotter against the soul" and "a cadaver and always dead." Our living bodies, for all their supposed sanctity, were seen as the source of shame and weakness, our inevitable failure to live up to the perfection of the Divine.

The Israelites thought otherwise. Throughout the Old Testament our bodies are seen not primarily as a source of impurity and sin, but as the first manifestation of life itself. The psalmist can feel only gratitude to God for having created his body:

> For you have formed my reins; you have knit me together in my mother's womb. I will praise you, for I am fearfully and wonderfully made: Marvelous are your works, and my soul knows that right well. My frame was not hidden from you, when I was made in secret, and curiously wrought in the lowest parts of the earth. Your eyes did see my unshaped flesh; for in your book all things are written. (Psalms 139:13–16)

Our bodies, though inscrutable and complex, are nonetheless a gift of God; physical life is to be appreciated, enjoyed, protected, and nurtured. Longevity, for example, is considered a blessing in the Bible, while martyrdom, which played such a crucial role in Greek and early Christian writing, is shunned. Whereas Socrates prematurely took his own life by drinking the hemlock rather than flee Athenian justice, and Jesus remained forever young by passing from this world at the age of thirty-three, the Old Testament's heroes were almost always rewarded

with old age and a natural death: Abraham died at the age of
175, Moses at 120; David died "in a good old age, full of days" (I
Chronicles 29:28), whereas Job was well into his second century
when he died, "old and full of days" (Job 42:17). There are in
fact very few cases where a favorable character in the Old Testament dies prematurely, and when it does happen—as with King
Saul's son Jonathan, killed in battle in the book of Samuel—it
is seen as a bitter loss, a violation of the natural order of life. As
opposed to romantic notions of early death that have captured
the Western imagination from Justin Martyr to John F. Ken-
nedy, the noble death in the Old Testament comes late and in
peace.

But beyond the question of longevity, the Old Testament over
and over affirms physical pleasure per se as part of its affirmation of life. "Go your way, eat your bread with joy, and drink
your wine with a merry heart," we read in Ecclesiastes, "for God
has already accepted your works. Let your garments be always
white, and let your head lack no oil. Live joyfully with the wife
whom you love all the days of your fleeting life" (Ecclesiastes
9:7–9). "Wine makes the heart of man rejoice," the psalmist
teaches (Psalms 104:15). "Hope deferred makes the heart sick,"
we read in Proverbs, "but desire fulfilled is the tree of life" (Proverbs 13:12). One who undertakes monastic-style deprivations,
such as forswearing wine, is required to bring a sacrifice later to
atone for the sin that such deprivations entail.[2] And while there
may be moments in life when fasting encourages a certain kind
of spiritual experience—such as the annual fast of the Day of
Atonement, or Moses' making do without food and water for
forty days on Mount Sinai—these are quite clearly the excep-
tion. For most people, we are told, "You shall eat, and be satisfied, and bless the Lord your God in the good land which he has
given you" (Deuteronomy 8:10).

The rabbinic tradition, for all its austerity and discipline, took the biblical affirmation of physical life even further. Because the commandments are meant to enhance life rather than deny it, the rabbis ruled that the entire system of Jewish law (with a tiny number of exceptions) is to be suspended when life or limb is in danger. Dietary laws, the Sabbath, prayer service, regard for property or ritual purity—all these vanish the moment a life is threatened, even if that danger is distant or indirect. In order to encourage people to save one another's lives, for example, the rabbis allowed firefighters, medics, and other emergency personnel not only to violate the Sabbath but to travel home after the emergency is over, in apparent violation of the law.[3]

The rabbis also expanded on the Bible's affirmation of pleasure. "In the world to come," the Talmud teaches, "a man will have to account for every good thing his eyes saw, but of which he did not eat." Mindful of this, Rabbi Elazar made a point of eating every available type of permitted food at least once a year. In describing the right way to celebrate the major Jewish festivals of Passover, Shavuot, and Succot, the rabbis interpreted the biblical verse "and you shall rejoice in your holidays" in a particularly carnal way: "There is no rejoicing," they taught, "without meat [and] wine."[4] They also instituted a whole range of blessings that were, and continue to be, recited by Orthodox Jews today, before or after pleasurable acts like eating or sleeping. They saw these pleasures not as sources of shame but as experiences of physical life that could be elevated through a show of gratitude. Even going to the bathroom is cause for praising the Creator:

> Blessed are you O Lord, King of the Universe, who has made the human with wisdom, and created in it orifices and hollows. Revealed and known it is before your throne of glory, that should any of these be opened or shut up, it would be impossi-

ble to live before you. Blessed are you, the healer of all flesh who does wondrous things.[5]

In the rabbinic view, physicality, both in its pleasures and in the fulfillment of its needs, is inherently positive, part of the celebration of life. We are alive when we are physical—when we play basketball or go for a drive in the country, when we smell perfume or taste ice cream, when we take in the grand vistas of the ocean or the valley far below us, when we invest in our health, when we experience the pleasures of food and drink and sex and sleep. All of these can be vices if allowed to overtake our judgment—but all begin as an affirmation of our basic physiology, the processes of life that are inherently good.

The flesh is beautiful, our bodies wondrous. According to the Bible, we cannot truly value life if we do not value living.

But this is only the beginning. The Bible is not an epicurean text, promoting pleasures of the flesh above all else. Rarely in the biblical or rabbinic traditions do we find the kind of rapturous praise of strength, endurance, speed, or virility that is so familiar in ancient mythology. There are no glorifications of intercourse and sexual organs of the kind we find in pagan antiquity. Sexuality is often spoken of through metaphor, as in the use of the verb "to know": "And Adam knew his wife Eve, and she conceived and bore Cain" (Genesis 4:1). Nor is desire always to be indulged: Joseph is tested by the advances of Potiphar's wife, and his rejection of her is a crucial step on his path to greatness; Samson's downfall begins with his lust for the duplicitous Delilah. And the Bible's numerous dietary restrictions suggest that appreciating life entails something more than gratification—an awareness that, as God famously tells the Israelites, "Man does not live by bread alone" (Deuteronomy 8:3).

But if not by bread alone, then by what else? We may say the "spirit," yet here again we need to be careful about what we mean. If some ancient Greeks and early Christians deprecated the body, it was because they believed that our real identity was in the "soul"—the true locus of wisdom, freedom, purity, and truth. The body was temporary and destined for the grave; the soul was seen as eternal, entering the body for a brief time but destined for an endless journey in another world. This radical separation between soul and body was mirrored by Buddhism and Hinduism as well, which taught of the soul as needing to detach itself from the world and merge with the universe, and it was eventually taken up to one degree or another by all the major Western religions, including Judaism, which described an eternal life after death, an ethereal world tailored to each according to his acts or beliefs during his life. Most important, this eternal soul was described as true *life,* whereas our actual physical lives are but an illusion, a "corridor to the World to Come."[6]

Thus it may come as a surprise to discover that the Old Testament makes almost no mention of heaven and hell, the afterlife, or any other kind of human experience detached from the body. This does not mean that the Bible rejects the possibility of life after death—there are a few places where it seems to be confirmed, such as Saul's summoning of the deceased Samuel through a diviner, or the multiple references to the death realm of Sheol. But in all such cases, the afterworld is never described in positive terms; it is a land of darkness about which we know nothing. "I go whence I shall not return," Job says. "A land of gloom, as darkness itself; and of the shadow of death, without any order, and where the light is as darkness" (Job 10:21–22).[7] If there is life after death, the biblical authors saw little point in describing it.

The spirit, on the other hand, is mentioned countless times. The Bible has many words for the spirit, including *nefesh, neshama, ruah,* and *lev,* each of which touches on a different aspect of the life that emerges beyond the mechanics of the body, from passion to wisdom to creativity to vitality.[8] Joshua, leader of the Israelites after Moses, is referred to as "a man with spirit in him" (Numbers 27:18), whereas God tells Moses that he has filled Bezalel, the architect of the Tabernacle, with "the spirit of God, in wisdom, in understanding, in knowledge, and in all manner of workmanship" (Exodus 31:3). Samson is driven by the "spirit of God," which enables amazing feats of strength, while it gives King Saul the ability to prophesy. "My spirit longs, indeed, it faints for the courts of the Lord," the psalmist sings. "My heart and my flesh cry out for the living God" (Psalms 84:3).

As a child I was told that the Eskimos have thirty words for snow. If a multiplicity of terms suggests a deep concern and awareness of nuance, then the spirit is one of the Bible's most important points of reference.

But if there is so much spirit and so little afterlife, then to understand the Bible's view of life we have to break out of centuries of thinking about our true living selves as otherworldly, and of the spirit as something pure, abstract, and antithetical to biology. In the Old Testament, the spirit is part and parcel of our daily lives, our psychology and our energy and our wisdom and our character, an extension of physicality rather than its antithesis, ingrained in our nature from birth, divine in origin but nonetheless central to what the Bible means in its praise of life.

The spirit is inseparable from the body. Our blood and bones are the source of our energy; our vitality depends entirely on our health. Every love, every calculation, every urge and its overcoming—all these are also neurons that fire up, hormones secreted, a heart that beats faster. We cannot be creative if we haven't slept, cannot think clearly if we haven't eaten, cannot take responsibility for others if we fall ill. The body is not the prison of the spirit, nor even its temple. It is its lover, its life partner, its inseparable being. It is the match from which the fire of spirit rises.

This unique approach to human life is expressed even in the most mundane aspects of daily life, such as the clothes we wear.

Whereas the Greek sculptors adulated the naked form as a human ideal, the Bible sees nudity as a regression to our animal state, an affront to man's spiritual uniqueness. The moment Adam and Eve taste the fruit of the tree of knowledge of good and evil—the key moment in their investment with human spirituality and moral discernment—their nudity becomes a source of shame, and God knits them loincloths out of fig leaves. Their shame is not of physicality itself, so much as an expectation that their physical state should reflect their new spiritual status, a marker that identifies man as different from the animals while being fully flesh. "Who told you that you were naked?" God asks (Genesis 3:11). Until you became truly human, you didn't know there was anything else to be; when you were just animals there was nothing shameful about showing off your genitals. It is your unique spirit that makes you so different from them. Look the part.

Of course, this does not mean that spiritual excellence is always expressed in increasing layers of clothing. Sometimes the spirit must let loose by shedding the confines of dress. Thus when King David, the epitome of the redemptive spirit, marches into Jerusalem bringing with him the Ark of the Covenant from its exile among the Philistines in the book of Samuel, he dances in the streets wearing little more than a linen vest—to the chagrin of his wife, Michal:

And David leaped about before the Lord with all his might; and David was girded with a linen efod. . . . And as the ark of the Lord came into the city of David, Michal, Saul's daughter, looked through a window, and saw King David dancing and leaping before the Lord; and she despised him in her heart. . . . And Michal the daughter of Saul came out to meet David, and said, "How glorious was the king of Israel today, in that he uncovered himself today in the eyes of the handmaids of his servants, as one of the low fellows shamelessly uncovers himself!"

And David said to Michal, "It was before the Lord, who chose me before your father, and before all his house, to appoint me prince over the people of the Lord, over Israel. Therefore will I play before the Lord. . . . And of the maidservants of whom you have spoken, of them shall I be had in honor." And Michal the daughter of Saul had no child to the day of her death. (II Samuel 6:14–23)

This is one of those moments where the Old Testament bares itself, like David dancing the dance of life. Like the half-naked, flag-bearing Lady Liberty leading the French people in Delacroix's famous painting, David's undress reveals a ferocious love and an overwhelming redemptive spirit. Michal is repeatedly referred to as the daughter of Saul, the first Israelite king who failed precisely because he lacked the spiritual fire that burned in David's heart. In David's view, the return of the Book of Life to the capital city of the Israelites could not be marked with august pomp. It required that he show his people that the greatest moments of life are moments of the spirit, in which we "play before the Lord," leaping about with all our might.

Michal's punishment, as cruel as it sounds, serves as the didactic punch line of the story: David's dance was the ultimate affirmation of life, the celebration of the spirit through the bared body, at the very moment when his people were being invested with the symbol of redemption, the ark bearing the Ten Commandments. By denying all this, Michal was denying life itself, and was punished with barrenness.

It is hard to overemphasize how crucial this story is for understanding the ongoing praise of life taking place throughout the Old Testament—and how far a cry it is from the dry, grimacing "book of the Law" that people have made it out to be for millennia. For every moment of anger in the Bible there is a moment of love, for every punishment there is a redemption, for every livid prophecy of doom there is a prophetic song of hope, for every wise proverb there is a psalm bursting with life. What binds all of these is not callousness to human frailty but an intensity of life that may live despite the possibilities of loneliness, thievery, murderousness, lies, slavery, abuse, and strife that forever threaten to drown us all as it did in the time of Noah. Without this kind of affirmation of life, we would have little idea what to do with passages like this one:

> See, I have set before you this day life and good, and death and evil; in that I command you this day to love the Lord your God, to walk in his ways, and to keep his commandments and his statutes and his judgments: Then you shall live and multiply, and the Lord your God shall bless you in the land into which you go to possess it. . . . I call heaven and earth to witness this day against you, that I have set before you life and death, blessing and curse: Therefore choose life, that both you and your seed may live. (Deuteronomy 30:15–19)

Here we find all the key ingredients to the biblical affirmation of life represented in the Sixth Commandment: First, that life and death are synonymous with good and evil—that man's goodness is also his greatest affirmation of life, and thus when God describes the creation of man on the seventh day as "very good," whereas everything else is merely "good," we can say that man, unlike animals, has life beyond life, the life of the redemptive spirit. Second, that the affirmation of life means to "walk in his ways," to imitate God's redemptive nature. And finally, that the life of the spirit is not contradictory to prosperity and the success of the flesh, but rather is inseparable from it. If we love and grow, we will also "live and multiply" and receive blessings in the land.

This is the life that the murderer takes away. Every human being is a story, a redemption in the making, a divine fusion of flesh and spirit that has no parallel in the universe. Every murder is the undoing of all Creation, an absolute repudiation of the value of human life that is the purpose of everything. "When someone takes the life of another," the rabbis taught, "it is as if he has destroyed the whole world."[9]

We are of two minds about life. There is always a part of us that finds comfort in the idea of life as sacred, miraculous, and absolute, an approach that tells us to refrain from killing but often makes us apologize for living. So much of modern life is built on hard work and discipline, of pleasures denied for the sake of achievement, that we often neglect the life that the Bible is trying to affirm, instead filling our days and nights with constructive toil and self-imposed duties, losing ourselves in a whirlwind of work, chores, emails, meetings, and the uniquely modern compulsions of fitness and diet. Even our family life is often seen first of all as a matter of responsibility rather than enjoyment of time with our spouse and children. In a culture that places responsibility and achievement above all else, our pleasures become "indulgences," our intellectual activities limited to studying for degrees, our vacations "getaways," which sound more like a criminal's escape than an essential life experience. We have not yet come to terms with the affirmation of life. It confuses us, gets in the way of success, makes us feel guilty.

The Bible is not suggesting that we quit our jobs and become life-affirming shepherds like Abraham, Moses, and David. But just as the Sabbath teaches us to focus on ourselves one day per week as a first step toward our affirmation of the self, so too does the biblical heroes' profession tell us something about the life that the Bible is affirming with the Sixth Commandment.

The shepherd's life is not without struggle. The constant search for pasture, the daily caretaking of beasts, and the warding off of predators is anything but the Garden of Eden. But it is a life with enough of its own pleasure, pleasures of body and spirit, that one need not be haunted by the constant questions of inner alienation, of subordination to the dictates of others, of whether we are being taken advantage of, of the fears that modern life continuously plants in our hearts. It is a life where our own physical and spiritual health is not a source of guilt, where the self-expanding love of others does not contradict our own success. It is a life where life, the spirit and body together, reigns supreme.

The life-affirming self, however, cannot rest in the confines of his own lonely existence. The redemptive spirit, as we have seen, wants to thrill not only in his own life but in another's as well. We turn outward, body and soul.

We turn to love.

7

Love and Ecstasy

You shall not commit adultery.

Of all the prohibitions of the Ten Commandments, adultery
is probably the hardest to talk about. First of all, it is complicated. You have the confluence of three sticky problems: The
problem of marriage, a formal, public bond with strong sacral
overtones, but that most nonreligious people take seriously nonetheless; the problem of sexuality, an animal urge whose origins
are in the deepest recesses of our biology and that often makes us
do things we know to be wrong; and the problem of love, which
is a real human, spiritual commitment to another, but which,
once ignited, can be so fierce as to destroy everything in its path.
In the quest for marital fidelity we find all three problems crash-
ing together like particles in a nuclear reactor.

Adultery is hard to talk about also because it is often traumatic and damaging, not just to the spouse who is betrayed but
also to the adulterer, to the extended families, and especially to
the children, who must carry the burden of one of their parents
betraying the other for the rest of their lives.

Finally, adultery is about sex, and sex is hard to talk about.

According to surveys, about one in every five Americans, and two in every five people around the world, have extramarital affairs. Because more people will hide their affairs when answering a survey than will falsely profess infidelity, we can assume the real numbers are higher. These are cold, unpleasant facts.

Partly as a result of these figures, we frequently hear talk about the collapse of marriage in modern society. Social critics point, in addition, to soaring divorce rates, premarital sex, and the growing legitimacy of "alternate" forms of marriage as clear indicators that something very precious is being lost, that the core of the family is unraveling as the anchor of social stability.

But the collapse of marriage might be too easily blamed on modernity and its promiscuities, its glorification of sex and moral dissolution, and not enough on the failure of most people to have a clear idea of what marriage is about. Sometimes marriages fail because of a momentary loss of control against the tide of temptation that washes over us from time to time. But just as often they fail because they have ceased to reflect a genuine and powerful bond of love between the two partners, and because people are far less willing to live loveless lives than they used to be. This is the real problem. If the love is there, sexual betrayal can often be overcome in fixing a marriage. If it is not, then adultery is often just a match being struck in a sealed house with the gas left on.

I am not trying to justify the casual attitude to adultery that many of us have. Rampant adultery is a blight on society, one that undermines the core of the family as an institution for stable relationships of love and for the raising of healthy children. But both adultery and the "softer" failures of marriage cannot be understood without looking at the deeper problem that leads to them. It is the problem of not knowing what marriage is for—and why it is so important to leading redemptive lives. If the Sixth Commandment showed us the value of life through the extreme case of murder, the Seventh brings us the most spectacular and devastating failure of marriage as a lesson about love.

Romantic love is not the first thing we usually associate with the Old Testament. For thousands of years, the Bible has been connected in our minds with the uncompromising subordination of spiritual aspirations to a hardened law; with the fire-breathing Moses spoiling the party by smashing the tablets and dragging the Israelites, kicking and screaming, to the Promised Land; with humorless prophets casting their rhetorical brimstone over the peoples of the world; with the cruel, primitive God slamming the quivering and fickle Israelites over and over again.

So it may come as a surprise for me to suggest that in Israelite thinking, the most important relationship two human beings can share is not between a prophet and his disciple, a father and his son, or a king and his subject. It is the love between a man and a woman.

The foundations of the biblical approach to love are found in the opening chapters of Genesis, when the first woman is created.

> And the Lord God said, "It is not good that the man should be alone; I will make him a help to match him." And out of the ground the Lord God formed every beast of the field, and every bird of the air; and brought them to the man to see what he would call them: And whatever the man called every living creature, that was its name. And the man gave names to all cattle, and to the birds of the air, and to every beast of the field; but for the man there was not found a help to match him.

And the Lord God caused a deep sleep to fall upon the man, and he slept: And he took one of his sides, and closed up the flesh in its place, and made a woman, and brought her to the man. And the man said, "This is now bone of my bones, and flesh of my flesh: She shall be called Woman, because she was taken out of Man." That is why a man leaves his father and his mother, and cleaves to his wife—and they become one flesh. (Genesis 2:18–24)

At this early stage we already find three powerful statements about the bond between man and woman. First, that woman is the answer to man's inherent loneliness, an intolerable state in which man faces the world solely from within the confines of his limited self. Man is born alone, makes his decisions alone, and faces death alone. Loneliness is the idiom of his life. According to some modern thinkers, who write as though loneliness were their own discovery, there is nothing man can do to escape this horrible truth.

The Bible, however, opens its exploration of the human condition with the problem of loneliness and offers a more optimistic response: love. Not the love of God, nor the love of Creation—neither of these is apparently good enough for Adam—but the love of a woman.

Second, we learn that the true love of a man and a woman is a kind of fusion, a sense of reunion, something that completes the missing parts of our body and soul, totally wrapping ourselves around and in one another, making the object of our love into a part of our inner being. We understand that by naming all the animals and Eve herself, Adam is extending his dominion over them, expanding himself to include them. Naming is a sign of possession, of intimate expansion, which creates a relationship that was not there before.

In the ancient world, a world that was overwhelmingly male-centered, the Bible spoke of Adam's possession of Eve and largely ignored the woman's side of love. Yet we should not dismiss the story just because it does not fit our modern, egalitarian sensibilities. Possession is not only dominance and hierarchy; it is also incorporating another into ourselves. The true love of man and woman is best expressed as a kind of mutual possession, including one another in who they are, giving each other names, embracing and caring and protecting as one flesh.

The story of Adam and Eve is not about the formal contract we call marriage but about a kind of relationship that marriage is meant to reflect or protect. This bond, we learn, is so strong and profound as to displace the connection we have with our own parents—a love stronger than any other. If parental love represents the one-directional imposition of our parents' being on our inner nature, then marriage represents the two-directional fusion at the level of our bodies and souls. This is what Adam found in Eve. It was the only satisfying answer to his loneliness.

Third, it seems clear from the story that the love of man and woman, while unique in the human experience, is also a kind of paradigm for the relations human beings are to have with one another more broadly. Adam starts out alone in the world; God gives him Eve as "a help to match him." Yet the result is the creation of all of humanity. Not only marriage, but the entire social reality of mankind is produced from the desire that man not be alone. Marital or romantic love is the ultimate answer, but it does not mean that the lesser loves, of friendship and family and community, are not important. They too are answers to loneliness, cut from the same cloth.

The Old Testament does not have many love stories in it. Nor are there a lot of discussions about the meaning of marriage. But the few that are there are unequivocal and decisive in Israelite history.

The first generations of the Lord's people appear not as individual teachers but as married couples: Abraham and Sarah, Isaac and Rebecca, Jacob (also called Israel) and his two wives, Leah and Rachel. Yet it is only with Jacob that the Israelite project gets off the ground. Each of the first two couples passes on the divine legacy to only one of their sons; Jacob, on the other hand, passes it on to all twelve of his sons, and the entire nation was named after the family he founded. There are no Children of Abraham or Children of Isaac in the Bible, only Children of Israel.

Jacob is also the first person in the Bible to fall in love. After he falls out with his twin brother Esau, Jacob's mother Rebecca sends him off to the East, where he will stay with her brother Laban. As he reaches his uncle's fields, Jacob sees Laban's daughter Rachel, who is tending her father's sheep. Without knowing who she is, he helps her by removing the heavy stone from the mouth of a well to water her flock. This one redemptive deed is, apparently, enough to bring them together. No words pass between them before they embrace. "And Jacob kissed Rachel, and raised his voice, and wept" (Genesis 29:11).

Jacob spends the next month in his uncle's home. Laban asks him what he thinks his wages ought to be, and Jacob offers to work for seven years in exchange for Rachel's hand. Seven years go by, and Laban arranges the marriage. A great celebration is held, but the next morning Jacob wakes up to discover that the woman in bed with him is not Rachel but her older sister, Leah. He is outraged by the last-minute switch, but Laban merely shrugs. "It must not be done in our country, to give the younger before the firstborn" (Genesis 29:26). Jacob discovers that in order to have Rachel, he must first have Leah, and then work another seven years.

The first thing we understand from the story of Jacob and Rachel is that love is something that explodes into our lives, existing prior to, and independent of, marriage. In the entire Bible, no love is as powerful, dominant, and lasting as Jacob's love for Rachel. Their love is desperate but patient; he is willing to sacrifice a decade and a half of his life, to carry the burden of marriage to a woman he does not love, and to endure subordination to a cretinous father-in-law, all in order to have her. And indeed, like all other true loves in the Bible, this one does not disappoint.

The Bible is exceptionally sensitive to genealogies. Over and over again, we hear long lists of who begat whom, and these lists often contain literary or moral significance. The Bible is always careful to couch its stories in terms that suggest that our descendants' lives are deeply affected by our own behavior, that "the acts of the fathers are a sign for the sons," as the rabbis put it.[1] For example, Levi, the son of Jacob, acts like a zealot to protect the purity of his family in killing the people who raped his sister Dinah, and then his descendants the Levites go on to join with Moses in zealously wiping out the supporters of the Golden Calf in the book of Exodus. The Levite Phineas famously kills the leader of the tribe of Simeon who is ceremoniously copulating with an idolatrous princess, and the Levites as a whole become the priestly class of the Israelites, where zealotry and purity are the most important measures of success—though without the killing. Similarly, we see in the behavior of another son, Judah, the makings of wise political judgment and integrity, and his descendants become the ruling dynasty of the Israelite kingdoms.

Both Levi and Judah are the children of Jacob's first wife, Leah. The firstborn of Jacob's true love, Rachel, however, is none other than Joseph—the most beloved of Jacob's children, for whom he makes the famous coat of many colors, and who runs into trouble with his brothers because of his father's preferential treatment. After he parades himself about with his coat one too many times, the brothers conspire to fake his death and sell him off to slavery in Egypt. From there, he relies on his cleverness, moral strength, and boundless confidence to work his way up from the dungeons of the guard to the imperial palace, where he attains the role of grand vizier, second only to Pharaoh himself. In this capacity, he saves all of Egypt from a massive drought that blankets the region—and also saves the lives of his father and brothers, who find their only source of food in relocating to Egypt under their brother's protective aegis. Joseph is by far the most redemptive of the twelve sons of Jacob, a model for the grand self whose self-assurance, creativity, and concern for others bring salvation to both God's people and his adoptive nation in Egypt. All this, we understand, is the result of Jacob's love for Rachel.

We see this pattern repeated later in the Bible: passionate love overcoming harsh obstacles and giving rise to children and descendants who go on to redeem. There is the story of Ruth the Moabite in the book that bears her name who, after the death of her Israelite husband, clings to her destitute and exiled mother-in-law, Naomi, traveling back to Bethlehem with her, and overcoming poverty and the stigma of being both a widow and a foreigner to earn the love of a local leader named Boaz. The story reaches its climax with Ruth's marriage to Boaz, and then strikes its final note with yet another genealogy—a long list that begins with the two of them and ends in the words "And Jesse begat David." Curtain.

With the begetting of King David ringing in our ears as the last words of the book of Ruth, we realize that the whole text has been overturned before our eyes, a sudden reversal worthy of an M. Night Shyamalan film. The point of the whole story, it turns out, is to tell us about David's origins: that the greatest redemptive soul in the whole Bible was the product of a romantic love that overcame exile, ridicule, and impoverishment; that true love redeems through marriage and the children it produces.

Love is so important in the Bible that even when it begins in scandal, its fruits are still incomparable to those of a marriage where love is absent. King David's love for Bathsheba is so strong that it leads him to have her husband, Uriah the Hittite, killed on the battlefield so that he can take her. This is David's worst sin, and ultimately it plants the seeds for the collapse of his kingdom. Yet of all his children from all his wives, the greatest by far is King Solomon, the sole surviving son of his union with Bathsheba. If the most sinful marriage in the Bible produces the wisest man on earth as its child, then there is something about that union that cannot be dismissed. The love of David and Bathsheba was radical, overwhelming, passionate, and in some awful sense ideal.

We always like to think that the products of evil cannot be good, for this helps us keep order in our minds and in our lives. But here the Bible is not giving us an easy way out, for where love is concerned, the simple answers are set aside. Was David wrong to take Bathsheba for a wife? Of course he was, for he had to murder for it to happen. The Bible makes no bones about this. But their love was real, and the child they raised was like no other. When love is found, it rides roughshod on human order and can cause us to do evil—but it is also irreplaceable and of the essence of the redemptive life. This contradiction cannot hold in our minds, but it is part of the foundation of humanity. "I believe that the most lawless and inordinate loves," writes C. S. Lewis in his theological masterpiece *The Four Loves,* "are less contrary to God's will than a self-invited and self-protective lovelessness."

It should not surprise us, therefore, that one of the most amazing works of love poetry in the ancient world appears in the Hebrew Bible. The Song of Songs is expressly attributed to King Solomon—the master of human wisdom, the man who according to tradition also wrote Proverbs and Ecclesiastes, but also the man whose own life was produced by the most scandalous love in the Bible.

Even the book's self-proclaimed title is indicative: It is the ultimate song, the most eloquent expression of the human spirit. "All the writings are holy," Rabbi Akiva said, "but the Song of Songs is the Holy of Holies."[2] And what a song! Eight solid chapters of excruciating longing between Solomon and his love, the first-person voice alternating between his and hers. Although almost the whole Bible reflects the male-dominated society in which it was written, the Song of Songs breaks the pattern by presenting love as mutual, as equally cherished between man and woman. And this song is unbearably intense—its first words are, "Let him kiss me with the kisses of his mouth; for your love is better than wine," and goes on to, "I am sick with love," "Turn away your eyes from me, for they have overcome me" (Song of Songs 6:5), and more and more. "For love is strong as death . . . its coals are coals of fire, which have a most vehement flame. Many waters cannot quench love, nor can the waters drown it" (8:6–7). The key word repeated for love is *dod,* which alternatively is used for sexuality and the lovers themselves, but which is also the etymological source of the name of the author's father, David, the greatest symbol of the redemptive spirit in the whole Bible.

Earlier I suggested that the Bible offers little support for universal love. In the Song of Songs it is utterly rejected: "There are sixty queens, and eighty concubines and young women without number. My dove, my undefiled, is but one" (6:8–9). Love puts all its focus on a single person, to the exclusion of everyone else.

• • •

The purpose of marriage is love. Not an abstract, impersonal, or universal love, but a specific, consuming, focused romantic love of two human beings. Only by affirming love of this kind can we truly recognize the potential of the redemptive self who embraces another in a lifelong envelopment of body and soul. Such a love changes the order of the universe, makes the galaxies rotate in reverse, recalls the moment of Creation, brings salvation to a people. It defies philosophy and religion and wisdoms ancient or new. It ruins everything and fixes everything and fills everything with scent and taste. When consummated, such a love can create children who are not merely raised in an atmosphere of infinite support and confidence, but whose very being is the ultimate fusion of two bodies and souls, the greatest expression of redemptive creativity.

God has a part in this kind of love. For many ancient Christians and Greeks and Buddhists, romantic love was inadequate, lowly, at times even wrong. In their view, the love of God, the highest love, was fundamentally different. In the Old Testament, however, we discover the opposite: The love of God can be grasped only with reference to the passionate, redemptive love of man and woman.

God must be loved, but when trying to explain what was really meant by "And you shall love the Lord your God with all your heart, with all your soul, and with all your might" (Deuteronomy 6:5), the biblical authors found themselves, over and over again, using romantic love and marriage as the central metaphor for describing the love of God. Idolatry is described by the prophets as a form of adultery; the Israelites likened it to a harlot who has bitterly betrayed her husband. But the reverse is true as well: "As a husband rejoices over his bride," Isaiah assures us, "your God will rejoice over you" (Isaiah 62:5). Later on, the Jewish mystical tradition would find the love of God in the erotic, with the Song of Songs becoming a metaphor for our relationship with the Divine, and with every good act of ours signifying the "union of the [male] Holy One and the [female] Divine Presence." Not only does romantic love not contradict the love of God, one cannot understand the latter without knowing the former.

Because we are mortal, because love often ends and life always ends, because love includes the biological urge of sex, and because it is so hard to find room for love in an orderly philosophical outlook, many people come to believe that love is a deception, a kind of drug or primitive regression that disconnects you from reality; that life is much better when we seek only stability, health, pleasant friendships, cold wisdom, and productive hobbies. Indeed, many ancient and modern wisdoms seek just this kind of passionless, timeless pleasantry, pure and unchanging and even claiming for itself the name of love. From the perspective of the Old Testament, however, such a love is like a waking death, neutralizing the core of what life is about. Perhaps one is bringing heaven to earth. But nothing grows in heaven. Heaven is sterile.

The central human axis of the Old Testament is a fiery, lusty, wild, insatiable half-animal-half-divine *human* love, the same love that our literature and film and music and art have been fixated on for more than a century, the love we moderns cannot get out of our minds. In romantic love, we find the expansive motion taken to its extreme, embracing another and setting our flags upon one another in an act of mutual conquest. All other loves, whether of friends or nation or family or even God himself, are mere reflections of this—limited love, constrained to certain parts of our lives or our personalities, all of them catching a glimpse of the expansion of the soul, all shimmering under the light of the redemptive ideal.

• • •

Very good, as God might say. But if love is the answer, why do we need marriage? The Seventh Commandment, after all, does not tell us to love—this appears elsewhere—but not to commit adultery, which is another way of saying that preserving the formality of marriage is in some sense essential to the love the Bible is advocating. In practical terms, the Seventh Commandment is talking about the sexual exclusivity of marriage. Just as murder is the ultimate symbolic rejection of human life, marital infidelity is presented here as the ultimate symbolic repudiation of love. But why is sex so important to this?

To understand the Seventh Commandment, we will need to understand a little bit more about sex—with help from a Talmudic parable.

The rabbis were having a hard time with sex. It was the source of so much human suffering, of adultery and incest and prostitution and unwanted pregnancy, of disloyalty and unclear paternity and immodesty. It was so destructive that they understood it to be the essence of the "evil inclination," the animalistic side of man taking over, trampling reason and creativity and judgment and contemplation of the Divine.

So they came up with a plan.

They hunted down the evil urge. When they found it, they put it in irons and chains. When it struggled, they placed it in a sealed container, of the kind we might use to store nuclear waste. Sexual evil would afflict people no more.

The next morning, the world had changed. Everything was calm. People walked with a new dignity, were unusually polite to one another, said their prayers and studied their texts with serene devotion.

But something was not right. One rabbi discovered that his

hens had stopped laying eggs. Soon it became clear that all the cows and sheep were barren as well. Within a few months, they were alarmed to find that the trees were showing none of the usual signs of bearing fruit. Women stopped getting pregnant.

The world was coming to an end. In trying to quell the source of human evil, the rabbis had undone the work of Creation.

Seeing they had no choice, they set the evil urge free, and the natural order of life was restored.[3]

For many centuries, Western society saw only the negative side of sexuality. Plato saw it as a lower, animal form of attraction, one that ultimately gets in the way of the intellectual union that alone is the highest kind of love. Ancient Christianity too saw sexuality as a curse. "It is well for a man not to touch a woman," wrote Paul, himself celibate. "I wish that all were as I myself am" (I Corinthians 7:1–7). Marriage was allowed, its advantages often considered, but it was never idealized. It was a concession to human frailty, to the sexual drive.

Of course, there is much to be said for the dangers of sexuality. The most important lesson I learned in my ninth-grade biology class is that every creature under heaven is driven by two basic drives: self-preservation and species preservation. Animals and plants have endlessly clever means of defending and perpetuating themselves or their kind. For man, species preservation is found first of all in sexuality. The desire to procreate is every bit as fundamental as the desire to eat and fight and flee danger. In our arousal we find hundreds of millions of years of species survival channeled in an instant into every fiber of our being. Sexuality can take over all our more docile mental faculties, like reason or sympathy. It can reduce us to panting, grunting, thoughtless creatures. Sexuality is not just an urge; it can be a fundamental physical need that upends every aspect of our judgment. Out of control, sexuality slips quickly into idolatry, ripping our focus away from everything we know to be good and right.

Yet there is another side to sex. In a worldview that disavows the body, we can understand why sexuality would be seen as unequivocal wickedness. But to the Israelites, the essentials of our biology are good, being a central part of the "very good" creation of human life. Regardless of the dangers that the sexual drive entails, the Bible cannot see it as inherently wrongful. As the rabbinic tale shows, it is life itself.

To understand the Seventh Commandment, and the sexual exclusivity it demands, therefore, we need to understand the inescapable role that sex plays in love. In sexuality we may find the most powerful and sensitive expression of mutual concern, affection, and redemptive joy. When the Bible says that "Adam knew Eve his wife, and she conceived and bore Cain," this "knowledge" is not a euphemism but a glimpse into the depths of their love, a complete fusion of the body that is also of the mind and spirit, of memory and the intellect and intimate knowledge of another. Any love that does not include the merging of souls and also of bodies is incomplete. Only in sexuality is loneliness fully resolved.

Nor is it enough to say that sexuality can be a spiritual experience, alongside but different from the biological one. These are not two different sides of sex: Its spirituality is intimately bound up in its biology.

The sexual urge is inherently creative. It exists in order to make new life, to replicate God's creation of man on the sixth day. When we share it with someone we love, we are doing more than giving each other pleasure; we are joining together in the most sublime and miraculous act of creation that a human being is capable of. Certainly not every act of intimacy is aimed at having children. Yet there is no getting away from the fact that the nature of sexual intimacy is still inherently procreative—on some deep level, sex will always be about making babies.

It is only in this light that we can fully understand the meaning of sexual exclusivity. In keeping faith sexually, we are saying two things.

First, that we recognize intimacy as an act of love, as the most intense expression of our humanity. By refusing to have sex where there is no love, we are refusing to relate to our sexuality as purely biological, and in showing this to our beloved, we infuse our intimacy with human meaning. As the enshrinement of sexual exclusivity, marriage is a tool to help us permanently channel our sexuality into love, spiritualizing sex and making it uniquely human. Sex becomes a form of expression, a way of telling another how much we love him or her. Yet as with any communication, the meaning differs from person to person, from moment to moment. In receiving sexual affection, we are taking our partner's love on faith. And how special is a gift of flowers when it comes from someone who never gives them to anyone else! A partner who sleeps around has ruined sex as a way of saying something true and deep and unique.

Second, we affirm the creative essence of sex as an act connected (even if not immediately or solely) with having children. Creating a child is one of the most profound acts of human love: Our bodies merge with that of the one we love, creating a human being who literally expresses that union. In sex we come together; in parenthood we fuse completely—and create something that can outlast even our own lives. We defy death not only in the eternal experience of love, but literally, physically, carrying ourselves over into the future. In dedicating our whole reproductive essence exclusively to one another, we establish our claim to the future, committing ourselves not just to having children but to raising them in love, imbuing their souls with the same fire that their parents shared, redeeming the generations to come.

The Seventh Commandment, in other words, is about the subordination of sex to love—the love of another, and of the children we will create together. It is the declaration, first of all, that just as our love is profound, exclusive, and everlasting, so too is our sexuality. That just as we saw that life is total, the entirety of body and soul celebrated as we "dance before the Lord," so too is our love. Our commitment to another is a commitment of everything we are.

Yet when put this way, we could still draw the conclusion that where there is no love, there is nothing wrong with adultery.

Marriage, however, is not merely love; it is also an institution, a public declaration, and a contract. Its purpose is love, but as an institution it takes on a life of its own. It may be the most important human institution ever devised.

Marriage is, first of all, a formal bulwark against the highs and lows of love. Love is never static, and as a result it inevitably has its phases. It is much easier to maintain passion in the first year or two of a relationship, or when we are young, than to keep love alive with the same person for ten or twenty years. As life moves forward, we may fail to invest the time and patience needed to make love stay. We discover that life at forty-five with children is radically different from life at twenty-five without. A relationship is far less stimulating when you feel that you've already had all the conversations, that you already know how your partner will answer every question, or when the drudgery of parenting and the stress of making a living leave no time for the hard work of love. If love is not a constantly renewing spring of creative growth for both sides, it quickly reveals itself to have been a flash in the pan, or settles into a protracted pattern of stale comity.

As a formal contract, marriage affirms how important love is to us, a binding public commitment of both partners to work hard at love always, to see beyond momentary lows, to permanently view their relationship as one where love must ultimately win out. In this sense, a marriage contract is not so different from other contracts we make: Like a major treaty between states, a marriage raises the stakes of the failure of love, forcing both partners to work much harder to preserve it.

Because sexuality is not merely spiritual but also powerfully biological, it needs constant supervision and a special set of reins: It is the easiest way for a low point in love to become a disaster, the weakest link of the marital chains. One night of weakness can undo many years of investment in a loving relationship and can shatter any hope of repair where love has gone stale. It can also cause irreparable harm to children, whose worlds have been shattered by the betrayal not just of the spouse but of the family as a whole—betrayal that can often be more easily forgiven by the betrayed spouse than by the children. By focusing on the sexual aspect of marriage as its linchpin, the marital commitment helps us overcome those moments where our biology blinds us to the consequences of our actions.

Yet the importance of marriage is not limited to protecting the love of the couple. By making marriage a formal institution and sexual exclusivity a public declaration, we proclaim the centrality of lasting love to the human experience. We make a stunning symbolic statement to the world, affirming our undying belief in the possibility of love and of the establishment of families and homes where children are to be raised as first of all an object of love.

We cannot underestimate the importance of such a declaration. If romantic love is the highest form of relating to another, it is also an ideal against which all other loves are measured. Every love, whether of friendship or family or even of God, is an expansion of the self to include another, seeing ourselves as responsible for his fate and committed to his success. If these loves are more limited, if they contain little or no physical element, if they lack the totality and spiritual abandon of romance, they nonetheless are a reflection, a kind of imitation, of the highest love.

If anything, the restraint against wanton sexuality demanded by the Seventh Commandment makes other, nonsexual loves all the more meaningful: Sexuality is so powerful that it can create confusion and trauma when it is allowed to spill out into nonmarital relationships. Sexuality must be severely limited without being crushed if we are to create safe places where proper relationships of family and friendship can grow and deepen without the threat of unintended, animal aims muddying the picture.

The redemptive spirit, in other words, needs both the possibility of total love in marriage, and the sharp restriction of sexuality anywhere outside it, for real relationships of friendship and family to develop in the fullest way possible. Just as with the Fourth Commandment we learned a great deal by asking what Creation would have looked like if God had not rested on the seventh day, we may reasonably ask what our human world would look like if there were no such thing as marriage. Quickly we would find that the very idea of permanent and complete love between two people, of redemptive love even among friends or family or community, had little in our experience to anchor it.

Most human relationships begin as purely instrumental. We look to pass the time with friends, to make money at work, or to find sexual release in the impersonal fling. Real spiritual bonds develop over time, through shared experiences and tests of loyalty, and require from the outset a kind of faith that such bonds are at all possible. To overcome loneliness, we need to believe that loneliness is a solvable problem, that it is not inherent to our nature. We need to believe in love.

Adultery shatters that faith. If marriage is a public symbol for the possibility of redemptive love, then adultery is the symbolic rejection of that possibility—just as the violation of oaths undermines the possibility of honesty in our world. Marriage is a formality, but a powerful and crucial one that safeguards and symbolizes love. If marriage is the archetype of love, then adultery is the archetype of betrayal. At least symbolically, adultery makes us alone again.

Understood properly, marriage is the singular institution that proclaims and establishes the possibility of complete and total love in our lives.

How many marriages today are really like this? We can't see what goes on behind the closed doors of marital relationships. We can see only the painful results of love's failure.

So often, people marry for the wrong reasons, or stay married without committing themselves to love. A friend of mine married a man who seemed like a pretty good guy at the time. Maybe he was no kind of soul mate, and their conversations were shallow and quirky, but she was reaching an age where the desperation to have children causes some women to make all the worst compromises. Within a few months of their marriage, it became clear that the man was not just alien, but abusive. All her considerable career achievements did nothing to make her personal life tolerable. She was fortunate to have a good friend tell her, over and over again, that she needed to divorce to save herself. Within a year of her marriage, it was over.

This marriage was doomed before it began, and divorce was the only thing that saved her from a life of abuse and misery, and kept her from raising children in an atmosphere of contempt and brutality.

Friends were helpless, however, in the case of a man I knew who married a woman whom we all knew was utterly wrong for him. He was brainy, arrogant, introverted, and disinclined to physical affection; she was warm, emotional, deeply insecure, and sought assurance through touch. But they both sought stability, felt ready to build a home, and saw marriage as a religious obligation. Marriage for them was less of a relationship than an ideology, something that gave them the faith and confidence that all their differences could be overcome.

For years, the couple fought bitterly—not productive fighting where problems are aired and addressed, but aimless, brutal, dehumanizing, incessant, and shallow fighting. They simply could not understand each other. There was no love.

At a certain point, they decided that in order to try to save their marriage, they would have a child. Their daughter was born, a warm and delightful child, and within a year they were divorced. They realized the futility of pinning their hopes on a baby—and how unfair it would be to her as well, to force her to grow up in a cauldron of acrimony and alienation.

Divorce is only the most obvious sign of a failed marriage. As common is the cold and loveless marriage that drags on for decades solely out of convenience, social and financial pressure, or misplaced concern for the well-being of children. The partners have consigned themselves to a spiritual imprisonment that offers no hope. Love, if ever there, has died. In such a relationship, one sacrifices the essence of life itself. But the real victims are the children, who not only miss out on the warmth and energetic concern of true love but often go on to replicate their parents' dead relationship in their own. Lovelessness becomes their model, the only kind of marriage they know how to have.

Of course, divorce isn't the only answer, especially when children are involved. There is much that can be done to heal a failing marriage. In some cases, love was there long ago, and fixing things requires rediscovering the original, powerful web of mutual affection, desire, and respect. In others, the key to renewal lies in focusing on the parts that work well, such as conversation or mutual ideals or physical attraction, and using that as a base from which to reinvent the rest of the relationship. Every marriage has its low points. These can be heartwrenching and, left untreated, can lead to adultery and other devastations. But with careful attention, often including outside help, many marriages can be saved if both spouses agree that the key to everything lies in committing themselves to the long and arduous path to sustained love.

The biggest problem with marriage today is that many of us look to it as a solution to a problem, rather than a framework for the project of love. After years of searching, we finally tie the knot and believe that we have cured, at long last, our existential loneliness. But the Bible, while recognizing the problem of loneliness, looks not to marriage but to love as the answer. Marriage is a crucial step in the trajectory of our love for another, but it is an early step, at its best creating the conditions in which love can prosper over many decades.

Love, on the other hand, requires a tireless investment in our partnership. We must constantly take inventory: Are we still lonely? Have we found the spiritual and physical companionship we seek? Is the relationship a continual source of growth for us? Have we, as redemptive souls, genuinely expanded to include another human being down to the core of our essence? The answers to self-aware questions like these are found through introspection and communication and time together: being able to adequately express what makes us happy or unhappy, to analyze what works and what doesn't, to know when it's time to seek help, and to take the time to deepen the good things and correct the bad.

We often speak of "saving our" marriages. While much of the advice we hear is right and helpful, the question is itself part of the problem. We should be more worried about saving our love.

8

Making Room for Others

You shall not steal.

T he redemptive spirit is expansive, life affirming, caring,
taking responsibility for others, imposing one's limitless
love and will for the good on a world that may not always be so
ready for it. Which brings us to an obvious problem.

Love casts a heavy net. How do we keep from overdoing it,
from dominating others, crushing *their* own independent selves
in our bear hug of redemptive affection?

This is not just a theoretical question. We all know people
who think they know what's best for others, involving themselves endlessly in people's private lives, often doing more harm
than good. Love can be stifling, especially for a young adult desperate for independence from her parents, or a spouse who feels
there is no room in the relationship for his own development.
But the problem becomes especially acute when taken to the
broader level of society and government. Under the totalitarian
regime of the Soviet Union, the government presumed to know
everything about what individuals needed, from the kinds of
products sold in stores to the size and shape of one's home. And

though at times we may take away the car keys of a friend who's had too much to drink, such regimes are built on the assumption that ordinary citizens are all of them drunkards heading for their deaths on the highway.

The Seventh Commandment taught us to expand ourselves to include another person with all our might; the Eighth moves us in the other direction, teaching that true redemption requires not just love but also respecting others as independent, free selves. In the words *You shall not steal,* we learn that other people also have a natural inclination to expand; that they have every right to control their own world, just as we do; that their freedom is essential to their humanity. If the ban on adultery taught us about love as the ultimate expansion, the ban on theft teaches us the opposite: the need to limit our self-expansion to allow our neighbors to thrive.

In the biblical view, this begins with respecting their property.

There is probably no subject that divides the Old and New Testaments more deeply than the question of property and wealth. For thousands of years, criticism of Judaism, including the most awful anti-Semitic expressions in the Christian world, claimed that the Jew placed his concern for money above all else. Part of this came from the fact that both the Old Testament and the rabbinic culture that embodied its teachings were indeed concerned with property and affirmed material prosperity far more than did classical Christianity, which taught us to overcome material concerns, to embrace poverty, and to look at the wealthy with suspicion.

Yet to dismiss the Hebrew Bible as primitive and materialistic is to miss out on one of its most unusual ideas, an idea that finds bold expression in the Eighth Commandment and has entrenched itself deep in the heart of Western civilization: For all the problems of wealth, for all the risks of selfishness and callousness toward the underprivileged, on the most profound level owning property carries spiritual significance.[1] It is through property that we discover ourselves, not merely as physical bodies whose extent in time and space is dictated by chance, but also as human beings, first-person actors with the ability to define ourselves, to grow and expand according to our own decisions, to influence the world around us. And it is through the respect for the property of others that we learn to see other people in a similar light, as spiritual selves with the power to redeem.

The Bible's teaching on ownership begins with Adam, and as with other aspects of the first chapters of Genesis, we should read this as a declaration about the nature of mankind as a whole. God's first words to mankind are as follows:

> And God blessed them, and God said to them: Be fruitful, and multiply, replenish the earth, and conquer it; and have dominion over the fish of the sea, and over the birds of the air, and over every living thing that moves on the earth. And God said, Behold I have given you every herb bearing seed, which is upon the face of all the earth, and every tree, on which is the fruit yielding seed: To you it shall be for food. (Genesis 1:28–29)

Man is put on this earth, we learn, to expand and spread and dominate the earth. He is not merely given permission to enjoy the earth's bounty; he is told to "conquer" and "have dominion." He is not told to take whatever he needs for food; from this passage, it seems that his diet is limited to grains and fruits. As for "every living thing that moves on the earth," he is told to possess, to own. The acquisitional instinct of man is presented in Genesis as not merely a fact of human nature, but a positive fact—indeed, one of man's first, God-given goals on earth, part of God's original blessing.

Recognizing the central role property plays in human life, the Bible is filled with laws and rules that concern the protection of our property and the consideration of others'. A robber who takes one's cattle, thereby depriving him of not only property but also the source of his livelihood, must not only pay it back but is penalized at four or five times its value. We learn about the liability of a paid guard who fails to protect the property of his boss, about what happens when we borrow an object and it is damaged, about what happens when we let our animals eat in another's field or we start a fire that spreads to our neighbor's property. We may not adjust the posts marking the borders of our field, effectively stealing our neighbor's land. We are also told that the respect for property outweighs any difficulties we may have with our neighbors. If we see our enemy's animal gone astray, we are commanded to go out of our way to bring it back to him. If we see his animal struggling under its burden, we are to help the owner set it right.

All these laws could easily lead us to think that respecting property is simply a matter of social order. We know that good fences make good neighbors, and there is nothing like solid, enforced laws clarifying where my stuff ends and yours begins to give everyone the stability, security, and clarity needed to live productive lives.

But the Bible clearly has something else in mind. This emerges not so much from the laws as from stories that point to a much deeper significance to ownership. When God decides to destroy the world in the time of Noah, the reason given is that "the world had become corrupt before God, and the world was filled with *hamas*" (Genesis 6:11)—an ambiguous term associated with thievery and avarice.[2] Here the disrespect for property seems to justify the wholesale destruction of mankind: "And the

Lord repented that he had created man, and he was saddened in his heart" (Genesis 6:6).

Later on in Genesis, we encounter Abraham mourning the death of his beloved wife, Sarah. In searching for a proper burial site, Abraham focuses on a cave at the edge of the fields of Efron the Hittite, on the outskirts of what is today the city of Hebron. There ensues a bizarre passage, in which Efron offers Abraham the cave for free, but Abraham insists on purchasing it "for the full price." Efron then names an astronomical price of four hundred shekels of silver, which Abraham accepts. For reasons unexplained by the text, Abraham would rather pay an extortionary rate for the grave site than get it for free. He wants this to be unequivocally his land and is unwilling to raise any doubts by taking it as a gift. Again, ownership is not just a matter of social order, but points to something deeper.

But what is probably the strangest story about property concerns the sin of Ahab, which appears in the first book of Kings. Ahab, the king of the northern kingdom of Israel, has his eye on a certain vineyard not far from his palace in the city of Samaria, which he wants to purchase and convert into a vegetable garden. The owner, Navot the Jezreelite, refuses to sell it, saying, "The Lord forbid it me, that I should give you the inheritance of my fathers." Ahab is thrown into a deep depression, lying in bed and refusing to eat. His wife, Jezebel, comes up with a plan and dutifully sends letters in Ahab's name to all the elders of Navot's city, telling them to falsely accuse Navot of cursing both God and Ahab. They promptly do so, and Navot is executed by stoning, his body left to the dogs. Thrilled by Jezebel's resourcefulness, Ahab gets out of bed and promptly makes his way to the field to claim it for himself—but is surprised to find Elijah the Prophet waiting for him there, with fire bolts in his eyes and an accusation on his lips:

Thus says the Lord: Have you murdered, and also taken possession? . . . In the place where the dogs licked the blood of Navot shall the dogs lick your blood. . . . Behold I will bring evil upon you, and will sweep you away, and will cut off from Ahab every male person. . . . Him that dies of Ahab in the city, the dogs shall eat; and him that dies in the field, the birds of the air shall eat. (I Kings 21:19–24)

Ahab's sin harkens back to that of King David, who had Uriah killed so that he could have Bathsheba. David's punishment was harsh—because of his deed, the kingdom of Israel was later rent in two, and he suffered palace intrigues for the rest of his reign. Yet Ahab's punishment is far more brutal: Not only is he destined to die without burial, but his entire line of heirs will be wiped out, and they too will remain unburied—perhaps the worst imaginable punishment for any king, who sees the creation of a dynasty as the most glorious expansion of himself into the future. The text concludes by asserting that "there was none like Ahab, who did give himself over to work wickedness in the sight of the Lord" (I Kings 21:25). Almost as an afterthought, the Bible then tells us of his incessant involvement in idolatry.

What is it about Ahab's sin that strikes us, and struck Elijah, as so grotesque? We know that in the biblical world, kings led armies in battle and regularly bloodied their hands, consistently indulging in what today we would call war crimes and atrocities. Another killing by a power-drunk monarch should not surprise us.

Yet Ahab does not murder someone out of rage, excessive militancy, or the blinding desire for a woman. He is driven to madness by his lust for a vegetable garden. There is something so deeply disturbing about wanting something so much that you will *murder* its owner to get it, that the more we think about it, the more we sympathize with Elijah's rage. True, Jezebel violated the Ninth Commandment as well, with her letters bearing false witness against Navot. But this does not seem to bother Elijah nearly as much as the fact that Ahab has "murdered, and also taken possession"—a formulation that makes it sound as though the two sins are somehow parallel, or that it is the combination of the two that makes it so heinous.

What emerges from the biblical stories is that property is in some way deeply connected with the essence of who we are, with our very presence in the world as human beings. In the time of Noah, God regrets having ever made man—for his disregard for others' property effectively undoes the elevation of humanity that stands at the heart of Creation. Abraham's purchase of the cave is not an untoward distraction from his mourning but an integral part of it: In his sorrow, Abraham wants desperately to show the world that Sarah has been a real part of himself, his true love, and he cannot bury her in a place that is not also an unequivocal extension of his being—titled land for which he has paid a very high price. Elijah shows Ahab that killing Navot for the purpose of dispossessing him constitutes a perverse and extreme form of dehumanization, more than ordinary murder out of anger or jealousy.

There is something about our property, our dominion over the world of things, that makes us human—and something about stealing that undermines the core of our humanity.

What does it mean to own something?

The right to property is usually described in negative terms: We forbid stealing, forbid the violation of an individual's belongings, forbid the restriction on their freedom to use an object or even destroy it as they please. Yet there is a positive side to property, a crucial affirmation that takes place every time we purchase something new, or pick up an old book or piece of jewelry we own, every time we drive a new car or fix something in our home. It is an affirmation of ourselves—a confirmation of our self-definition, not so different from looking in a mirror.

Ownership is the most basic form of self-expansion. Young children might not yet know what it means to take responsibility for others, to love others or take them under their wing. But they know what it means to own something. "Mine" means "me." Take away a toddler's toy, and more likely than not he will respond with the ferocity of the injured. Our things are an extension of ourselves, the first case of dividing up the world between us and everything else. When we purchase something new, we feel a thrill of life; we begin to imagine what we might do with it, explore new possibilities before us. We attach sentiments to objects, so that when we lose them, we feel a sliver of death. We can recall exactly how we acquired almost everything of value we own—the acquisition being an important memory that we cannot erase. And when our home is broken into, we feel not merely frustrated or disgusted, but *violated*—someone has attacked us personally, has taken away a part of us by force.

Ownership, moreover, is the embrace of an object not only as an extension of ourselves, but also as the embodiment of our freedom. Our things define our options: As soon as we know something is ours, we begin to rethink what we may do. A sudden infusion of money focuses our attention on repaying debts, upgrading our lifestyle, or investing it to make more money; a sudden loss of capital hurts us precisely because of the limitation on our choices. Nor is this just about money, which is little if not the quantification of freedom. A new pen offers us the newfound freedom of writing easily or beautifully; a new oven or lawn mower usually has advantages over the old one, "features" that open new, if mundane, possibilities in our lives.

Whereas our bodies are forever limited in their extent, the idea of property means that our borders can always change: We may expand to a limitless degree. If redemption means expanding our souls, property is the first lesson that teaches us such expansion is even possible.

But for this very reason, when we violate the property of another we are not just committing an act of violence against his extended self; we are denying his fundamental right to expand, and thus assaulting his very humanity. The feeling of violation that accompanies being robbed is not limited to the injury itself; it resonates throughout our world, leaving us insecure about everything else we own as well. Our homes are the most salient expression of our expanded selves, a place where who we really are is felt in every piece of furniture, every poster on the wall, every dish left unwashed or pair of pants tossed on the bed. It is our solace in a world that is largely beyond our control. Being robbed often makes us feel like our own home is no longer on our side, no longer reliably *us*. We are no longer who we thought we were, and this shakes us to our foundation.

The deep connection between property and freedom, identity, and humanity was of intense interest to the ancient rabbis. Unlike the early Christians, who saw the lack of property as a path to spiritual elevation, the rabbis never took vows of poverty—even though they sometimes embraced other forms of asceticism, such as voluntary fasting or refraining from alcohol. "Profane your Sabbath," Rabbi Akiva tells us, "but do not become dependent on others." So committed were the rabbis to a strong concept of property rights that they insisted that the only way to atone for the sin of theft is by returning the property to its rightful owner—even when it seems impossible. "Even if someone stole a wooden beam and built it into the city capitol,

the capitol must be torn down and the beam returned to its own-
ers," they taught. The connection between property and spirit
was most vividly expressed by Rabbi Yohanan, who declared
that "anyone who steals a *shave pruta* [that is, the smallest possible unit of value] from his friend, it is as though he has taken
his soul from him."[3]

Yet when it comes to the Eighth Commandment itself, the
rabbis throw us for a loop.

According to rabbinic tradition, the Eighth Commandment
is not about stealing, but rather about kidnapping. Now, there
is almost nothing in the text to suggest that *You shall not steal* is
anything other than what it sounds like. Throughout the Bible,
the Hebrew verb "to steal" (*ganav*) is used almost exclusively to
describe theft of belongings. The justification the rabbis gave
for such an unintuitive reading is forced, in a manner familiar
to students of the Talmud: The ban on stealing is covered elsewhere, they insist, in any number of verses that include explicit
prohibitions on theft; so if it appears again in the Ten Commandments, it must be talking about something else.[4] That
something, they asserted, is stealing one's person.

Here as elsewhere, it is fruitful to assume the rabbis were trying to get at something deeper. Kidnapping is an ultimate case
of violating another person's self. Stealing is deeply connected
with kidnapping, because property is literally an extension of
ourselves and an expression of our freedom that lies at the core
of our humanity. By subordinating the other's property to our
own material expansion, we rob him of his soul, in a way that is
not as different from kidnapping as we may at first think.

That this is their intention becomes even more clear when we
consider other rabbinic statements that further restrict the case
of the Eighth Commandment: According to one source, it refers
specifically to the case of a man who kidnapped someone for the

express purpose of selling him as a slave. Another rabbi added that you truly violate the Eighth Commandment only when you take possession through one of the formal acts of acquisition recognized in Jewish law—that is, when you treat him as if he were your own property.[5]

We can see where this is going. From the simple words *You shall not steal,* the Eighth Commandment has transformed in the rabbinic imagination into the complete subordination of another human being to your own expanded self. You have come to believe that he is not human at all, but a thing to own.

One of the things that strikes us most about raising children is the difficulty they often have, at every age, recognizing that the universe does not revolve around them. Whether it's the toddler who has a tantrum about a toy that has been returned to its rightful owner, or the teen who flies into a rage because you won't buy her clothing for which she has no conceivable need, or the odd habit of kids of all ages to burst into a quiet house, fill it with noise, and then just as easily sweep out again, leaving epic destruction in their wake—parents often just shake their heads in wonder at the utter obliviousness that kids have to the existence and feelings of people outside themselves.

Yet this is a natural state. We are hardwired to survive, to satisfy our desires, to exist within and for ourselves. Kids are like this by nature, and the first step in emerging beyond their animal state is learning to recognize that other people are worlds unto themselves as well—and that they have rights, feelings, dreams, and belongings of their own.

One rabbinic story captures this idea beautifully:

Mar Zutra the Pious had a purse full of silver stolen from him at the guesthouse. He saw that one of the students washed his hands and then wiped them on the clothing of his friend. He said: "That is the one, for he does not care about the property of his fellow." They bound the student, and he confessed.[6]

There is obviously something outrageous about wiping your hands on a friend's shirt. But what exactly is the problem? Surely it is not the cost to property—he neither stole nor damaged his friend's clothing. Rather, it is the brazen dehumanization of his friend, who is suddenly reduced to a towel in his eyes, that sets off Mar Zutra's alarm bells and leads him to his thief. Ultimately, what the student did to his friend was of the same kind, if not the same degree, as what Ahab did to Navot. He dehumanized him.

Many of us will feel uncomfortable with a biblical approach that glorifies property and wealth to such a degree. Unlike the destitute figures of Jesus, Socrates, or Buddha, all of whom shunned material success for success of the soul, the Old Testament heroes were frequently wealthy, and the Bible goes out of its way to describe the riches accumulated by Abraham, Jacob, Solomon, and others. Jesus famously teaches that it is "easier for a camel to go through the eye of a needle than for a rich man to enter the kingdom of God."[7] The Old Testament, on the other hand, seems to see no inherent contradiction between wealth and righteousness. Should this not bother us?

There is something very appealing about sweeping away all our material commitments and repudiating property. We are, after all, talking about things, not people, and it is easy to look at the self-extension in property as a kind of deception, or at least a bad set of priorities in our life. Aren't people more important than things?

Yet there are very good reasons why the Israelite approach to property has stood its ground over time. Overwhelmingly, the

Western world has remained faithful to it, and not because it is dominated by greedy, immoral people. Rather, there is something intuitively true about a worldview that sees material prosperity as central to the affirmation of life, and sees respect for property as the foundation stone for respecting the humanity of others. We don't have to be master economists to recognize that societies where property is respected and the freedom to gain and dispose of wealth as we choose is assured are everywhere more prosperous than those where thievery is rampant or economic decisions are left to distant experts whose interests are presumed to be more altruistic and objective than they ever really are.

Indeed, we may venture to say that the Israelite approach to property would have long ago eviscerated all these other anti-material approaches were it not for a single, overwhelming, horrible fact about our world.

For all the spiritual goods that affirming property seems to give us, we know this is not the whole story. We know that for every material success we achieve, there is someone else who has failed. We know that all around us there are poor people, people we encounter in the street of every city, or people we never see who nonetheless endure hardships we can't even imagine. Or perhaps we have been there ourselves and still have the taste of destitution in our mouths, the sense of knowing just how sharply the suffering of the poor clashes against the sanguine accumulations of so many wealthy people. And when we succeed, we know that our financial success comes against the backdrop of so many others who fail.

The pain of poverty is unique in our experience. The unpayable bills, the need to turn to friends or family for support, the humiliation before indifferent bank managers or creditors, the mental wreckage of unemployment, the shelving of dreams and plans, the need to say no to our children about things we always assumed we could give them, the constant tightening and retightening of expenses, the inability to think about anything else, the lost sleep, the massive fights with spouses or lovers, the temptations to escape into gambling or drugs or drink, though we know it will only make things worse, the temptation to steal. . . . In poverty comes the reduction of ourselves, the erasure of our self-expansion for which we worked so hard, the depletion of the self. It dehumanizes us, evoking the fear of the animal in the wild who thinks of little other than survival, and it threatens to undermine not only our vacations and luxuries but our basic self-image as good, confident, loving, moral people.

For everything we want to achieve in life, poverty stands in the way. Poverty is not just suffering, like physical pain or rejection or the loss of a loved one. It is different, a calamity coupled with the constant terror of how much worse things might get, a thick fog of fear that seeps into every choice, every human interaction, and for some people is so traumatic that it never fully disappears even when they have reestablished themselves financially—a fear that they pass on to their children and grandchildren. Poverty digs its fangs of fear all the way to the bone of our being.

This is not to say that wealth carries no danger. Just as one can become obsessed with health, spending endless hours in the gym or poring over nutrition websites, so too can the accumulation of wealth become a fixation that drowns out other human realities. The affirmation of wealth in the Bible serves two purposes: to promote our basic financial health akin to physical health, and to express the human need for expansion in the inanimate world. Yet all too often, the pursuit of money serves neither of these purposes. Instead of being driven by an inner spiritual strength, it is driven by greed and fear—the fear of poverty, of losing public status, of disappointing others. Instead of material expansion being integrated with a self-expansion on the human level, it comes at its expense, undermining true friendships, causing already wealthy people to dedicate too much time at the office and too little at home, or preventing them from developing real relationships with others or helping those in need.

The Bible offers a response to poverty, less glamorous and optimistic than those of other approaches, but perhaps more compelling for it.

Our encounter with poor people fills us with complex emotions. Here the parallel to physical health is limited: While we may feel guilty about our own health when in the presence of the ailing, we know such guilt is unfounded. Having less health of our own wouldn't contribute an iota to the health of others. With wealth, however, most of us are not so confident: We can part with money, we can put it toward easing the burdens of the poor, and deep down our own wealth poses a challenge to us whenever we see the suffering of others less fortunate.

Probably the most common response, and the most despicable from the biblical perspective, is to retaliate against the poor in our minds, judging them harshly for their failure to ground themselves financially, convincing ourselves that as mature adults they are responsible for their fate, that their poverty is essentially their own fault. We may even take this further, asserting that any help we give them provides a disincentive for them to get out of their structural anguish through their own hard work. *Get a job,* we say under our breath, and walk on.

The Bible anticipates this line of reasoning and offers a powerful answer. According to the biblical law, once every seven years, all loans are to be forgiven, as a kind of amnesty that constitutes part of the Bible's relief to the poor. Yet there is an obvious problem: As the Sabbatical year draws near, people will be far less likely to lend money to someone whose ability to pay them back quickly is suspect. Here is the Bible's response:

> Beware that there not be an unworthy thought in your heart, saying, "The seventh year, the year of release, is at hand," and your eye be evil against your poor brother, and you give him nothing. . . . You shall surely give him, and your heart shall not grieve when you give to him. . . . For the poor shall never cease out of the land. Therefore I command you, saying, you shall open your hand wide to your brother, to your poor and to your needy, in your land. (Deuteronomy 15:9–11)

Two statements here jump out of the page. First, *and your eye be evil against your brother.* In invoking the fact that poor people are our "brothers," the Bible is using the full force of its rhetoric. Like a real brother, for whom we are responsible regardless of who he is or what he has done, the face of the poor person presents an absolute call for help and care. His suffering is never to be ignored, regardless of how different he seems to us, how far beyond our capacity to help, how alien his needs or ailments. The fact of his suffering overrides our calculated estimations as to its causes, calculations that usually come more from our ignorance than familiarity with his history.

Second, *For the poor shall never cease out of the land.* Once we allow ourselves to ignore the suffering of the poor, it becomes easy to adopt a high-horse approach to poverty: By giving them money, I encourage the flaws of character that led to their poverty; if everyone were simply to stop giving charity, then all the poor people would be forced to learn to take care of themselves instead of begging in the streets, and poverty would disappear. The poor would cease out of the land.

The Bible says, no, they wouldn't. And even if there were a measure of truth to this line of thought, the harm done to each of us by habitually turning a blind eye, the dehumanization of our souls resulting from saying no to the real poor person standing before us, is far worse than any possible gain in "incentivizing" self-sufficiency in this way. This is what the rabbis mean when they teach that in receiving charity, "The poor man does more for the rich man than the rich for the poor."[8] We cannot know how wisely a poor person will spend our charitable dollar. But we can guess what will become of us if we, as a matter of principle, refuse to help him.

For this reason, the Bible relates to the poor as, first of all, real people who need to be treated with both respect and sensitivity—neither as children who have no standing as citizens nor as irresponsible adults who have made their own beds. In instructing judges on how to keep an impartial eye, the Bible forbids distorting justice not just to favor the rich but also to favor the poor: Before the law, all are equal, and this equality is essential for preserving the sense of mutual respect within society. At the same time, however, we are told never to take a poor person's coat as collateral on a loan and never to delay the day laborer's wages even for a single night.

The rabbinic tradition took this dual approach even further: On the one hand, charity is hailed as one of the highest forms of righteousness—to the point where one is obligated, according to the rabbis, to give away a tenth of one's income to the poor. On the other hand, even the poor person who himself receives charity is obligated to give charity as well, for in giving we establish our own humanity, and this is something even a poor person must do.[9] The assumption is that helping others is a universal obligation, and that no matter how poor one becomes, one never loses his fundamental status as a human being capable of redemption.

Charity, in other words, is an expression of our self-expansion, not of our self-negation. This is very different from the ancient Christian concept of charity, which was seen as a form of "grace," by which the individual gives as an act of self-negation, transforming himself into a vessel for the transmission of the divine into the world. The rabbis, on the other hand, prescribed not only a minimal level of charity, but also a maximum—usually seen as one-fifth—lest the giver reduce himself to poverty. They also taught that the greatest form of charity is in teaching a poor person a trade—giving him not just money but the tools he needs to stop taking charity in the first place.[10]

Just as respecting property means respecting another's humanity, so too is the highest form of charity that which maximizes the recipient's humanity, his ability to earn and give and take part in the flow of economic life just like us.

In expanding ourselves materially, many of us all too often neglect the duty to expand ourselves on the human level as well. We submit, like Ahab, to the idolatry of wealth. Wealth is good in that it trains us to be greater than our limited bodies; but this training is meant to encourage us to expand on the human level as well, to teach us to love and protect people the way we love and protect our things. The moment we see our wealth as the main focus of our expansion, and consider those in need as a threat to our wealth instead of an opportunity to care, we have dehumanized our fellow man—and, in the process, missed the entire point of being wealthy.

In my work with nonprofit organizations, I have had the good fortune of meeting exceptionally wealthy people who understand this very deeply. Financiers who earned hundreds of millions by the age of forty, and give away tens of millions each year to charities, often anonymously; women and men who made their money in real estate, in software start-ups, in banking, or the not-quite-as-rich doctors and lawyers, all of whom take time out of their lives to find charitable organizations where their money will do the most good, or to help individuals in their community who are caught in a deep financial bind. Most of them can afford any luxury they want, but many keep relatively modest homes. I met one man who, nearing the end of his career, decided to give only a small percentage of his vast estate to his children, for fear that endless wealth would spoil them. Nor did he trust the judgment of the lower-level managers who would give away his money if he left behind a sizable philanthropic foundation. Instead, he spent the last years of his life just giving away his money, researching and interviewing one organization after another, giving only to those he felt would spend it efficiently and help the most people in the most important ways.

How many lives have been saved or eased by the hospitals, immense charitable organizations, and legal aid groups that are built by the wealthy? What right do we have to judge them harshly for having been so successful and then channeling their wealth to helping others? Could such hospitals exist if these people had instead become writers or journalists or failed businessmen? There is a kind of antiwealth rhetoric that insists that rich people are inherently bad, and that where there is more wealth, there is more poverty—not just because money is limited and, if you get it, you must have taken it from someone else, but because by encouraging people to make money, we champion selfishness. Surely this is true for some people. But how do we account for the existence of the enormous nonprofit sector, where hundreds of billions of dollars are given away each year to care for others?

Obviously, spending time with philanthropists can give you

the misimpression that all rich people are like this; you don't meet many sickeningly greedy people at fund-raising events. Philanthropy does not flow naturally from wealth. It is, rather, the product of a specific cultural attitude, a way of relating to money as something that, beyond a certain point, is earned in order to be given away. The donors I've met often saw their parents struggle yet remain committed to caring for others no matter how bad things got, and now their children are determined to help where their parents could not. They are humble people who know their good fortune could easily have been bad. They recognize their wealth as a blessing from heaven, one that cannot be taken lightly.

Earlier I suggested that the Eighth Commandment moves in the opposite direction from the Seventh: As opposed to the ever-expanding, embracing love that is implied by *You shall not commit adultery,* the commandment *You shall not steal* restrains our love to make room for others.

Yet it should be clear that these do not actually contradict each other but rather work in tandem. The most difficult problem of love is the sense of superiority, the feeling that having embraced someone else and taken responsibility for his well-being, we crush his independent self rather than encouraging him—that like property, we feel we own the people we love. The Eighth Commandment reminds us that a central part of love is respect, that we cannot really love another until we take responsibility for not only his material and physical welfare but also for his growth, spiritual independence, and well-being. "If you love someone," the Bible sings with Sting, "set them free."

But if love without respect is crushing, respect without love is alienating. If the Eighth Commandment gives the Seventh its direction and maybe even its legitimacy in the affirmation of the other as a free human being, the Seventh gives the Eighth its possibility of redemption. What we learn from the biblical attitude toward wealth and poverty is that for all its concern for proper borders and mutual respect between individuals, there is still a mandate to love—to care sincerely about our neighbors; to respect their decisions but make it clear we will be there for them if they are in trouble; to give generously of our time and money to those in need, letting them know they are never alone, but giving them the respect and honor due every human being.

But there is still a final step that must be taken before this ideal of interpersonal relations can be translated into an ideal for society as a whole. The Seventh and Eighth Commandments set the stage for building powerful, thriving, loving relations between strong individuals capable of redeeming. But for this to translate into redemptive communities and a redemptive society, we need to understand what community and society are all about. We need the Ninth Commandment.

9

Our Communities, Ourselves

You shall not bear false witness against your neighbor.

At first glance, the Ninth Commandment looks like another ban on lying. Indeed, throughout history many religious authorities put the biblical prohibition on falsehood here, rather than back in the Third Commandment. The thirteenth-century Franciscan theologian Ramón Lull even went so far as to physically relocate the Ninth Commandment just after the Third. So convinced was he that they are essentially saying the same thing, he just rewrote the text.

There are reasons to think Lull was wrong, and that the Ninth Commandment has little to do with lying per se. We know enough about the Ten Commandments to recognize that each of them is an extreme case of a broader moral principle. Lying is a sin first of all against the self, something we do in order to get out of trouble or to gain some advantage—but not necessarily out of spite or malice for others, the way it's presented here. The false oath, not the false witness, is the true epitome of the lie.

The Ninth Commandment, on the other hand, is part of a string of commandments that appear as a single verse, Exodus 20:13: *You shall not murder, you shall not commit adultery, you shall not steal, you shall not bear false witness against your neighbor*—all in one breath. This is the fourth in a series of "you shall nots" that are not really about our inner selves so much as the attacks we commit against others.

What is it about the false witness that merits putting this sin into the Ten Commandments alongside the values of life, love, and freedom? The case at hand seems clear enough. It prohibits knowingly testifying in court that someone committed a crime when he did not. This is obviously a terrible thing to do to someone.

But the false witness, I suggest, attacks not only his victim but his entire community. He is, in fact, the paradigmatic destroyer of communal life. Here is the first time we encounter the phrase "your neighbor" in the Ten Commandments, the first time man is presented not just as an individual but as part of a collective, a neighborhood.

To understand what the Ninth Commandment is really after, we need to take a closer look at the meaning of community and how the false witness strikes at its very heart.

The redemptive spirit longs to go beyond his closest friends and family, and to extend his love to ever-expanding circles. But every time he tries, he discovers that success or failure depends largely on something that has preceded him, something not fully in his control, a veil of preexisting impressions, some false and some true, that people already have of him.

We call this his "reputation." A good reputation turns people toward us instinctively, as if they have been waiting for us all along. A bad one makes it nearly impossible for others to accept our support and love. Reputation is like a force field that surrounds us, extending far beyond ourselves, reaching people's minds before we get there and remaining long after we go. It is our presence in the human community.

From childhood we are told to ignore what other people think about us, to make sure we are good and right in our own eyes, or those of God. But anyone who has tried to run a business, start a social club, run for office, or otherwise play an active role in the community knows that success depends to a large degree on one's reputation for honesty, effectiveness, or quality of work. In a society where people work together to achieve larger goals, the protection of reputations is every bit as crucial, if not more so, as the protection of property. Community depends on mutual responsibility, which in turn depends on mutual trust, which in turn depends on reputation. By fostering a discourse of slander, the false witness threatens the foundations of community.

The Bible is deeply aware of the incredible power of speech to tear down and destroy trust and respect. In addition to the Ninth Commandment, we read that "you shall not go as a tale-bearer among your people" (Leviticus 19:16), a prohibition not so much against lying as against gossip, the self-serving stream of negative stories about others that seems to flow endlessly from the mouths and pens of so many of us. Again, "among your people" suggests that the problem of talebearing goes beyond the individual hurt and affects everybody. Moses' sister, Miriam, is stricken with leprosy because she bad-mouthed her brother after the latter married a beautiful Cushite woman. The link between false witness and negative speech is emphasized more broadly by the Proverbs, where we read of the "six things that the Lord hates, seven that are an abomination to him," a list that ends with "a false witness who breathes out lies, and one that sows discord among brethren" (Proverbs 6:16–19).

The rabbinic sages took an extremely strict attitude toward the way we speak of our fellows. Gossip is called *lashon hara,* "the evil tongue," and the rabbis believed it to be one of the worst crimes against society. According to the Talmud, "Anyone who speaks the evil tongue, God says of him: He and I cannot live in the same world." One legend describes the evil tongue as the source of all plagues. Another says that anyone who speaks it loses his place in heaven. The evil tongue is described as being worse than the shedding of blood, sexual immorality, and idolatry—the three sins that Judaism holds that one ought to die rather than commit. "Anyone who embarrasses his friend in public," the rabbis taught, "it is as though he has shed his blood."[1]

This understanding of the Ninth Commandment wasn't exclusive to Jewish interpreters. John Calvin, the Protestant founder who lived in sixteenth-century France and Switzerland, wrote, "The reason why I am prohibited from bearing false witness against my neighbor is because God intends for friendship to be established between men and for no one to be tormented with regard to his honor." This, he goes on to argue, is the central purpose of speech in general, which was given to us by God "for the purpose of nurturing tender love and fraternity with each other, may we not abuse it in order to gossip and hustle about here and there, so perverting our speech as to poison ourselves against each other."[2] Martin Luther took an especially harsh view of gossip and slander in his own commentary on the Ninth Commandment:

> Knowledge of sin does not entail the right to judge it. I may see and hear that my neighbor sins, but to make him the talk of the town is not my business. . . . Those are called backbiters who are not content just to know but rush ahead and judge. Learning a bit of gossip about someone else, they spread it into

every corner, relishing and delighting in it like pigs that roll in the mud and root around in it with their snouts. This is nothing else than usurping the judgment and office of God, pronouncing the severest kind of verdict and sentence, or the harshest verdict a judge can pronounce is to declare somebody a thief, a murderer, a traitor, etc. Whoever therefore ventures to accuse his neighbor of such guilt assumes as much authority as the emperor and all magistrates. For though you do not wield the sword, you use your venomous tongue to the disgrace and harm of your neighbor.[3]

Turn on any cable news channel or visit any public-affairs website, and you are likely to find an effervescent flow of evil tongues. I am not speaking of disagreement and the clash of values and ideas, or of the careful look that is taken at a public figure's record—all these are not just legitimate but essential to any democratic society. I am speaking of the ease with which motives are impugned, lifestyles derogated, name-calling condoned, individuals and groups demonized.

These things draw attention and therefore are often in the commercial interest of any forum that survives on the strength of ad revenues. They are legitimized by citing the need of the public to know, but ultimately they destroy our confidence and faith in other people, and push us closer to an overarching cynicism that is the antithesis of community and the redemptive vision. Instead of assuming from the outset that people are fallible and therefore accepting as human their weaknesses, we look for imperfections in every politician, pundit, or pro athlete, and when it is discovered that they are less than perfect, we yell "Gotcha!" and assume they have nothing positive to contribute to society. Yet in many cases it is we, not they, who have revealed a weakness.

It's amazing how little heed we pay to so many centuries of Christian and Jewish teaching about the evils of derogating others. While we have fairly well committed ourselves to the value of life and the respect for property, the inclination to demean runs wild. Why?

The most obvious reason is that whereas in crimes like murder and theft the harm is evident and well-defined, with negative speech it is easy to convince ourselves that there are no bad results, especially when the words are spoken in private. Gossipers may argue that they mean no ill. The information they pass is usually a form of entertainment, meant to build their own status in the eyes of their listener. By showing they have exclusive access to interesting information, they make themselves important. As for the potential harm, they convince themselves that what they say will remain in confidence or have little impact.

The fallacy of such reasoning should be obvious. The individual speaking "in confidence" is, in fact, the most important conduit of rumors, and confidences about such things are rarely kept in full—for if the teller did not restrain himself, then why should the listener employ a higher level of discretion? But until we have fallen victim to false or embarrassing rumors, most of us do not think twice about what we are doing. Our mongering of gossip is the kind of irresponsibility we ordinarily associate with children: It is mostly innocent in its intentions yet small-minded, and it does not reflect a sense of responsibility for others. "The gossiper," the rabbis taught, "talks in Rome and kills in Syria."[4]

There is a second reason. It is often hard to distinguish the evil tongue from legitimate, constructive criticism. The number of situations in which it is appropriate, even important, to say something negative about another is not small. If we have been harmed by someone's dishonesty or rapaciousness, do we not have a duty to warn others? Our wisdom of the world, more-over, grows through mutual consultations over the pluses and minuses of people and institutions. From an economic perspective, the whole system of competitive markets and the improved goods and services they bring *begins* with the efficient transmission of comparative opinions about them. Surely we would not go as far as to say that a negative restaurant review or an unfavorable estimation of a plumber violates the Ninth Commandment?

Let us go further still. In a democracy, the free flow of information about public figures, and especially political leaders, must necessarily include no small measure of negatives. Indeed, it is precisely these negatives that create a system of public accountability without which there can be no informed democratic choice. "No body politic is healthy," the journalist Heywood Broun said, "until it begins to itch." This democratic tradition of open criticism finds its roots in the Bible as well. The prophets Moses, Isaiah, Jeremiah, and Nathan risked their lives to publicly rebuke political leaders. The Ninth Commandment is clearly not meant to still the voice of moral outrage.

For these reasons, however, we often allow ourselves far too much leeway in slamming the reputations of politicians, cultural critics, or opinion makers—the very people who have taken responsibility for the broader well-being of society. What does it mean when books with titles like *Michael Moore Is a Big Fat Stupid White Man* or *Rush Limbaugh Is a Big Fat Idiot* become bestsellers? Call me a curmudgeon, accuse me of being tone-deaf to camp humor and literary slapstick—I can't help feeling that something has gone wrong when we elevate the grotesque potshot to an art form. Such book titles cross a line of bad taste precisely because so many people agree with them in all seriousness. No matter what one thinks of Moore's films or Limbaugh's radio show, no matter how much each of them may have contributed to the culture of nastiness itself, we are talking about individuals who have dedicated their careers to protesting evil (in their view) and trying to correct things. By indulging our lowest expressions of hate, we legitimize the most vicious kinds of verbal assaults on others and make it that much more risky for ordinary people to take responsibility for others, knowing what kind of attacks await them.

Successful communities require a different way of relating to our friends and peers—from a standpoint of responsibility rather than enmity. People in formal positions of responsibility usually know this intuitively: A good manager doesn't take an employee to task in the presence of others; a good coach doesn't criticize a player to the ears of others; a good parent doesn't reprimand his child in the presence of another. Such people recognize that their task is to maintain the sense of mutual regard, excitement, and support necessary for collective achievement— and that if they don't, the entire enterprise might fail, bringing ruin far beyond what we may realize.

The Talmud tells of a certain man named Kamtza, who lived in the land of Israel at a time when relations with the Roman imperial government were tense. A close friend of his threw a dinner party, inviting all the leading rabbis. The friend told his servant to invite Kamtza as well, but the servant accidentally invited someone named Bar-Kamtza instead—who happened to be a bitter enemy of the host.

When the host discovered Bar-Kamtza seated at his party, he told him to leave. Bar-Kamtza, trying to protect his good name and avoid a scene, offered to pay for his share of the meal, but the host refused. He offered to pay for half the feast, but the host insisted he leave. He offered to pay for the whole thing, and the host threw him out the door.

"Since the rabbis were there, saw the whole thing and did not protest," Bar-Kamtza thought to himself, "they clearly had no problem with my humiliation."

He went to the Romans and told them the Jews had rebelled against their rule. As proof, he suggested that they send the Jews a calf to offer as a sacrifice at the Temple in Jerusalem, and to see whether they accepted it. As the calf was being delivered, however, Bar-Kamtza deliberately disfigured it, rendering it unfit for sacrifice. The rabbis refused to perform the service, and the Romans took it as proof of their rebellion—setting off a chain of events that ended with their burning the Temple to the ground, destroying Jerusalem, and bringing an end to the Jewish commonwealth.

Rabbi Elazar concludes from the story: "Come and see the disaster that can come from embarrassment, for God helped Bar-Kamtza and destroyed his Temple and burned his Sanctuary." According to Rabbi Yohanan, however, the problem was not only with the host of the party but also with the rabbis, who did not protest Bar-Kamtza's humiliation, and who put the purity of their sacrifices above the dignity of their peer.[5]

The rabbis of the Talmud lived in the shadow of Jerusalem's destruction, which took place in the first century C.E. Inevitably they drew comparisons with another destruction, six centuries earlier, when the Temple of Solomon was sacked by the Babylonians. They looked for theological explanations and found them in the Jews' own sins. Whereas the First Temple, they taught, was destroyed as God's punishment for the sins of murder, idolatry, and sexual immorality that were rampant among the Israelites, the Second was destroyed because of "baseless hatred" among the people. This sin, we learn, was worse than the others, for while the first destruction was followed by a brief exile and the Jews' return to the land seventy years later, the second brought an exile that would last indefinitely.[6]

The worst forms of immorality, we learn, can bring the collapse of society. But even this can be repaired more easily than the communal rot that results from mutual hatred. Slander, gossip, and attacks on others strike at the heart of society's very existence.

The false witness, however, is not just slandering an innocent person. He is doing it in a court of law. The case of the Ninth Commandment is carefully chosen: Beyond his failure to uphold his friend's good name, the false witness commits a second crime, directed squarely against a community's most concrete manifestation: its institutions.

The court is the paradigmatic communal institution. While our police and prosecution and prisons are needed to maintain order and fight crime, and our schools and churches help families nurture the norms and values of our children, it is the courts that make justice real in our day-to-day lives, establishing a moral baseline of behavior and giving citizens the confidence that their society is, in essence, a safe and just one. Even if we rarely set foot in a courthouse, it is the court's effectiveness that allows us to buy a car, to walk down the street, to speak our minds, to save for the future.

As I write these words, I am confident no one will attempt to kill me for having written them; no government will put me in jail; no one will plagiarize this text; and my publisher will not violate our contract. Such things happen, but I'm not worried. My confidence arises not from the inherent good in man—there are many places on earth where I *would* be worried. Rather, it flows from my sense that such acts are sufficiently deterred by a justice system that enforces laws governing free speech, intellectual property, and contracts. Good courts make communities work even when trust and friendship are lacking; they give us the security we need to live without the constant fear of being eaten alive.

In the biblical view, creating a court is an act of delegation, of making sure that as a community we can live in peace and freedom. In the ancient world, adjudication of disputes often took place more or less ad hoc. While there were always courts appointed by the rulers, in many cultures there were also local judges who attained prominence in a more organic fashion, as people recognized their wisdom and turned to them for counsel and resolution; they, in turn, accepted the greater authority of others, who became judges of wider geographical areas.[7] In a modern democracy, the judiciary represents a conscious act of responsibility taking on the part of society, where judges, appointed by elected representatives or directly elected themselves, interpret written laws and judicial precedent to ensure the effective, consistent application of justice throughout society.

The courts, in other words, are *ours,* an essential part of how we as a community take responsibility for one another. But they can do their job only when the public feels confident in their fairness and effectiveness. The false witness pulls the rug out from under that confidence, exploiting the court for the precise opposite of its purpose: for inflicting injustice. He hijacks the community's essential institution to amplify his power, enlisting it against itself—and against the community as a whole.

What is true for the courts, of course, is true for every communal institution—formal ones, like government, schools, and the military; and informal ones, like clubs and volunteer organizations or even the weekly bridge game in our neighbor's home. Each and every one of these is a tool for the advancement of communal life. But each can also be commandeered by unscrupulous, opportunistic people. When a police officer takes a bribe from criminals and turns a blind eye to their crimes; when an ambassador "goes native" and puts the interests of his host country above those of his government; when a well-off person fraudulently arranges to get taxpayer-subsidized benefits meant for the poor—in all these cases, the Ninth Commandment is violated. Our government, our schools, our civic institutions—all of these belong to all of us, and we have a duty to help them succeed.

Leaving aside my ill-fated term as class president in seventh grade (a tale I will leave for another time), only twice have I ever run for anything resembling public office. Both times, I was responding to bad situations I thought I could help fix. In one case, my kids' elementary school had been taken over by a nonprofit religious organization that three of my friends and I suspected of serious improprieties. The four of us ran for the seven-seat school board, and all of us won, making it possible to extricate ourselves from the nonprofit's clutches and restore to his post the principal whose vision had guided the school for years, but had been forced to quit by the new regime.

That was easy, however, compared with the time I ran for the board of my synagogue, which had been mired in endless disputes about whether the rabbi was doing a good job. Some people thought his amazing oratory and creative scholarship were a blessing for the community and a source of pride; others thought he should talk less and spend more time on communal needs and pastoral care. I thought I might help heal the rift. Such was the poverty of my community's enthusiasm for the synagogue, however, that I ended up running unopposed. I quickly found out why: The acrimony was so deep, the gap in visions so wide, that my contribution was useless. Within a few months, I resigned. Not long after, the rabbi quit as well.

What do you feel when you take responsibility for others? In both cases, my decision to run came with a transformation of how I felt toward the whole community. Instead of receiving services in exchange for dues or tuition, I now saw the enterprise as an extension of myself. Instead of being a member, I was, in a sense, an owner. Responsibility means staying up late at night, attending meetings or just failing to fall asleep, directing our creative energies toward the project because we care about what happens to these people or that organization, because we know that if things go wrong, it is our own failure—because they are, in some real sense, us.

We often think of "community" as something we participate in, are members of, benefit from. But the point of the Ninth Commandment is that community begins not with involvement but with taking responsibility. Community is alive when the redemptive self turns outward beyond his loved ones and best friends, caring for and nurturing and protecting the people and institutions that community is made of.

For thousands of years, the Jewish people faced an almost inhuman pressure to create cohesive, successful communities. Judaism is not just a faith but a comprehensive way of life, and often Jews had to circle their wagons in order to fend off governments and non-Jewish religious institutions that actively tried to get them to abandon their unique practices. Such was the case in Judea under the occupation of the Seleucid Greeks in the second century B.C.E., under the Spanish in the time of the Inquisition in the fifteenth century, under the French in the time of Napoleon in the nineteenth, and under the Soviets in the twentieth. In every age, Jews felt a need to protect their communal life, to help one another, to develop institutions and attitudes that made sure that every member survived with his dignity and identity intact.

The result was that over time, Jews developed a powerful

sense of communal responsibility—a feeling reflected in formal and informal institutions, funded by charity, and usually run by volunteers. Many of today's traditional communities continue this through innumerable charitable organizations, started by redemptive individuals taking responsibility for others: free loan societies and help for the poor; tuition subsidies for religious education; specialized free-lending shops for wedding dresses and other bridal costs, and for children's clothes and toys; breast-milk banks for mothers having difficulty feeding their newborns; welcoming committees for new families in the community, offering food, babysitting, and other services to families who have just moved in; organized meals for families who have just had babies; discounted or free child care for working mothers; organized visits to hospitals for sick members of the community; and more and more.

Such was the community I had the honor to serve. Perhaps the most amazing thing about it was that even as the synagogue was being decimated by competing visions and appraisals of the rabbi, in all other respects the community continued to thrive, with most of the organizations, aid societies, and educational programs going strong. As soon as it came to helping one another in their ordinary lives, the debates about the rabbi were forgotten.

Such a communal life is not for everyone. Many people find it stifling, and it has a darker side to it as well: Founded on classical strictures and traditions, many communities turn their backs on people who do not accept the basic religious attitudes or styles of family life that are the ground rules of acceptance. Communities can also be a seething cauldron of gossip and invasion of privacy, a weakness that often sets the stage for infighting, evil tongues, and eventual collapse.

Yet these communities offer a powerful example from which

we can learn. They still thrive throughout the West, mostly in a religious context, and people who participate in them enjoy a human richness, a sense of belonging, and the benefit of the kindness and wisdom of others that are rarely found anywhere else.

One of the biggest problems with community today is that most of us think we do not need it. We no longer need church functions and local politics, school board meetings and bake sales, we tell ourselves, to be successful or happy people. So much of what used to be handled by the community can be found elsewhere—government programs take care of the poor; the workplace gives us human contact; television gives us our news. Moreover, technology has made the whole idea of community seem somewhat outdated: We are more mobile than we used to be, friendships rarely are built over many years, cell phones and the Internet reduce direct human contact, replacing it with fleeting, casual, shallow interactions. Life is too busy for community. Or is it?

True, a Facebook friendship is usually more impersonal or shallow than one that emerges from working together in a soup kitchen. Yet to blame the Internet for the loss of old-fashioned communities is like blaming the telephone for the loss of the art of letter writing, or the internal combustion engine for the loss of concern for horses. Technology changes the way we interact, but it need not change the essential values and goals that guide these interactions.

If anything, technological advances give us infinite opportunities for taking responsibility for others. Today, friendships can be maintained even after friends move apart; lovers can text each other touching reminders throughout the day; and communities can coordinate their activities and make last-minute changes, sending notices out by email and issuing urgent calls for assistance. It's up to us to fill our new modern life with content, to find creative new ways to take responsibility for others.

For the redemptive self, community is neither a luxury nor a hobby. It is a need, a fulfillment of our expansive urge that goes beyond our closest circles. Just as with a lover, where we long both to caress and to be caressed, to love and be loved—the mutuality of love being a simultaneous act of giving and receiving, of selfishness and selflessness that fuse into a single moment of self-affirming redemption—our communal involvement is about giving and receiving, mutually and simultaneously. It is about joining others who are like us and embracing them precisely because of what we share, offering them our uniqueness as a gift and enjoying theirs.

But how? With whom? One thing that *has* changed in our modern lives is that while our community was once chosen for us—where we lived, our religious affiliations, our trade—today we share so many different things with so many different people, and it is so much easier than ever before to connect with them, it becomes unclear what is or is not a community for us. Living in a major city, do we create community with the other tenants of our apartment building? Our fellow sweat-soakers at the gym? Fellow Pentacostals or Jimi Hendrix lovers around the world?

To make the final transition from the redemptive life to the redemptive society, to understand what the Ninth Commandment is really after, we need to focus on who we are—and to say a few words about our hopelessly complex identities.

Who are you?

I am a Bostonian. I am an alumnus of Brookline High School, in Brookline, Massachusetts. I spent many good years in and around New York and count myself as a New Yorker as well.

I went to Columbia University and Yeshiva University and Hebrew University. I am a Jew, and I am also an Israeli, not just because I moved to Israel as an adult but also because I grew up in a Hebrew-speaking, Israeli immigrant home in central New Jersey. I love music and grew up playing the piano and singing in choir and even had a rock band in high school. I live in Israel and pay its taxes. I am a writer.

All these descriptions of me are legitimate candidates for basing my self-expansion and communal involvement. For every one of us, there is a similar set of statements that speak to our experiences, our birth, our ethnic or religious affinities, our training and native talents. Each of these is a potential starting point for reaching out to others like us and taking responsibility.

The first step in true, honest community in the modern world is asking ourselves who we really are and which of all these identities we are most committed to. There is no use adopting false identities or trying to force ourselves to care deeply about things that are not streaming through our blood. Identity is not a canvas we can splatter with whatever media are at hand. I can look back and cherish my years in high school, loving the part of myself that connects with it, and reach out to others who share that experience by creating an alumni association. I will put in all the effort to try to track down my classmates, starting a website where we can share our memories, organize reunions, and encourage mutual support. But would I do it for someone else's high school?

One man with the right attitude toward identity showed up at a baseball game in late September 2001. As a lifelong New York Yankees fan, I've done my best to keep up even after leaving the United States. Their first game after the terror attack that devastated New York just a few weeks earlier was in Chicago. In all of sports, no team is as reviled as the Yankees, and at any other time, this would have seemed unthinkable: A Chicago fan was holding a big sign that read, WE ARE ALL YANKEES.

There was no mistaking the intention behind the words in the wake of 9/11. Sports allegiances are wonderful but extremely limited and in some sense false, based entirely on who we are when we are taking a break from being who we are. When genuine tragedy strikes, the fan was saying, we have to remember that we are Americans first. The Yankees are not merely a sports franchise but also a group of real people who have just suffered a personal trauma that is more important than baseball. We won't stop rooting for one team or another, but we want you to know that all of this is just a show—in truth, we identify with the victims and those whose nightmare could have just as easily been our own. We include them and care for them. They are a part of us.

Finding community in the modern world means constantly asking ourselves what is or is not a real part of us, and how to prioritize these parts, dedicating time to some and shedding others, always looking at our activities and asking, "Is this really me?" Frequently we find, as did the fan at the ballpark, that the largest, most comprehensive religious and national identities are also among the most important in our lives. Jewish identity, Catholic identity, French identity, American identity—all of these represent not just shared ideals and beliefs but also centuries of shared history, and as a result they express themselves as a connection to others over the whole spectrum of life's experiences, including our most painful tragedies. These larger collective commitments are an incredibly powerful force in human affairs, capable of inspiring intensive and lasting redemptive activism on a huge scale. These are the greatest communities we have.

But can't they, because of how powerful they are, also be the basis of strife, conflict, and endless violence? There is a myth out there, like the one that claims that property itself is to blame for poverty, that blames identity itself for the horrors of war—that if we all were to stop seeing ourselves as proud members of a country or religion and just embrace our humanity, there would be peace on earth.

This is a fantasy. Redemptive societies emphasize these kinds of wider identities, turning communal self-expansion into the basis of a mutually supportive, coherent civilization. They look not for war but for the richness of life. Every redemptive identity ultimately affirms humanity, even if it is sometimes exclusive of others, even if at times it must respond to threats, because it makes an argument that a certain way of life is good for all people and tries to prove it through the inherent attractiveness of its members' lives. It claims to possess a unique wisdom about how to live and in this sense offers itself up as an irreplaceable gift to mankind. What does a purely universal identity offer that can compare?

This does not mean, of course, that we should ever forget we are also human beings, that the tragedies that unfold around the globe are, on some level, our own tragedies as well. A crucial part of our identity is our humanity, and one of the biggest tests of whether our identities are worth pursuing is if they push us to hate people whose identities are not our own. Because the redemptive spirit is inherently constructive, the best way to tell whether we're on the right track is to ask ourselves whether the exclusion of others is merely a matter of focusing on our own and protecting ourselves from genuine threats, or whether it has become a force of destruction, demonization, or inhuman neglect.

At the risk of sounding hopelessly idealistic, I really do believe that the key to ending most of the bloodshed and war in the world comes down to the question of how to allow such redemptive identities to thrive, affirming them in genuine love. Americans should love America, should love their nation's pragmatism, its entrepreneurial energy, its youthful creative spirit; the French should love their country's aesthetic taste, its appreciation and creation of beauty, its human complexity. Muslims and Christians and Jews should love their own traditions without turning in hatred toward others.

For many years, political scientists have been pointing out that democratic states almost never go to war against one another. There is a reason for this. It is not that they have abandoned their own symbols and values, or that they are all really the same. In affirming themselves, rather, they do not need all the hate that is the precondition for violence. When every individual has the freedom to chart his own course, to build communities and society that are truly part of himself, when every person can look to his government as a locus of responsibility rather than a focus of fear, and when every leader has to account for failed policies and does not have the luxury of blaming external enemies for his mistakes, then a civilization has the human breathing space, the room for the self, needed to focus on building rather than destroying, on affirming and enriching its citizens' lives rather than asserting their superiority through force. A truly redemptive society knows how to make room for others.

The Ninth Commandment tells us to protect, defend, and advance the community as a whole, and every individual in it, as if they were our own. Not just to involve ourselves, but to take responsibility—for the reputations of others, for our communal institutions, for our towns, our schools, our courts, our coreligionists, our broader societies and nations, and anything else we love about ourselves and share with others.

If all of us were to see our communities as part of ourselves, civic life at every level would change. Perhaps the debates would still be intense and rancorous, but they would spring from a greater concern and mutual affection, and would reflect a deep regard for the reputations of others and the institutions we share. The ranks of the volunteers would swell, and the most difficult domestic problems would be those of organization rather than alienation, of efficacy rather than apathy. Society would thrive, and national pride would grow, while always remaining focused on affirmation and humanity and love. But all this begins with a basic attitude toward those around us, which comes from seeing our friends and peers—especially those we disagree with—as a part of ourselves.

This, in turn, has to come from somewhere. Creating a redemptive society requires a certain frame of mind, a psychological disposition, a spiritual poise and self-affirmation. People who are hesitant to take on the commitments of community often are too busy protecting their jobs and families and achievements and resources, or too afraid of what unknown burdens the commitments of community might entail.

To address this problem, the final obstacle to the redemptive vision, we must take one last step inward again. It is back to our inner selves that the Ten Commandments make their final turn.

10

Peace

You shall not covet your neighbor's house. You shall not covet your neighbor's wife, nor his man-servant or his maid-servant, his ox or his ass, or anything that is your neighbor's.

The peak of a mountain looks small to one who has reached it.

At first blush, there is something petty about the Tenth Commandment. One of the world's greatest moral works, which opens with the overwhelming declaration of *I am the Lord your God* and over nine earth-shaking pronouncements presents a whole vision of God, man, and society, now comes to a close with a trifle about our stuff. *His ox or his ass*—do we really need a list of mundane longings for other people's belongings?

But like the summit of a soaring mountain, the Tenth Commandment is anything but trivial. It stands for a new principle reflecting back on the previous nine but adding a dimension, touching on a uniquely human evil, widespread and alluring, a sin of the spirit so egregious as to warrant closing on this note, so deeply hidden as to have to wait until the end.

There is a literary element here as well, giving us further clues as to the Tenth Commandment's importance. Like the First, the Tenth is not about our actions, but focuses on our thoughts, emotions, or ideals. The first and last commandments are like bookends, a psychic framework without which the inner eight cannot stand alone. We also hear an echo of the Fourth Commandment, the only other place where we are given a list of concrete examples of this kind: *Neither you, nor your son or your daughter, your man-servant or your maid-servant, your beasts or your stranger in your gates.* The Tenth Commandment reads like a deliberate reference to the Sabbath, the pivotal moment where the self is discovered, the core of our redemptive lives spelled out for the first time.

The ban on coveting is a rejection of a single personality flaw so destructive as to be the source of many other sins—the sin behind sin, the inner evil without which, in the biblical view, all the other sins would be committed far less often. In understanding this sin, we find the key to turning the Ten Commandments from an abstract vision into something concrete and pragmatic, into a real-life worldview that we can undertake immediately, changing who we are into something better.

It is the sin of insecurity.

We do not usually speak of insecurity in moral terms. The word is vaguely clinical, associated with psychological counseling and problems that need to be fixed, with a malfunction in the mechanism of our mind, but one that does not necessarily reflect wrongfulness—more like bad cholesterol than bad character.

The Tenth Commandment, on the other hand, imbues the problem of insecurity with all the weight of God's moral approbation. It directs our attention to the source of our greed and unbridled want that leads us to take what is not ours, to the dis-

torting fears that lead us to strike out against others, to our failure to affirm ourselves and act with courage. To covet is to have
lost our inner peace, our baseline satisfaction about who we are
and what we have. "Who is rich?" the rabbis ask. "One who is
happy with his lot."[1]

Covetousness is the deflation and failure of the self. Instead
of feeling happy with our lot, we grab for more in the hope that
this will restore our status in our own eyes. Instead of judging
things as they are, we twist the world to respond to our fears and
the perceived intentions of others, convincing ourselves that we
have a right to things that are not ours. Instead of redeeming, we
do evil. Instead of loving, we hate.

Throughout the biblical stories, insecurity is found lurking
behind the greatest of man's failings.

As the Israelites wander through the desert, Moses is constantly left dumbstruck by the complaints and hesitations of his
people. Having been shown in every conceivable way the benev-
olence and reliability of God, who was willing to break even
the laws of nature to take them out of slavery and lead them
to freedom, to destroy their enemies, and to provide for them
in the wilderness, who has given them every reason to feel that
the universe itself is on their side and that nothing can stand in
their way, the Israelites nonetheless repeatedly call into question
not only their own prospects for survival but also the wisdom of
Moses' and God's leadership.

Something went wrong with the exodus.

In looking at the stories of Israel in the wilderness, we are
struck by two facts. One is that the Israelites are congenitally
incapable of overcoming their deepest insecurities, coming up
with the most absurd claims against Moses and God, twisting
reality in a way that only abject fear can explain, and never learn-

ing from their experience. The second is that these outbursts of insecurity are taken by God and Moses not as acute psychological disturbances but as moral failings that raise questions about whether they really deserve to be redeemed in the first place.

Moses' impatience is evident from the beginning of the journey. With their backs to the Red Sea and Pharaoh's armies bearing down on them, the Israelites lodge their first complaint, setting the tone for a cavalcade of cavils to come:

> And they said to Moses, "Because there were no graves in Egypt, have you taken us away to die in the wilderness? Is not this the thing that we did tell you in Egypt, saying, 'Leave us alone, that we may serve Egypt?' For it had been better for us to serve Egypt, than that we should die in the wilderness." And Moses said to the people, "Fear not, stand still, and see the salvation of the Lord, which he will show you today.... The Lord shall fight for you, and you shall hold your peace." (Exodus 14:11–14)

Of course, the people did not beg to stay in Egypt. Although they gave Moses the cold shoulder at first, before he showed up in Pharaoh's court with his plagues and miracles, there is nothing to suggest that the exodus was anything but voluntary. Indeed, the rabbinic tradition suggests that a great many Israelites in fact chose to remain behind, emphasizing that those who made it to the Red Sea had decided to go with Moses of their own accord.[2] Yet they are now allowing their fear to turn their hearts against him, as if the whole thing were his fault.

The miracle of splitting the Red Sea seems to calm their anxiety for a bit, long enough for them to sing a great song in God's praise. Three days pass, however, and again they complain. When they find a spring where the water is bitter, God miraculously sweetens it, to show them again that inner confidence and faith in the redemptive God were the keys to this journey. This keeps them for about a month and a half. In the wilderness of Sin, however, they start up again, responding to the struggle to find food. "Would that we had died by the hand of the Lord in the land of Egypt, when we sat by the flesh pots, and when we ate our fill of bread; for you have brought us out into this wilderness, to kill this whole assembly with hunger" (Exodus 16:3). Moses takes offense at this rant, but God ultimately gives them both manna from heaven and a massive supply of quail meat.

Even after the titanic events at Mount Sinai, when days of thunder and otherworldly sensations, sounds and smells and lights signified God's overwhelming intervention in human affairs—even then, insecurity drives them to create the Golden Calf. "This man Moses . . . ," they titter, "we know not what is become of him" (Exodus 32:1). Again, this makes God so angry that he threatens to destroy them all and begin again with Moses as the new patriarch—a threat that disappears only when Moses talks God out of it. Yet as the Israelites make their way through the desert, their fears seem only to grow, with each successive act of grandeur on God's part quieting their troubled spirits only briefly, before fear and angst turn again into anxiety, loathing, and rebellion against those who had rescued them from slavery.

These stories are usually read through the prism of religious faith, and they are presumed to carry a simple and clear message: Only through unbending dedication to the Lord may we make it through the difficult trials that life gives us.

Yet there seems to be something else going on here, a more subtle message about the relationship between insecurity and evil. The Israelites' problem is not so much that they lack faith in God—indeed, they often affirm it even as they grumble against Moses—but that they lack faith in themselves. As we have seen,

the key miracles in the exodus story required the direct partici-
pation of human beings in bringing redemption: From the need
to wipe the blood of the Paschal Lamb on their doorposts while
still in Egypt, to Moses' putting out his staff to split the sea (and,
in the rabbinic reading, Nachshon's venturing into the water),
to having to gather the manna themselves, we are constantly
reminded of man's role in redemption.

But this is even more true on the negative side of the coin:
The Israelites' fears and complaints are looked down upon by
God and Moses. It is through their expressions of dissatisfaction,
even anger at the Israelites, that we can get a glimpse of what
the alternative might have been: A bold Israelite nation, under-
taking this trek as their own, pushing Moses to hurry them to
their destiny, preparing for battle, and diving into the Promised
Land with all the redemptive fervor of those anticipating freedom, peace, and a righteous sovereign life.

This also explains why the miracles fail to solve the problem.
With every successive display of divine prowess, the Israelites,
rather than believing in themselves and their mission, instead
further internalize their own slave mentality: God and Moses,
not they, are doing the heavy lifting, and as a result the Israelites still cannot believe in themselves. On a deep level, God has
taken Israel out of slavery, but not slavery out of Israel.

Ultimately these stories set the stage for the greatest failure of the Israelite spirit, the moment where the Children of
Israel are finally overcome with fear to the point where God
and Moses can no longer help them. And it comes at the most
crucial juncture, just as they are about to undertake the colos-
sal self-redemption that was the point of it all, just as they are
getting ready to mount their great military assault on the land
of Canaan, the land their shepherd forefathers promised them
centuries before.

This moment is known as the Sin of the Spies, and it is the turning point in the entire story.

God tells Moses to prepare for the invasion of Canaan. Moses sends twelve men, one from every tribe, to reconnoiter the Promised Land, charging them to "see the country, what it is; and the people who dwell in it, whether they are strong or weak, few or many; and what the land is that they dwell in, whether it is good or bad; and what cities they dwell in, whether in tents, or in strongholds" (Numbers 13:18–19). The aim is to gather intelligence as the first step in conquering the land. There is no question about whether to invade, only how.

Yet things do not go as Moses wants. When the spies return, they bring the following report:

> "We came to the land where you did send us, and indeed it flows with milk and honey; and this is the fruit of it. But the people are strong that dwell in the land, and the cities are fortified, and very great. . . . We are not able to go up against the people, for they are stronger than we."
>
> And they spread an evil report of the land that they had spied out to the Children of Israel, saying, "The land, through which we have gone to spy it out, is a land that eats up its inhabitants; and all the people that we saw in it are men of great stature. . . . And we were in our own sight as grasshoppers, and so we were in their sight." And all the congregation lifted up their voice, and cried; and the people wept that night.
>
> And all the Children of Israel murmured against Moses and against Aaron. And the whole congregation said to them, "Would that we had died in the land of Egypt! Or would we had died in this wilderness! And why has the Lord brought us to this land, to fall by the sword, that our wives and our children

should be a prey? Were it not better for us to return to Egypt?"
(Numbers 13:27–14:3)

Moses had not asked for the spies' opinion as to whether the
Israelites could or could not defeat the Canaanites. That they
offered this was bad enough; far worse was their spreading anxiety among the people, whipping them up into a frenzy of horror
at the possibility of fighting. Their obsession with the memory
of Egypt—as if slavery had been a golden age—is meant to show
us just how skewed their judgment had become. So is the fact
that two of the spies, Joshua the son of Nun and Caleb the son
of Yefuneh, reject the majority report and insist that Israel could
easily prevail. The Canaanites, they announce, "are bread for us.
Their defense is departed from them, and the Lord is with us:
Fear them not" (Numbers 14:9).

God wants nothing to do with this. Just like after the Golden
Calf, he tells Moses he's had it with them and wants to wipe
them all out. Moses again talks him out of it, citing how bad it
would look in the eyes of the nations if God led his people out
of Egypt only to kill them in the desert. The Sin of the Spies, we
learn, is of the same degree of depravity as the Golden Calf. God
once again recants from his instinctive response, but this time
the punishment is harsh beyond words:

> Your carcasses shall fall in this wilderness; and all that were
> numbered of you, according to your whole number, from
> twenty years old and upward, who have murmured against
> me, shall by no means come into the land. . . . But your little
> ones, who you said should be a prey, them I will bring in, and
> they shall know the land which you have despised. But as for
> you, your carcasses shall fall in this wilderness. And your chil-
> dren shall wander in the wilderness forty years, and bear your

backsliding, until your carcasses be consumed in the wilderness.
(Numbers 14:29–33)

In the Bible, punishments are not always matched against the cruelty or wickedness of a crime. Sometimes, a deeply troubling situation demands correction, a wrong must be righted. There is something psychotic about the terror of the spies and their followers, about believing that so vast a people, with as many as six hundred thousand fighting-age men, would fail to conquer the puny populations of Canaan. With a minimal motivation to fight among the Israelites, all of Canaan's fortresses and men of bearing would not last an hour against an army so vast. But in their hearts, the Israelites are still slaves, their thoughts dominated by insecurity rather than courage, preferring the comfort of the harsh yet familiar desert to the unknowns of battle and freedom.

What suddenly becomes clear is that this generation of Israelites is a lost cause. As long as they live, God now seems to realize, they will be grasshoppers in their own eyes, harboring nothing but anxiety in the base of their hearts, no matter how many miracles have saved them in the past. Someone born into slavery, living his entire childhood and early adult life in abject terror of the master, cannot be expected to become a warrior overnight, perhaps never. An entire generation will have to pass before the people possess the inner strength needed to fight for their freedom.

The Israelites' punishment makes no sense at all if we read it simply as a response to their inadequate faith, or if we look at their fear through the clinical eye of the therapist. As we saw in the story of Ahab, the symbolism of death without burial represents the loss of one's humanity. By repeating the imagery of their carcasses decaying slowly in the desert, God is telling the

Israelites that through their fear, they have reduced themselves to cowering animals at precisely the time when human, redemptive boldness is needed. If they cannot be redeemers, what was the point of delivering them at all?

The Bible is telling us that the Israelites' fear was not merely unfortunate. It was profoundly wrong. There is no greater depravity, we learn, than the self-dehumanization that comes with succumbing to our demons. When courage is called for, fear is a sin.

That the sin of the deflated spirit, rather than the lack of faith in God, is the true message of the story of the spies is verified by a second aspect of their punishment: the wandering. The Israelites will now spend the rest of their days in the desert, taking forty years to complete a trip that today can be done by car in a couple of hours.

Where else have we seen this wandering, homelessness, a life of indigence and impotence as punishment for a singular sin? To understand what is actually at stake, we need to look back to the only other time such a punishment was meted out: in the story of Cain. There too we learn about the sin behind the sin. Hidden behind the crime of murder, there lies in Cain's act an acute commentary on the connection between insecurity and evil that is the real message of the Tenth Commandment.

When Adam and Eve were expelled from the Garden of Eden, humanity was born. Thrust against their will into a world of toil, shame, and pain, they were like newborns forced out of the womb, leaving the amniotic sanctuary of the life-giving garden into the harsh Middle Eastern wild. Into real life.

Adam and Eve thrive despite the hardship. They bring two sons into the world, Cain and Abel. Theirs is the first story of the real world—and also the first time the word "sin" appears in the Bible, setting the stage for a thousand pages of good and evil deeds.

Again, the professions are crucial. Cain is a "tiller of soil," a farmer like his father; Abel is a shepherd. As we know, the Bible favors the free-spirited shepherd over the farmer, who is permanently dependent on his land, the seasons, and the weather. So we should not be surprised that when the two of them bring their bounty to God, Cain with his produce and Abel with his meat, Abel's sacrifice is accepted while Cain's is not.

This may seem unfair. Cain, just like Abel, brought God a gift. We may chalk the judgment up to God's arbitrary character, or the difference between the gift of the free shepherd and that of the dependent farmer. Or we may read more closely, with the rabbis, and discover that whereas Abel brought the "firstlings of his flock," Cain merely brought a gift "of the fruit of the ground," making the former more generous, more self-expansive.[3] It matters little to what happens next, for it is Cain's disappointment and ensuing spiritual collapse that bring him to murder his brother.

Cain is devastated and furious ("And Cain was very angry, and his face fell"), and God tries to cheer him up:

> Why are you angry, and why are you crestfallen? If you do well, will you not be accepted? And if you do not, sin crouches at the door, and to you will its desire be—but you may rule over it. (Genesis 4:6–7)

In this awkward yet crucial passage that is the last thing said before the crime, God tries to teach Cain about the harshness of life and the danger of the swirling tempest of rage and disappointment that engulfs him. Forget about the unearned pleasures of the Garden of Eden, he tells Cain. In this world, you will succeed on the basis of your actions, and you will be judged in ways that do not always seem fair. Your failures, however, carry the risk of undermining your sense of self, leading you to evil. Do not let this happen, for you can always overcome sin through the power of your redemptive spirit.

Cain says nothing. Consumed by humiliation, suspicious that life is failure, unwilling to meet God's challenge in the eye, he looks to retaliate. If God favors Abel, he reasons, then I will kill him, and show that I too can judge and reject. In order to commit the act, Cain must first ignore Abel's humanity and reduce him to the level of a symbol—a symbol of his own failure. He arranges to meet his brother out in his fields, and slays him.

Cain's descent into evil begins with his disappointment at his failed sacrifice and the collapse of his spirit that follows. This collapse, however, is not expressed in fear, the way it was for the Israelites in the desert. Instead, it turns into a catastrophic self-loathing, a deterioration of the structure of his psyche that threatens not just to bring him down but to make him take everything else with him. God tries to prevent his slide, warning him that "sin crouches at the door," but Cain, like the child who smacks his sister even though her only crime was to be praised by her parents for doing something good, ignores the warning and tries to reassert himself in the most shallow and reprehensible way. If I am garbage, he reasons, then why should anyone have expectations of my moral state? If I am garbage, at least I can show you that Abel is too.

The ensuing dialogue with God bears this out, as well. Immediately after the crime, Cain hears God's voice:

And the Lord said to Cain, "Where is Abel your brother?"
And he said, "I know not. Am I my brother's keeper?"
And he said, "What have you done? The voice of your broth-

er's blood cries to me from the ground. And now, cursed are you from the earth, which has opened her mouth to receive your brother's blood from your hand; when you till the ground, it shall not yield to you her strength; a fugitive and a vagabond shall you be on the earth." (Genesis 4:9–12)

When God asks Cain where his brother is, we may assume that the One who knows all knows this as well. The question is rhetorical: The redemptive soul should know where his brother is—in a sense, that is what makes him our brother in the first place. The strong self seeks to love, and to love is to expand to include another, to see his "place" as our vital concern. When Cain answers "I know not," he is lying on the literal level, but the lie reveals a deeper truth. Cain has failed to know where Abel is.

The second half of Cain's answer to God, "Am I my brother's keeper?" merely drives the point home. We cannot ignore the wordplay: The word "keeper" (*shomer*) has already appeared once in Genesis in its verb form, when Adam is put into the garden "to work it *and to keep it*" (*ul'shomro*). Cain tilled the land like his father, working it to produce his own food; but he has failed to understand that the central commandment of the redemptive spirit is to be a keeper, a caretaker of humanity, to expand beyond our own selves and see to the flourishing of our world, beginning with our brothers. Cain's insecurity and the collapse of his spirit have led him to abandon his central moral charge.

Finally, we learn of Cain's punishment. No longer can he be a farmer, but must instead roam the world—not the way a life-affirming shepherd does, but as a lifeless vagabond. Had God merely struck him dead, or abandoned him to the next brigand to come along, his demise would have been just another turn of the pinwheel of life and death, and the world would have continued on its way. But the descendants of Adam and Eve are meant to represent something else, the possibility of humanity rising above the clash of claws and teeth of the wild. God will not kill Cain, but instead leaves him to roam the world, a ghost, living on only as a symbol—just as Cain turned Abel into a symbol.

The parallel between the punishments of Cain and the Israelites, the wandering until death, shows us that underneath the most obvious differences between their crimes, they shared a deeper wrong. The archetypal sin in the Bible is, we see, the sin of dispiritedness, of self-deflation that inevitably leads to more horrible sins. Like the spies in the desert, Cain had become a grasshopper in his own eyes. Like the Israelites, he let insecurity destroy him.

In this kind of spiritual self-destruction we find a scourge at once so dire and yet so common that among character flaws it is in a class by itself. The Tenth Commandment contains a central key to understanding evil, and to working our way toward something better.

Why do people do bad things? Two answers have been handed down to us from the ancient world and continue to dominate much of our thinking today. Each of them has its merits, but ultimately cannot satisfy.

One is temptation. This is the main theme in classical Christian thought dating all the way back to the New Testament. "Lead us not into temptation," we find in the Lord's Prayer, "but deliver us from evil" (Matthew 6:13). The assumption here is that our natural drives and desires (often described as Satan, or the "tempter") conspire against us, constantly pushing us to do wrong. The paradigmatic sin, in this view, is that of Adam and

Eve in the Garden of Eden: They ate the delicious-looking fruit of the tree of knowledge because they failed to follow God's command and resist the tempter, who appeared in the form of a snake. As a result, they fell from their angelic, primordial state into a sinful existence that has plagued mankind ever since. By this view, man is forever racked by temptation, and though he must try to overcome it, he may never be fully redeemed without the miraculous intervention of God, who forgives us despite the fact that we do not deserve it.

There is much to be said for such a view. The animal kingdom is indeed a wicked place, and if we always give in to our native impulses—our appetites, our jealousy, our violence— then we cannot emerge beyond the state of nature, and morality has no hope.

There is also something troubling about this answer, in some sense begging the question by ignoring the deeper issues of what kind of person has the strength needed to defeat temptation and to do right. As a reading of the Garden of Eden story, it falls short as well: Again, the Bible does not introduce the word "sin" until the story of Cain. It is unclear why eating the fruit of knowledge of good and evil would be such a monstrous sin, not to mention symbolic of sin more broadly, even if God did tell them not to do it. God's biggest problem with eating the fruit, it seems, is not that there is something inherently wrong with it, but that, when it happens, "man is become like one of us, knowing good and evil" (Genesis 3:22), that, having risen suddenly above the animal plane, he risks becoming arrogant, comparing himself to God. This seems more like a metaphor about the tragic burden that moral awareness places on man's shoulders, about how much easier life might have been had we all remained animals without the enormous, explosive potential of the redemptive spirit. At the end of the day, don't we want to know about good and evil—doesn't *God* really want us to know?

Much more problematic, however, is the outcome of such a doctrine: the psychological effect of being told all your life that your natural drives are inherently wrong, your pride and desire and healthy appetite the marks of the wicked. One wonders whether the focus on temptation as the essence of sin has not contributed greatly to the West's enduring neurosis about physical life and its pleasures.

A second view, which begins in ancient Greece and has come to dominate modern secular thinking since the eighteenth century, is that evil comes from ignorance. If morality begins with recognizing the humanity of others, the reasoning goes, then the wrongdoer's problem is one of perspective: He has not learned to step outside himself and look at things objectively; he has not sufficiently internalized the teachings of reason, that we should always act according to whatever would be best for all people to do. The more we educate people, the more they will come to recognize the irrationality of their behavior—and change their ways.

There is much truth to this too. We are indeed blinded by irrationality just as we are blinded by temptation. The ability to think coolly about right and wrong, to weigh the interests and just claims of others, is indispensable to just behavior.

But here again, a mistake is made when this becomes the exclusive focus when talking about evil. As with temptation, the question is begged: What kind of person has the inner calm required to suspend his claims and step outside himself? And again, this view of immorality renders shameful much of what we know to be crucial for living vital, healthy lives. Our passions, our loves, our affirmations of life—all these irrational things are not just not always wrong; in many cases we cannot be good without them. We know that supremely rational beings, like Mr. Spock in *Star Trek,* may have risen above many of man's natural iniquities, but they are not necessarily the best people to follow. We still need Captain Kirk. Being good is not just about having the right perspective but also taking redemptive action, and this requires a fiery soul, a creative energy, an irrational, expansive motivation that reason can never fully account for, much less provide. We can imagine that Kirk ate well.

As against these partial answers, the Old Testament offers a third view, as symbolized by the Tenth Commandment. Sin, according to the Bible, flows not so much from temptation or ignorance, as from the weakness of spirit that precedes them both.

Not all of us have committed idolatry or murder, but when we read the words *You shall not covet,* we have all been there. Our desire takes over our thoughts. We may convince ourselves that a woman's or a man's love is all that separates us from happiness; or that a new car, a new house, a certain object will satisfy our most acute needs. To covet is to focus all our desire on something we do not have, perhaps cannot have.

Why do we do this? You don't have to be a psychologist to recognize that coveting is the product of insecurity. We lack a self-sufficient soul, a psychic peace that would spare us such distortions, and instead of looking inward, facing the real sources of our angst, we look to easy answers, convincing ourselves that release can be found in the external world, in radical and often wrongful forms of self-assertion.

Insecurity. The child who cries for attention by breaking every rule and ignoring every command. The gifted student who refuses to study because she does not believe she can live up to her parents' expectations. The good-looking boy who cannot ask a girl on a date. The unwillingness to believe in one's talents and the failure to develop them, choosing instead "safe" professions where our mediocrity is guaranteed. The braggart who, always unsure of his inner worth, prattles endlessly about his wealth, his sexual encounters, or his great plans. The fear of others that makes us believe we have no right to voice our concerns, to fight for our rights, to assert ourselves in a world where we never stop feeling like a child among adults, like a slave among masters. The mental avoidance of hard questions that leads us, again and again, into tragic situations of neglect—about money, about our children, about our relationships, about our careers, about our souls. The avoidance of talking to the people we fear, even when it is urgent, even when there is nothing to fear at all. The neglect of our parents' needs as they age, because we cannot bear to see them as needful. The channeling of our fears into nastiness—the hatred of another, acting out against our world, taking things that are not ours. Insecurity undermines our creativity, for we cannot think creatively when we're afraid. It undermines our judgment, for it skews our reason and undercuts our desire to gain wisdom. Insecurity is thus the antithesis of redemption.

Every single one of us, to one degree or another, in one area or another, at one time or another, slides down the spiral of fear and anxiety, of deferring to the judgment of others even in our most personal decisions, of avoiding problems, of twisting reality, of justifying our wrongs rather than admitting them, of cheating or lying or stealing or running away. Call it fear, call it self-hatred, call it the deflation of the spirit—whatever we call it, these are the expressions of insecurity, of an absence of the inner peace that is an irreplaceable ingredient in the redemptive person. They are a fundamental part of what it means to be human, but they are also a searing moral problem that will not go away by ignoring either insecurity's wrongfulness or its humanity.

Fear itself is not always a sin, of course. There are many real dangers in life that must be faced, and fear begins as a natural response that helps us recognize danger. But danger, once recognized, needs to be addressed through quiet courage rather than self-deflating terror, or, alternatively, rather than the overweening acts of the falsely bold, like the karate novice who gets himself killed when all he needed to do was give the mugger his wallet. Or like the Israelites in the desert who, upon hearing that they have been sentenced to a life of wandering more hideous than death on the battlefield, try to mount a desperate and futile headlong assault against the well-prepared Amalekites, an attack that fails utterly.[4]

The Tenth Commandment does not say "You shall not fear" but *You shall not covet*—meaning you shall not allow the things you fear to become demons controlling the core of your psyche, like a virus commandeering a cell and reproducing itself a thousandfold, changing the very essence of the self into a machine for the production of more fears, more loathing, more sins, blindly and wildly groping in our world, convincing ourselves that with one more object, one more pay raise, we will somehow find release from our agony. Coveting is the paradigmatic case because it is so transparent to the outside observer, so readily recognized in ourselves, so easy to define and present as an archetype.

There may be no image more absurd in the entire Bible than that of Ahab bedridden with despair over Navot's refusal to sell him his vineyard, a king so besotted with greed that he will allow a vegetable garden to stand between him and any shred of inner peace, so much so that he will ultimately resort to murder to expand his estate—but so devastated as he lies in that bed that it doesn't even occur to him to kill the man until Jezebel comes up with the idea, like a mug of chamomile tea, to calm his nerves. Ahab was one weird cookie, but all of us know a sliver of his stupid agony.

• • •

Despite all this, some readers will still have difficulty giving so momentous a role to insecurity. To call it a sin, after all, is to make all of us sinners.

Yet consider:

1. An insecure person cannot accept the redemptive vision. He can master neither creativity nor judgment. Insecurity, moreover, makes him lower his expectations of himself: God becomes a source of resentment rather than a model of emulation. There can be no leaving Egypt when insecurity is in control.

2. An insecure person, instead of searching for moral truth beyond the easiest answers, will look for the total, complete, sweeping solution to all things. Not having truth in his hands makes him feel inadequate and lonely, and he overcompensates by grabbing at whatever gives him clarity. This is why young people, less secure in their place in the world, are so taken by simplistic ideologies. The source of idolatry is the insecure impatience with the arduous path to truth.

3. An insecure person will resort to dishonesty, for he cannot trust in the validity, legitimacy, and efficacy of his own truth. He looks instead for words that will manipulate the world. The liar cannot imagine people will love and respect him for who he is, and instead must conjure up something better. Insecurity is the enemy of integrity.

4. An insecure person will despise his own self and refuse to invest time into deepening and enriching it. His fears of financial and professional failure will cause him to work endlessly, never take time off, never experience a true Sabbath. Insecurity posts a massive roadblock on the path to the self.

5. An insecure person will resent his parents for his flaws rather

than cherishing their gifts. Instead of loving them and their teachings, he will live within the permanent, residual childhood fear of their disapproval, hating their intervention in his life, in the end rejecting their wisdom of the heart.

6. An insecure person will, like Cain, resort to violence to try to establish his self-worth.

7. An insecure person will fail to love, lacking the inner strength from which true love must flow. He will instead fear his spouse and fail to grow together with her, looking outside the marriage for an escape. Or the opposite may happen: In his insecurity he will fail to respect her own humanity, stifling her and forcing her to look elsewhere for *her* escape. Adultery is almost always the product of deep insecurities of one or both of the spouses.

8. An insecure person will disrespect other people's property, resenting their wealth and independence, ultimately justifying theft and undermining their humanity.

9. An insecure person will attack the reputations of others and the institutions of community, twisting the world in order to hurt his neighbor and show his own importance. A community of insecure people, moreover, will look for external enemies to blame for their problems rather than blaming themselves or their leaders—eventually leading to war and destruction. Peace in the world stands or falls on the inner peace of its individuals.

All of us suffer from insecurities of one kind or another, and in this sense it is difficult to put insecurity into the same weight class as murder and stealing. The point here, however, is not to brand all of us irredeemable sinners but to recognize that insecurity is, at its heart, a moral problem, and not just *a* problem, but one that lurks behind so many others that it merits its own separate commandment, at the end, as the capstone of all that has been said, and as the key to moving forward.

And it is an immediate problem, for the entire possibility of a redemptive society rests, as a first step, on overcoming our insecurities, feeling a deep and abiding confidence in ourselves, and incorporating the habits of creativity and judgment in our lives. For every one of our failures, no matter how trivial, it is worth asking how things might have been different had we acted out of inner peace. Would we have communicated our feelings to our spouse early enough to prevent the collapse of the marriage? Would we have ignored the wealth of our friends as a measure of our own life success? Would we have reserved judgment when everyone else was enthralled by this fashion or that political leader? Would we have boldly set forth in life, choosing careers and lives that fit our needs and talents? Would we have had the strength to know ourselves and bring our fullest love into the lives of others?

For every moment we grasp what might have been, we allow ourselves a glimpse at what might yet be.

Reaching the summit of a mountain is not merely an achievement. It also marks a new beginning, as we stand on the understated peak and take in the breathtaking vista we have earned. Having reached the top, we look not only back to where we came from but also ahead to a world we see as if for the first time.

As we begin our descent, we know that we are changed, as was Moses when he descended Mount Sinai, and a new light shone from his face, a light of inner peace, and everyone who saw him recognized him as a changed man.

The Tenth Commandment puts the entire enterprise of the Ten Commandments into a different perspective. The critique of our insecurities gives us a path to move forward, a new light shining from our faces, even if we have yet to make a single change in our lives.

For each of us this will be a unique light, showing us a different path down the mountain. Each of us harbors particular fears, inhibitions, habits of avoidance that stand between us and the redemptive life; each of us must undertake a painful and lonely struggle to overcome them, and will find some of them easier to correct than others.

But having been on the mountaintop, we have the tools we need to take them on. Tackling each insecurity one by one, learning to relax, to believe in ourselves, to identify and overcome fears, to benefit from the Bible's wisdom, to rise and breathe deeply, to forgive our own mistakes as we move forward, relentlessly correcting them, improving, going beyond insecurity and turning toward our higher goals, learning, loving, expanding to include others, our spouses and children and parents, our friends and communities, our nations and the whole world—this is the promise that the Tenth Commandment offers us; indeed, that the Ten Commandments as a whole offer us: a vision of redemption that each of us, in our own situation, has in hand as we reach our close.

Do we have room for this in our lives?

The Human Element

One of the most startling bits of rabbinic lore is the claim
that every major figure in the Bible sinned.[1] Adam and Eve
sinned when they ate the forbidden fruit. Noah, after the flood,
got himself good and drunk and passed out naked in his tent.
Abraham wrongfully risked the life of his wife, Sarah, by telling
the Egyptian king that she was his sister, for fear that the king
might otherwise kill him to have her. Moses was forbidden from
entering the Promised Land because he whacked a stone with
his staff in order to extract water from it, when God had told
him merely to speak to it. King Solomon got mixed up late in life
in riches and women and idolatry; Jonah ran away from God's
call to prophecy; Samson tragically fell for Delilah; and so on.

Why does the Bible go out of its way to tell us about the sins
of its heroes? The overriding sense in the Old Testament is that
nobody is perfect—and that the divine message being handed
down is aimed not at angelic beings but at real people.

In Genesis, God destroys the whole world he created by
means of a great flood, taking the very best person, Noah, and
preserving him and his family and two of every animal in a sea-
worthy ark of wood, hoping to rebuild humanity through him
as a sweeping answer to the imperfections of man.

It doesn't work. These are the first words after Noah descends from the ark into the new, desolate world.

> And Noah built an altar to the Lord. And he took of every pure beast, and of every pure fowl, and brought offerings on the altar. And the Lord smelled the savory scent, and the Lord said in his heart, "Never again shall I curse the earth because of man. For the inclination of man's heart is evil from his youth. Never again shall I destroy all life, as I have done." (Genesis 8:20–21)

God is moved by the sacrifice and swears never again to destroy humanity. Yet locked between two expressions of this promise is a sentence that points in a very different direction. *For the inclination of man's heart is evil from his youth.* What appears at first as a touching moment of grace reveals itself to be a searing commentary on the human condition, the incorrigibility of man, and the futility of high expectations. It is almost as though God is saying, Now that I have smelled the sacrifice, I have seen that even after the destruction of the world, man at his very best is forever a lusty, flesh-devouring, rough-and-tumble shepherd type, scarcely more than an animal. My biggest mistake, it turns out, was to hope for perfection in the first place, to imagine man as an angel who has no need for such pleasure. Instead I get more barbecue.

Like a pet cat who leaves a dead mole on your doorstep, man expresses his love of God not through perfection, but through the imperfect nature of his being.

A similar message comes through in a rabbinic legend about the Ten Commandments. When Moses was up on Mount Sinai, the rabbis teach, he ascended all the way to heaven. The angels, however, were not too pleased to see him.

They said to God, "What is this child of woman doing among us?"

He said to them, "He has come to receive the Torah."

They said, "Your precious secret you have kept hidden since 974 generations before the creation of the universe,[2] now you plan to give it to one of flesh and blood?" . . .

God said to Moses, "Answer them." Moses said, "I am afraid to answer, lest they burn me with their breath." God said, "Hold on to my throne, and give them an answer."

Moses said, "Master of the Universe, what does the Torah you give me say? *I am the Lord your God who took you out of Egypt.*" [Moses said to the angels,] "Did you go down to Egypt, to Pharaoh? Were you enslaved? Why do you need the Torah? What else does it say? *You shall not have other gods.* Are you among the nations, who worship idols? What else does it say? *Remember the Sabbath day, to sanctify it.* Do you toil, that you need to rest? What else does it say? *You shall not take* [*the name of the Lord in vain*]. Do you have business dealings? What else does it say? *Honor your father and your mother.* Do you have a father or a mother? What else does it say? *You shall not murder, you shall not commit adultery, you shall not steal.* Do you have jealousy among you, or the evil urge?"

Immediately they conceded to God.[3]

The Ten Commandments are the Bible's most poignant symbol of both the complexity and the possibilities of life. Far from being a call for perfection, they embrace the nuance of humanity, the spectrum of real experience, the challenges of weakness and hope, and the need for human beings always to take responsibility for their lives. The angels here represent all the ideals, the possible perfections that man can delude himself into thinking he can attain—ideals whose very breath threatens to burn us to oblivion.

God, for this reason, cannot be the one to answer their arguments. It must be Moses, the real human being, taking command of the debate and clinging to the redemptive ideal with all his might, defying the angels and making the astoundingly audacious claim that it is man's very imperfection, his enslavement and toil and evil inclinations, that makes him not just in need but also worthy of God's gift.

One of the biggest problems with a great many of the belief systems, both religious and secular, that have dominated our world over many centuries is their assumption that people should strive to be perfect, and might actually succeed: that their imperfections, their lusts and desires, their efforts to increase their wealth and power are all just wrong—and that the only good human being is maybe not a dead one, but an angelic one, which is close enough. Human nature always ends up being painted with a dark brush. We are told to try to escape who we really are and rebuild ourselves from scratch.

The problem with such attitudes is that they have little to do with reality. By building absurd expectations of what we can be and how we can shed our animal selves, by offering dreams of escape, they inevitably depict the world in sharp terms of good and evil, right and wrong, rational and irrational, always dividing between those who are presumed to have attained perfection and those who have not. But since none of us ever will, the true result is to instill cynicism and disillusionment among the most sensitive and truthful souls, and to encourage others to fake a pristine righteousness that they and God, at least, know to be a lie.

Of all our ancient textual traditions, the Old Testament is

probably the one most sympathetic to the imperfect nature of mankind. While many of our revolutionary ideologies spring from relatively short manifestos or philosophical treatises, the ancient Israelite worldview is spread out over a thousand pages of stories, laws, prophetic speeches responding to real human situations, poetry and song. More than anything else, the Hebrew Bible respects the richness of human experience, the wide variety of motivations and psychological states and situations, affirming all of these as true life—and insisting, in spite of everything, that redemption is possible in our fragile human world.

At its heart, the Hebrew Bible, with the Ten Commandments as its centerpiece, is a deeply optimistic text, and its optimism flows not in spite of human imperfection, but from it. For every failure of its heroes, there is also achievement, improvement, expectation, and hope. While the ancient Greek playwrights presented us with stories of tragic fate, of King Oedipus' inevitable decline that he could not avoid no matter how much he tried, the Israelites believed that each of us has the power to overcome fate, to rule over the sins that crouch at our door.

Such a promise, however, begins with an unremitting commitment to ourselves. So much of our modern culture pressures us to suppress our natural selves, to embrace the most shallow expectations of what we are "supposed" to be—to look a certain way, to act or feel or behave a certain way—that we end up pouring our best energies into meeting an image of success that is not really us. Instead of investing in our real interests and talents and intuitive affections for others, instead of developing true, loving relationships, we chase after false gods of power, beauty, and wealth, and listen too carefully to the endless stream of prescriptions assaulting our senses, promising us that redemption will come only if we act now, credit cards ready.

But real life is complex and long, and entails no small measure of suffering, failure, and the daily struggle of health, financial stability, raising children, building our communities, and
personal growth. This is a struggle to be embraced, not avoided
through cults and drugs and ideologies or through the fanatical
pursuit of career or beauty or even wisdom itself. To assume that
someone out there has easy answers that will relieve our burden
and all we have to do is find him, is to squander the fleeting, precious moment that is life. This is the real meaning of the famous
words of Deuteronomy:

> For the Commandment that I give you this day—it is not
> beyond you, nor is it far away. It is not in heaven, that you may
> say, "Who will go up to heaven and bring it to us, and we will do
> it?" Nor is it across the sea, that you may say, "Who will cross the
> sea for us, and bring it to us, that we may listen?" For the thing
> is very near to you, on your lips and in your heart, that you may
> do it. (Deuteronomy 30:11–14)

This passage spells out for us something we by now already
know: that all the grand words of commanding normative over-
lords, of the teachers and preachers and even the Ten Commandments themselves, are as nothing if they are approached
as alien, sublime, distant, and otherworldly, an escape from life,
a plane ticket to heaven.

The only way to understand them, rather, is as potential keys
to the gates of ourselves, as a signpost for our inner truths that
no one can ever show us, but that we may find only through
lonely, painful, and stubborn exploration. This is the only life
we have, the only truth worth finding.

The redemption of our world, in other words, begins with
the redemption of ourselves—with a relentless, churning, pow-

erful effort of honesty and self-investment, endlessly stoking the fire of love that burns in every one of us as surely as we breathe, expanding its warmth, including, exciting, inspiring, providing, loving our families and friends and communities and beyond, never stopping as long as we live.

ACKNOWLEDGMENTS

This study, nearly four years in the making, could not have happened without the generous help of many good people. Lorena Avraham, Mem Bernstein, Rabbi Shmuley Boteach, Rich Cohen, Nitsana Darshan-Leitner, Rabbi Dov Peretz Elkins, Sam Freedman, Arthur Fried, Mark Gerson, Fred Gorsetman, Ruth Hazony, Mark Helprin, Roger Hertog, Rabbi Isaac Jeret, Danny Klein, Yossi Klein Halevi, Neal Kozodoy, Martin Kramer, Liel Leibovitz, Avi Leitner, Ze'ev Maghen, Rabbi John Moscowitz, Michael Oren, Marty Peretz, Dan Polisar, Shmuel Rosner, Assaf Sagiv, Rabbi Shalom Schwartz, Saul Singer, Bret Stephens, Joshua Weinstein, Ken Weinstein, and Evy Zweibach all offered crucial comments, inspiration, research, or support at different stages.

My astute and delightfully deadpan agent Jennifer Joel gets a lot of credit for bringing this book into the world, holding my hand and deftly managing my expectations throughout. Colin Harrison, my editor, and Susan Moldow, publisher of Scribner, showed their acute literary wisdom, and their unblinking faith in the project, at every turn.

Three people were decisive in helping me develop the ideas in this book. Ethan Dor-Shav was the first person to suggest to me that the Ten Commandments have been seriously overlooked both as a focus of study and as a guide to modern life. Although we do not agree on everything, I have learned a great deal from his creative readings of biblical texts. In the places where his influence is most keenly felt, I've mentioned it in the notes.

Yoram Hazony, my older brother, first showed me the potential in analyzing the Old Testament for a modern readership in his book *The Dawn: Political Teachings of the Book of Esther,* as well as in essays he wrote in the journal *Azure*. He also played a crucial role in my decision to write this book and gave important criticisms at its earliest stages. Finally, he created the Shalem Center, which offered me a community of scholars that was irreplaceable for developing my thoughts early on.

Rabbi Joseph Isaac Lifshitz, my teacher and mentor, known to his students as Rav Yitzhak, has been for me both a scholar and a dear friend over nearly two decades. In teaching me to read rabbinic legends with a philosophical eye; in encouraging me to continue this project at a crucial juncture when I thought I couldn't do it; in helping me track down a great many of the rabbinic texts I have quoted; and in setting a personal example of the best kind of rabbi—his contribution has been invaluable, my gratitude infinite.

My appreciation for the inspiration, love, assistance, wisdom, and support I have received from others unmentioned, human or divine, will be expressed in private.

NOTES

INTRODUCTION:
Can You Name All Ten?

1. *McCreary County, Kentucky, et al., v. American Civil Liberties Union of Kentucky, et al.*, 545 U.S. 844 (2005). *Van Orden v. Perry, et al.*, 545 U.S. 677 (2005).
2. *Van Orden v. Perry,* Souter dissent, p. 2.
3. *McCreary County v. ACLU,* Scalia dissent, pp. 2–4.
4. For data on removing the Ten Commandments from public places, see "How 'Christianized' Do Americans Want Their Country to Be?" www .barna.org/barna-update/article/5-barna-update/192-how-qchristianizedq-do-americans-want-their-country-to-be. For polling on familiarity with the Ten Commandments, see Bill McKibben, "The Christian Paradox: How a Faithful Nation Gets Jesus Wrong," *Harper's,* August 2005, harpers.org/ExcerptTheChristianParadox.html.
5. Exodus 34:28; cf. Deuteronomy 4:13 and 10:4. Deuteronomy 9:11. Deuteronomy 10:8 and throughout; Joshua, Judges, and Samuel.
6. In rendering the biblical text in English, I have relied on the Jerusalem Bible, trans. Harold Fisch (Jerusalem: Koren, 2000), as a base, but I have modified the translation as I thought appropriate for either readability or accuracy. Translations of rabbinic texts are my own, unless noted otherwise.
7. Menahot 99b.
8. John 18:36; Yom Kippur liturgy, *vidui* confessional prayer. Ethan Dor-Shav has argued, impressively, that Ecclesiastes' intention is altogether different, and that a common misconception arises from a mistranslation of the Hebrew *hevel* as "vanity." See Dor-Shav, "Ecclesiastes, Fleeting and Timeless," *Azure* 18 (Autumn 2004): 67–87.
9. Cf. Ibn Ezra on Exodus 34:1.
10. Mishna Tamid 5:1. For a full discussion of the recital of the Ten Commandments in Jewish Temple, and later synagogue, services, see Ephraim E. Urbach, "The Status of the Ten Commandments in the Temple Service

and in Liturgy," in Ben-Zion Segal, ed., *The Ten Commandments in the Eyes of the Generations* (Jerusalem: Magnes, 1986), pp. 127–45 (Hebrew).
11. Shabbat 88a.

CHAPTER 1:

Redemption

1. Genesis 46:3; cf. Genesis 35:11: "A nation and a company of nations shall be of you"; Isaiah 42:6.
2. Genesis 1:26; Genesis 3:22; Deuteronomy 28:9; Genesis 5:22, 24; Exodus 33:11.
3. Hagiga 12b.
4. Exodus 32:9–14.
5. Shabbat 10a.
6. See, for example, Yeshayahu Leibowitz, "Religious Praxis: The Meaning of Halakhah," in Leibowitz, *Judaism, Human Values, and the Jewish State* (Cambridge, Mass.: Harvard University Press, 1992), pp. 3–29.
7. Moses Maimonides, *The Guide for the Perplexed*, trans. M. Friedländer, 2d ed. (New York: Dover, 1904), part II, chap. 45, pp. 241–42.
8. Sota 37a.
9. Berachot 25b.
10. Sota 5a.

CHAPTER 2:

Morality and Loneliness

1. On Egypt, Rudolf Anthes, cited in Henri Frankfort et al., *The Intellectual Adventure of Ancient Man* (Chicago: University of Chicago Press, 1946), p. 99; on Mesopotamia, ibid., pp. 202ff.
2. Sifrei Numbers 22:33; Nedarim 25a; Megilla 13a; Sanhedrin 103b.
3. Ecclesiastes Rabba 9:11.
4. Genesis Rabba 38:13.
5. That this is the real intention behind the rabbinic tale is made even more clear by an epilogue in the story. Abraham was accompanied by his brother Haran. The legend tells us: "Now, Haran was there watching the debate. He said, 'Whichever way you look at it: If Abraham wins, I will say I was with Abraham; and if Nimrod wins, I will say I was with Nimrod.' When Abraham survived the fiery furnace and was saved, they asked him [Haran] which side he had been on. He said to them, 'I was with Abraham.' They took him and threw him into the fire. His innards boiled, and he came

out and died at the feet of his father Terah." Having witnessed his brother's miraculous survival, Haran declares his loyalty to Abraham's God and is immediately thrown into the furnace as well. Yet because he made his decision purely on power considerations, he has failed to learn the very lesson Abraham meant to teach—the rejection of the concept of power as the determinant of righteousness. Haran dies at the feet of his father, Terah, who, we learn elsewhere, was not merely an idolater but actually made idols for a living—a true master of idolatrous power-logic.

6. Berachot 57b; Derech Eretz Zuta 4.
7. Jean-Luc Marion, *God Without Being* (Chicago: University of Chicago Press, 1991), pp. 10–11.
8. Leviticus Rabba 21:10.
9. Menahot 99a–b.

CHAPTER 3:

Our Lies Destroy Us

1. Shabbat 119b; Sota 42a; Sanhedrin 92a; Bava Metzia 48a; Pesachim 113b.
2. Shabbat 31a; Jerusalem Talmud, Maasarot 2:4; Mechilta, Mishpatim; Jerusalem Talmud, Demai 7:3.
3. Rashi on Makot 24a, s.v. "Rabbi Safra."
4. Mechilta Vayisa 1, quoted in Joseph Telushkin, *Jewish Wisdom* (New York: Morrow, 1994), p. 46.
5. Ketubot 16b–17a.
6. Genesis 47:29–31, 50:2–14, 50:24–25; Exodus 13:19; Joshua 24:32.
7. Still, promise keeping has its limits. In the story of Jephtah in the book of Judges, Jephtah takes an oath to God that if he helps him defeat the Ammonites in battle, Jephtah will offer a sacrifice of whatever creature emerges first from his house. The first creature, however, is his daughter, his only child, and in his zealotry to keep his promise, he decides to sacrifice her nonetheless. The text takes a critical and tragic view of Jephtah's action (though it is unclear whether his iniquity is in making the oath, honoring it, or both), and it appears in a context of overall decline of public order at the time of the judges. Judges 11:30–40.
8. Cf. Targum Onkelos on Genesis 38:18.
9. Rashi on Genesis 38:26, cf. Sota 10a.
10. Berachot 28a, Yoma 72b.
11. Francis Fukuyama, *Trust: The Social Virtues and the Creation of Prosperity* (New York: Free Press, 1995), p. 7.

CHAPTER 4:

The Redemptive Self

1. Ezekiel 22:26; cf. Shabbat 119b.
2. Mishna Shabbat 7:2.
3. Yosef Yitzhak Lifshitz, "Secret of the Sabbath," *Azure* 10 (Winter 2001): 85–117.
4. Beitza 16a, Deuteronomy Rabba 1:21.
5. Numbers Rabba 10:1; Zohar III Raya Meheimna 272b, cited in Dovid Wax, ed., *The Encyclopedia of the Taryag Mitzvoth, Introductory Volume: The Ten Commandments* (Lakewood, N.J.: Taryag Legacy Foundation, 2005), p. 199; Yalkut Reuveni, Vaetchanan, in C. N. Bialik and Y. H. Ravnitzky, *Sefer Ha'agada* (Tel Aviv: Dvir, 1987), p. 385:73 (Hebrew).
6. Maimonides, *Mishneh Torah,* Laws of the Sabbath, 24:12.
7. Beitza 16a, Yalkut Shimoni Genesis 2:16.
8. Mishna Avot 5:19, Berachot 62a.
9. Mishna Avot 1:6; Maimonides, *Mishneh Torah,* Laws of the Foundations of the Torah, 4:18.
10. Maimonides, *Mishneh Torah,* Laws of Torah Study 1:8, 10, in Telushkin, *Jewish Wisdom,* p. 339.
11. Pesikta Rabati, Ten Commandments, chap. 3; Bava Batra 134a.
12. Abraham Joshua Heschel, *The Sabbath: Its Meaning for Modern Man* (New York: Farrar, Straus, 1951), p. 29.
13. Avot Derabi Natan 6:2.
14. Tosefta Berachot 3:4; Mishna Avot 4:17.
15. Tanhuma Vayakhel 1; Mishna Sanhedrin 4:5; Succa 20a.
16. Mishna Avot 1:13.
17. Shabbat 31a, Jerusalem Nedarim 9:4.
18. Yoma 54b; cf. the *Zohar*: "The divine Presence rests on the marital bed when both male and female are united in love and holiness." For further discussion of sexuality in Judaism, see Eliezer Berkovits, "A Jewish Sexual Ethics," in Berkovits, *Essential Essays on Judaism* (Jerusalem: Shalem Press, 2002), pp. 103–28.

CHAPTER 5:

Wisdom of the Heart

1. Tana Debei Eliyahu Rabba 26:26; Kidushin 31a, Kidushin 32a; Jerusalem Kidushin 1:7; Jerusalem Pe'ah 1:1.
2. Kidushin 31b.
3. Midrash Mishlei 1, cited in Bialik and Ravnitzky, *Sefer Ha'agada,* p. 367:13.

4. Ecclesiastes Rabba 1:4.
5. Succa 46b.
6. Cf. Deuteronomy 4:40, 11:9.

CHAPTER 6:
The Meaning of Life

1. Mishna Avot 3:2. Plato and Philo cited in Daniel Boyarin, *Carnal Israel: Reading Sex in Talmudic Culture* (Berkeley: University of California Press, 1993), p. 31.
2. Ta'anit 11a.
3. Mishna Rosh Hashana 2:6.
4. Jerusalem Kidushin 4:12; Pesachim 109a.
5. Boyarin, *Carnal Israel,* p. 34.
6. Mishna Avot 4:21.
7. See Ethan Dor-Shav, "Job's Path to Enlightenment," *Azure* 32 (Spring 2008): 102–48, esp. p. 116.
8. See Ethan Dor-Shav, "Soul of Fire: A Theory of Biblical Man," *Azure* 22 (Autumn 2005): 78–113.
9. Mishna Sanhedrin 4:5.

CHAPTER 7:
Love and Ecstasy

1. Nahmanides on Genesis 12:6, based on Tanhuma Lech Lecha 9.
2. Mishna Yadayim 3:6.
3. Based on Yoma 69b.

CHAPTER 8:
Making Room for Others

1. See Yosef Yitzhak Lifshitz, "Towards a Jewish Economic Theory," *Azure* 18 (Autumn 2004): 34–58.
2. Cf. Genesis Rabba 31:5, Rashi on Genesis 6:11, s.v. "*hamas.*"
3. Shabbat 118a; Taanit 16a; Bava Kama 119a.
4. Sanhedrin 86a, Mechilta Yitro 8.
5. Mishna Sanhedrin 11:1.
6. Bava Metzia 24a.
7. Matthew 19:24, Mark 10:25, Luke 18:25.

8. Ruth Rabba 5:9.
9. Gitin 7b.
10. Ketubot 50a; Maimonides, *Mishneh Torah,* Laws of Gifts to the Poor 10:10.

CHAPTER 9:
Our Communities, Ourselves

1. Arachin 15b; Deuteronomy Rabba 6:8; Pirkei de Rabbi Eliezer, 53; Arachin 15b; Bava Metzia 58b.
2. Benjamin W. Farley, ed. and trans., *John Calvin's Sermons* (Grand Rapids, Mich.: Baker Books, 2000), pp. 206, 216.
3. Robert H. Fischer, trans., *The Large Catechism of Martin Luther* (Philadelphia: Fortress, 1959), p. 45.
4. Jerusalem Peah 1:1.
5. Gittin 55b–56a, 57a.
6. Yoma 9b.
7. See Raymond Westbrook, "Judges in the Cuneiform Sources," *Maarav* 12, nos. 1–2 (2005): 27–40.

CHAPTER 10:
Peace

1. Mishna Avot 4:1.
2. Exodus Rabba 14:3.
3. Genesis Rabba 22:5.
4. Numbers 14:40–45.

AFTERWORD:
The Human Element

1. Shabbat 55b. Technically the rabbis assert that "four died because of the Serpent" rather than their sins: Benjamin son of Jacob, Amram the father of Moses, Jesse the father of David, and Caleb the son of David. These are all minor figures in the Bible, and in the rabbinic context, Ephraim E. Urbach is correct to point out that "the meaning of this [passage] is unambiguous: All men die on account of their sins; and there is no death without sin." Urbach, *The Sages: The World and Wisdom of the Rabbis of the Talmud,* trans. Israel Abrahams (Cambridge, Mass.: Harvard University Press, 1979), p. 427.

2. We may speculate about the number. According to rabbinic numerology, the number is represented in the word *tit'aked,* which means "you shall bind yourself." The whole universe is presented as being bound in the primordial Torah, a design and plan for all existence. For another explanation, see Rashi on Shabbat 88b, s.v. "974 generations."
3. Shabbat 88b–89a.

INDEX

ABOUT THE AUTHOR

David Hazony has written about religion and politics for *The New Republic, Commentary, The Forward, The Jerusalem Post, The Jewish Chronicle, The New York Sun,* and *Policy Review,* and is a regular contributor to the weblog *Contentions.* The former editor in chief of the Israeli public affairs journal *Azure,* he has also edited three volumes of Jewish and Israeli thought. He studied rabbinic and biblical thought in Orthodox seminaries in the United States and Israel, and is pursuing a doctorate in Jewish philosophy at the Hebrew University in Jerusalem. His one translated novel, Emuna Elon's *If You Awaken Love,* was a finalist for the National Jewish Book Award in 2007. He lives in the suburbs of Jerusalem.